Ean Higgins grew up in Texas and Quebec, before moving to Australia. He has worked as a reporter, section editor, chief-of-staff and foreign correspondent for Australia's three national news-papers over nearly four decades. He was the *Australian Financial Review*'s first New Zealand correspondent, then moved to the Fairfax group's investigative newspaper *Times on Sunday*. Higgins joined *The Australian* in 1988 where among other roles he served as Foreign News Editor, *Inquirer* Editor, Europe correspondent and Sydney Bureau Chief. In recent years he has returned to reporting at *The Australian*, focusing on crime, corruption and politics. Having learned to fly as a young man, he also has a long interest in aviation, in recent years leading the world media's coverage of the MH370 mystery. Higgins lives and works in Sydney.

THE HUNT FOR MH370

THE MYSTERY. THE COVER-UP. THE TRUTH.

EAN HIGGINS

MACMILLAN

Pan Macmillan Australia

*To those who hunt for MH370 including the families
of the disappeared whose quest continues.*

CONTENTS

PROLOGUE   1

ONE: 'GOOD NIGHT, MALAYSIAN THREE SEVEN ZERO'   9
   Theory One: Rogue Pilot to the End   18
TWO: **INTO THIN AIR**   37
THREE: **THOUGHTS AND PRAYERS**   47
FOUR: 'STILL, THERE WAS NOTHING. TOTALLY NOTHING'   56
   Theory Two: Elope by Parachute   70
FIVE: **A PING FROM THE DEEP**   75
SIX: **NOWHERE TO HIDE**   105
   Theory Three: Onboard Fire   131
SEVEN: *'GRIEF RETURNS WITH THE REVOLVING YEAR'*   135
EIGHT: **AN INCONVENIENT TRUTH**   159
   Theory Four: Terrorist Hijacking Gone Wrong   171
NINE: **'X' MARKS THE SPOT**   175
TEN: **NO CURE, NO FEE**   186
ELEVEN: **KING AIR, A WING, A PRAYER**   210
   Theory Five: Rapid Decompression   236

TWELVE: 'YOU CAN ALWAYS GO IN WITH A KNIFE'   · 239
THIRTEEN: **REACH FOR THE SKY**   257

EPILOGUE   277

GLOSSARY   289
FURTHER READING   295
ACKNOWLEDGEMENTS   296

PROLOGUE

Somewhere out in the southern Indian Ocean, maybe in one of the underwater canyons of Broken Ridge but beyond the Seventh Arc, lies the answer to the world's greatest aviation mystery.

Malaysia Airlines Flight MH370 was on its way from Kuala Lumpur to Beijing when some very strange things happened on the Boeing 777. They caused a pilot to turn around, fly a zigzag course back over Malaysia, up the Straits of Malacca, then south to vanish literally in the middle of nowhere, all without a word from anyone on board.

Five years after it disappeared, the aircraft is still there, probably in very deep and cold water, well preserved along with the 239 souls, but just not yet found. Once it is discovered – and most aviation experts believe it will be one day – the mystery can be solved. The flight data recorder, the cockpit voice recorder, the identity and disposition of anyone in the cockpit at the controls, the configuration and nature of damage to the different parts of the aircraft, and, macabre though it is, the pathology of those on board, will provide the clues.

We will learn why the aircraft turned around about 40 minutes into the flight. We will glean insight as to why at that time the secondary radar transponder was turned off, the aircraft flew a deliberate route back over Malaysia roughly following the Malaysia-Thailand airspace border, over Penang, then north-west, and finally on the long track south.

Over the years since MH370 went missing on 8 March 2014, there has been no shortage of speculation about what happened – some theories wild and outlandish, some well informed and within the realms of the possible. Some believe it may have been a hijacking gone wrong. Others think there may have been a fire on board, possibly caused by the combination of cargo including lithium-ion batteries and a massive supply of the tropical fruit mangosteens, which have a hard, deep-purple casing outside, and inside succulent white segments which are little explosions of sweet delight.

There are those who look at accidental depressurisation, in which the pilots became a bit hypoxic, or light-headed because of a faulty oxygen supply – not enough to pass out, but enough to make silly and illogical decisions and fly the aircraft in a strange way. It's happened before – some air accidents have been recorded where the pilot is conscious but drunkenly happy with the reduced amount of oxygen.

Then there are the more extreme theories: that a rogue nation such as North Korea hacked into the aircraft's control systems and electronically 'captured' it, perhaps making use, ironically, of a new remote system said to be designed to counteract a hijack. Even more out there, something like a scene from the old US television series *The Twilight Zone*, some suggest MH370 was taken over by aliens.

Others, including some families of the Chinese passengers on the flight, say the official interpretation of the direction the aircraft took on the last leg is wrong, and it was in fact hijacked and flown north-west over the Maldives to central Asia and landed at an Islamic rebel airbase, its passengers and crew still held hostage to this day.

And there is one theory that the captain, his marriage having collapsed, took a parachute on board in his flight crew bag, and depressurised the aircraft to kill all else on board. He then set the aircraft on a course on automatic pilot, bailed out, and was picked up in a boat by his mistress. He and the mistress, so promoters of this theory say, are living happily under new, stolen identities in another country, maybe Australia.

Most professionals in the aviation business, though, believe the evidence best points to the flight's captain, Zaharie Ahmad Shah, having hijacked his own aircraft in a complex and cunning act of mass murder–suicide. The only debate there is whether, as the Australian Transport Safety Bureau (ATSB) maintains, MH370 was a 'ghost flight' by the end, flying on autopilot with no-one conscious, and crashing down rapidly after fuel exhaustion. Or did Zaharie fly the aircraft to the end, making a controlled ditching to try to keep as much of MH370 intact as possible and sink it with a minimal debris field?

If the ATSB had worked on the premise that a pilot flew the aircraft to the end, they would effectively have had to say they believed MH370 was most likely hijacked by its captain, Zaharie. By saying instead, as they did, that MH370 had an 'unresponsive crew' and was not controlled by a pilot at the end, they could avoid making such a call publicly – whatever they themselves thought had happened earlier in the flight.

Many veteran airline captains and top air crash investigators suspect the ATSB, even if subconsciously, came up with what became known as their 'ghost flight' and 'death dive' theory to avoid having to publicly embarrass the Malaysian government and its government-owned national flag carrier airline.

Did the ATSB, even without realising it, look for anything that might support a theory which would mean they would not have to say a trusted Malaysian pilot hijacked his own aircraft and took himself and 238 innocent people from around the world to their deaths? Did they, again subconsciously, read that bias into the later evidence as it came in, including when parts of the aircraft washed up on the other side of the Indian Ocean which many experts believe point to a controlled ditching?

The ATSB says, emphatically, no: the bureau's officers have told Senate Estimates they worked objectively on facts, science and logic, consulting the best Australian and overseas experts in the field to establish their target search area, without bias or subjective influences.

The debate is not academic; it has a fundamental impact on working out where the aircraft might be, and where to look. If the ATSB is right, the aircraft came pretty much straight down after it ran out of fuel, producing a relatively narrow search zone. If Zaharie flew the aircraft to the end and ditched it, either under power or gliding it after it ran out of fuel, he could have taken it a much longer distance, perhaps 100 nautical miles or more according to the ATSB, and well outside the search area the bureau defined. In that case, the ATSB-led undersea hunt never had a serious chance of success, and it blew almost $200 million of Australian, Malaysian and Chinese taxpayers' money on what was always going to be a lost cause.

In my efforts to get to the truth of MH370 as a reporter for *The Australian*, the ATSB, and the federal government's Joint Agency Coordination Centre (JACC), which was set up to orchestrate the MH370 search, engaged in some repressive media practices not usually consistent with public sector agencies in a democracy. They tried to have me taken off the story for persisting with questions they didn't want to answer, an attempt the editors rejected as an unacceptable bid by a government agency to undermine their independent authority and hobble freedom of the press. Eventually, as it became more desperate to suppress *The Australian*'s reportage of criticism of its search strategy, the ATSB hired a top law firm to issue warnings to the editors to 'refrain' from its style of coverage – warnings the editors tossed aside and exposed.

The ATSB and the JACC have usually, but to their credit not always, declined Freedom of Information requests about MH370.

These actions raise serious questions about the integrity of Australia's democratic system, of which key elements are transparency in government, freedom of speech and freedom of the press.

It adds to the mystery of the hunt for MH370. The families of the MH370 victims, and many in the international aviation community, have asked: why would federal bureaucrats, who are paid by taxpayers to serve the interests of the general public, behave in such a defensive and secretive way and engage in what to some looks like a cover-up? What agenda, and whose agenda, are they serving?

This book is the story of the international effort to work out what happened on board MH370, and the four hunts so far to find it. It's also the story of the individuals involved, many courageous and well intentioned. It's the back story of Australian authorities' progression towards a conclusion on what happened on MH370 which many professionals in the aviation sector believe to be predetermined and wrong, and possibly motivated, if only subliminally, by international political concerns. And it's an insight into the restrictive media tactics taken by the ATSB and the JACC to try to put a lid on such coverage by targeting the commentators who make such claims and the journalists who canvass them.

The public appetite, both in Australia and internationally, for MH370 remains insatiable – it's a mystery, and mysteries become addictive. Substantial stories on MH370 tend to go straight to the top of the most read online lists, and often stay there for a day or more – they go viral and are read voraciously by thousands of people internationally. The Nine Network's *60 Minutes* program ran two one-hour specials on MH370 in May 2018, more than four years after the disappearance. That same month, the Melbourne Theatre Company staged 'Hungry Ghosts', a live production based on the MH370 mystery. Reviewing it in *The Age*, Cameron Woodhead described it as 'a polyphonic piece'.

'For starters, there's the disappearance of the plane and all the fallout – from wild conspiracy theories to the desolated voices of grieving families, and the interminable search for the wreckage and the clickbait it generates.'

Any significant news story about MH370 gets taken up by news websites around the world. An international community has developed, a sort of MH370 addicts club, which includes professional airline pilots, aerospace engineers, air crash investigators, and a host of fascinated amateur tragics. In various online forums and email exchanges, the MH370 club analyses and debates every new development in the saga, with everyone in the club knowing what the Seventh Arc is and where Broken Ridge is located.

I'm a member of that international club of MH370 addicts. I have been ever since the day I was assigned to check out a story in the *Sunday Times* about a British angle on the search for aircraft. The mystery got me immediately, along with the extraordinary technology and detective work that had gone into the hunt, like the satellite data producing the Seventh Arc. Since then, I have followed every twist and turn of the MH370 saga, writing many, many news stories and features. Perhaps a further interest for me was that I spent a bit of time in Malaysia as an adolescent, including going to a local school in the peninsular east-coast town of Kuantan, and have been back since.

I have been fortunate to get to know some of the families of those missing on MH370; they are fine people still struggling with their loss, haunted by not knowing the truth of what happened on board the flight, and where their loved ones lie.

This book aims to inform and explain, taking the reader through the known facts. It's a piece of long-form reportage journalism: it recounts what is established, and reports the alternative views of credible, well-versed professional people about what those facts might mean and what conclusions might logically be drawn.

Four searches, the first on the surface, the second a combined surface/undersea operation, and two sea-floor surveys – all mammoth efforts – have failed to find MH370. But the Malaysian government, for one, has vowed to not give up. In some of his first remarks to journalists after newly elected Malaysian Prime Minister Mahathir Mohamad appointed him transport minister, Anthony Loke said 'a major issue for the ministry . . . is to continue searching for MH370 . . . this I think is very important not only for family members but also the aviation industry'.

The pattern of history in big lost-at-sea enigmas is that governments, companies, associations, adventurers and wealthy individuals with a passion will over time mount new searches until the source of the mystery is found. Examples include the German battleship *Bismarck*, the Australian cruiser HMAS *Sydney*, and, of course, the ill-fated British cruise liner *Titanic*. *Bismarck* and *Sydney* were sunk in combat in the Second World War, and found in 1989 and 2008 respectively. The *Titanic* went down, famously, when it had a run-in with an iceberg in the North Atlantic on the ship's maiden voyage in 1912, and was found in 1985. Intriguingly, the discovery of famous shipwrecks has tended to be led by private individuals or organisations rather than governments. Both *Bismarck* and *Titanic* were found by expeditions headed by Robert Ballard, a retired US Navy officer and a professor of oceanography.

The fact a long period of time had passed between the sinking of these ships and their discovery – and the fact they were found at all – reflect several dynamics. There is no question that earlier generations of wreck-hunters would have loved to have found these vessels whose loss was hugely famous, or infamous, at the time and thereafter. It took decades for the right undersea search technology to develop. But also, in each case, it took generations for the hunters to develop the right analysis of what was known about the circumstances of the ships' disappearance to work out just where the vessels ended up.

Many keen and highly trained observers in the aviation, engineering and scientific professions believe the ATSB officials relied on the wrong theory of where MH370 lies, and that's why they didn't find it. Those aviators, engineers and scientists also think they know the relatively narrow area where the aircraft and the 239 souls aboard do rest, where the ATSB did not look even when it was extensively briefed by proponents of the theory and had the chance. That's based on a vision of what happened different from the one employed by the ATSB. That chilling, but well-evidenced, scenario is outlined in the coming chapter. It's the first of five theories canvassed in this book about what might have happened to MH370, those theories selected as being the most credible, internally consistent, and possible against the known facts.

We don't know for sure what happened to MH370, the same way we don't know for certain what fate befell American aviator Amelia Earhart in 1937 over the Pacific Ocean. We won't know until MH370 is found. But we know a lot, and this book outlines that which we do, and the shocking possibilities which stem from it.

ONE

'GOOD NIGHT, MALAYSIAN THREE SEVEN ZERO'

Zaharie Ahmad Shah loved flying.

Growing up in Penang in a big family in a country which, while getting more affluent was still not rich, he'd considered himself fortunate to get a traineeship as a pilot with Malaysia Airlines.

By 2014, after 33 years as a pilot, Zaharie was flying Boeing 777-200ER airliners. They are big, wide-bodied, twin-engine beasts with extended range, boasting a wingspan of 61 metres, and a length of 64 metres. They can carry up to 300 passengers, with a maximum take-off weight of 300 tonnes.

But that wasn't enough flying for Zaharie. He flew model airplanes for fun, and went paragliding. He set himself up at home with a fairly sophisticated flight simulator using his desktop computer. He flew various simulated routes on the home computer, including one which was rather odd: it started out in Kuala Lumpur, headed north-west up the Straits of Malacca to the Andaman Sea, then turned left on a long track south to finish in the southern Indian Ocean.

The zigzag route made no sense – there was no logic to it and it ended up far from anywhere one could land an aircraft, in a very remote stretch of ocean. But to many airline pilots who have studied MH370, the imaginary flight on Zaharie's home computer flight simulator made absolute sense in relation to what they believe to be his cunning, malevolent intent. The professional aviators think it was a route Zaharie wanted to practice, to make a Boeing 777 with him at the controls vanish, along with its passengers and crew, to never be found.

Zaharie was politically active. He had in recent years joined the political party of opposition figure Anwar Ibrahim who had been deputy to former Prime Minister Mahathir Mohamad. Zaharie also happened to be distantly related by marriage to Anwar. Anwar had fallen out with Mahathir, and then faced a long prosecution on sodomy charges which were widely regarded as politically motivated and trumped up. In a Kuala Lumpur courtroom on the afternoon of Friday, 7 March 2014, Anwar's acquittal in an earlier trial was overturned, and he was convicted.

That night Zaharie arrived at Kuala Lumpur International Airport at 10:50pm, appropriately an hour or so before he was to board a Boeing 777, this one carrying the registration 9M-MRO. He was to take it to Beijing as pilot-in-command of Malaysia Airlines Flight MH370. It's not known whether he had kissed his wife goodbye, or one of the mistresses his sister told *The Australian* he took up with from time to time. Zaharie reported in to Malaysia Airlines' operations centre, and received the computerised flight plan for the trip, and read through any relevant Notices to Airmen, known as NOTAMS, relating to weather or other issues of concern.

Zaharie commanded considerable respect among his colleagues at Malaysia Airlines. At 53, he had clocked up 18,423 hours of flight time, including 8659 on the Boeing 777. Because of his experience and excellent flying record, he was designated as a Type Rating

Instructor on the 777, and a Type Rating Examiner, meaning he could train, and test, other pilots seeking to qualify to fly that type of aircraft.

So, when he ordered the ground staff to load extra fuel for the flight, no-one thought twice about it. The planned flight time to Beijing was five hours, 34 minutes. A fuel reserve of an hour would have been standard to allow for contingencies, such as if there were bad weather or air traffic congestion at Beijing and Zaharie had to go into a holding pattern or head to an alternative airfield.

But there's a trade-off with aviation fuel: the more fuel, the more weight, and the more power and hence fuel consumed to keep the aircraft in the air. Zaharie ordered 49,100 kilograms of fuel, giving MH370 an endurance of seven hours and thirty-one minutes, or almost two hours of what pilots call 'contingency fuel'. This was a lot, especially considering there were no particular weather concerns in Beijing at the time he planned the flight.

The first officer on flight MH370 was, compared to Zaharie, a youngster and a rookie. Fariq Abdul Hamid was just 27 years old, and had everything to live for. He was engaged to be married to his sweetheart, who was also a pilot, whom he had met at flight school on the resort island of Langkawi. Fariq had been a pilot with Malaysia Airlines for seven years, and had clocked up 2813 flying hours. Fariq was going through the process of qualifying to fly 777s – he had 39 hours on the type, and on this trip Zaharie, as Type Rating Instructor, was to guide him through his final training flight before his 'check ride' on his next scheduled flight.

Around midnight, either Zaharie or Fariq would have boarded the aircraft to start running through pre-flight procedures from the cockpit, while the other would have done a walk around the aircraft making sure it all looked in order. The 10 cabin crew came on board, and then the 227 passengers took their seats. There were 14 nationalities among the passengers: 153 Chinese, 38 Malaysians, seven Indonesians, six Australians, five Indians, four French, three

Americans, two each from New Zealand, Ukraine, and Canada, one each from Russia, Taiwan, and the Netherlands; finally, there were two Iranians – travelling on stolen Italian and Austrian passports.

Among those 227 passengers, New Zealander Paul Weeks, 39, having the previous day kissed goodbye to his wife Danica and young sons Lincoln and Jack in Perth, where they lived, slid his way into window seat 2K in business class on the aircraft's right-hand side. He was on his way to a new fly-in, fly-out mining job in Mongolia.

In economy, Australian Li Yuan, 33, took his place in the central set of seats at 14E, while his wife Gu Naijun, 31, settled in to hers in 14H. The couple, who divided their lives between Sydney and China, were on their way to re-join their two young daughters, who were staying with extended family.

In a cluster of four seats on the left-hand side of the aircraft, four Queenslanders from Brisbane got ready to fly out on a holiday of a lifetime. Rodney Burrows, 59, sat in 20A, his wife Mary, 54, in 20C beside him. Behind them were Catherine Lawton, 54, in 21A, and her husband Robert, 58, in 21C.

When they were both in the cockpit, Zaharie and Fariq would have continued through the pre-departure checklist. One would have read out the item on the list to be checked; the other would check the action had been done and all was in order. The 'Pre-Flight' Boeing 777 checklist starts with 'Oxygen', and the correct response is 'Tested, 100 per cent'. Zaharie and Fariq would have each got their oxygen masks out, made sure they were working, and put them back.

Next would have been the 'Before Start' checklist:

One of the pilots would have read out 'Flight Deck Doors' to which the other would, after checking, responded 'Closed and Locked', meaning no-one could enter the cockpit without permission from the pilots.

Zaharie and Fariq would then have gone through some procedural checks to make sure the computerised flight settings looked right, like take-off speeds, and ticked off that the taxi and take-off

FIGURE 1: MH370 SPECIFICATIONS AND SEATING PLAN

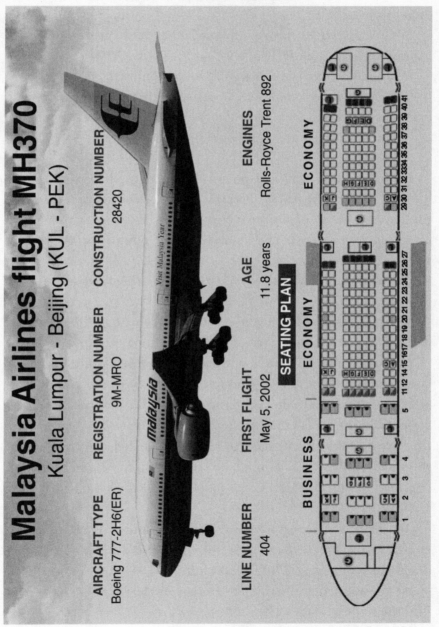

briefing had been done and that the plane's bright taxi anti-collision beacon was on.

With the engines now running, Zaharie and Fariq would have run through the 'Before Taxi' checklist:

'Autobrake?' one of them would have prompted.

'RTO,' the other would have confirmed, meaning the automatic braking system was set to heavy, in case of a 'Rejected Take-off'.

'Flight Controls?' one pilot would have asked.

'Checked.'

In the old days, and still on smaller aircraft, pilots would move the yoke and rudder pedals and look out the windows to see that the rudder, ailerons and elevator were working; today pilots make that check against computer displays showing the positions of the control surfaces.

'Ground Equipment?' would have been the next prompt on the list.

'Clear.' That hasn't changed – just a visual check that the aircraft is not still attached to any piece of equipment and nothing's in the way.

Malaysia Airlines' standard operating procedure requires that radio communications on the ground are handled by the first officer. So, at 27 minutes past midnight, Fariq requested a pushback and start clearance from Kuala Lumpur Area Control Centre. After completing the 'Before Taxi' check, Zaharie and Fariq taxied the plane to the threshold of runway 32 Right. The last item on the 'Before Take-off' checklist would have been:

'Flaps?'

To which the other pilot would have responded 'Set', meaning confirmation that the flaps on the wings were lowered to the correct degree to provide extra lift for take-off.

At 40 minutes past midnight, controllers cleared MH370 to head into the sky.

'370 32 Right for take-off,' is the recorded interchange between the pilots and the control tower.

The pilots pushed the throttles forward.

At 42 minutes past midnight local time on 8 March 2014, Malaysia Airlines Flight MH370 lifted off, its wheels never to touch the ground again.

Once comfortably airborne and with a check that the rate of climb was positive, the pilots would have raised the landing gear, and brought the flaps back to the retracted position in line with the rest of the wings. They would have gone through the two-item 'After Take-off' checklist:

'Landing Gear?'

'– Up.'

'Flaps?'

'– Up.'

Just after take-off, Kuala Lumpur control cleared MH370 to climb to 18,000 feet, and to track for waypoint IGARI in the South China Sea. Waypoints are part of the complex international air traffic control and navigation system that keeps aircraft flying safely without danger of smashing into each other. The waypoints, whose names all consist of five capital letters made up to be easily pronounceable, exist only on air-navigation maps; they are just points of latitude and longitude, placed on official airway routes which are numbered and which commercial airliners are generally required to follow.

At 43 minutes past midnight, with MH370 in the air, Kuala Lumpur controllers rang Ho Chi Minh Area Control Centre in Vietnam relaying the estimated time of arrival of MH370 for waypoint IGARI at 1:22am, and the secondary radar transponder code A2157.

There are two basic types of radar in air traffic control: primary and secondary. Primary radar is the original which dates back to the

Second World War: it bounces electronic pulses off objects to create a 'blip' on a screen – it does not tell the controller which aircraft is which.

Secondary radar involves an aircraft emitting an electronic signal via what's known as a 'transponder' which identifies it by a unique code, and the transponder relays the aircraft's altitude, speed and position in real time to air traffic controllers. With this tool, controllers can know exactly where each aircraft is at any time as the coded signals move steadily over their big display screens.

Primary radar is still used, including by the military because a hostile foreign aircraft pilot planning an attack during a conflict would be disinclined to tip off their position, altitude and speed to an enemy air traffic controller by emitting a transponder signal so they could be picked up by secondary radar. Military primary radar was to have a critical role in the MH370 drama.

The communication from Kuala Lumpur controllers to Ho Chi Minh controllers was important because IGARI was close to where the handover of responsibility for MH370 from Malaysian air traffic control to Vietnamese control was to take place. The world's airspace is divided up into different air traffic control sectors know as Flight Information Regions, and pilots and controllers are required to acknowledge each other when the aircraft moves from one sector to another.

A couple of other routine communications between Kuala Lumpur controllers and the pilots of MH370 took place: at 47 minutes past midnight the flight crew was cleared to climb to 25,000 feet, and a minute later got clearance to 35,000 feet. At 56 minutes past midnight the flight crew said they were maintaining that altitude.

At 1:19am, the official Malaysian safety investigation report into the loss of MH370 says the pilots were 'instructed to contact Ho Chi Minh Air Control Centre on the radio frequency 120.9 MHz'.

Four seconds later, Zaharie acknowledged the instruction with 'Good night, Malaysian Three Seven Zero'.

'This was the last recorded radio transmission from MH370,' the report says. In fact, it was the last time anyone on the aircraft was heard from.

A minute later, MH370 passed through waypoint IGARI.

From that point, 40 minutes into the flight, some things are known about what happened on Malaysia Airlines Flight MH370, but many are not, which is why the ultimate mystery of the lost aircraft remains unsolved. What follows is one possible scenario – like other theories to be outlined later in this book, it is a dramatised reconstruction of a theory based on fact, detective work, deduction and informed speculation. It is not purporting to be what happened, but one version of what *could* have happened consistent with what is known about the flight and the aircraft.

THEORY ONE:
ROGUE PILOT TO THE END

A couple of minutes before signing off with 'Good night, Malaysian Three Seven Zero' MH370 pilot-in-command Zaharie Ahmad Shah sent his co-pilot Fariq Abdul Hamid out of the cockpit on an errand.

'Hamid, would you mind getting me a cup of coffee while I attend to some paperwork? Many thanks.'

Zaharie would, as per standard operating procedure (SOP), have locked the cockpit door once Fariq was out. But what would not have been SOP was the series of actions Zaharie initiated next.

The minute after the acknowledgement 'Good night, Malaysian Three Seven Zero,' Zaharie reached to the central console and turned off the secondary radar transponder, making the aircraft vanish from air traffic control screens.

The Malaysian safety investigation report released in July 2018 says the symbol for MH370 dropped off from radar display at 1:20am. 'The Malaysian military radar and radar sources from two other countries, namely Viet Nam and Thailand, also captured the disappearance of the radar position symbol of MH370,' the report says.

At the same time, Zaharie turned off the aircraft's automatic transmission of flight data to ground stations. The report shows the final Aircraft Communications Addressing and Reporting System (ACARS) transmission was made through the MH370 satellite communication system just 13 minutes earlier, at 1:07am.

Then Zaharie took out his flight crew bag, containing a few ostensibly innocuous items of clothing – a jumper, scarf, insulated jacket, light gloves and wool cap. Nothing odd there – Beijing can still be very cold in early March. But then, in what was at that stage a comfortable warm cockpit, Zaharie put those items of clothing on.

Then, Zaharie donned his oxygen mask which had hours of oxygen supply in case of depressurisation or fire. Moments thereafter,

Zaharie turned off the electrical circuit for the cabin lights, plunging the passenger cabin into darkness in the middle of a moonless night. Zaharie then quickly reached up above his head to the upper control console and pressed a button to turn off the cabin pressurisation system, which is run by power from the engines and keeps the air in the cabin at near ground level pressure.

With the pressurisation turned off, the aircraft went into rapid decompression – this option is available for pilots to deal with an onboard fire by sucking out the smoke and exposing the cabin to the lack of oxygen and cold of high altitudes. Immediately after that, Zaharie took the aircraft off autopilot, and made a brief right-hand turn followed quickly by a sharp but long left-hand turn, turning the aircraft almost 180 degrees back towards Malaysia. The safety investigation report says that at 1:21am, a playback of Malaysian military radar 'showed the radar return of MH370 turning right but shortly after, making a constant left turn to heading of 273 degrees'.

The Malaysian investigators later determined the turn was too abrupt to have been made on autopilot, and had to have been performed by a pilot with his hands on the yoke manually moving the controls. The turn was so sharp, with such a high angle of bank, that it set off alarms and required Zaharie's full concentration as a highly skilled pilot to accomplish. The turn took two minutes and eight seconds, and Zaharie negotiated his way through it despite an audio 'bank angle' warning and 'stick shaker' stall warning.

The rapid combination of Zaharie's actions sent the 238 souls in his charge into mortal fear and in many cases outright panic. The oxygen masks dropped automatically due to the loss of cabin pressure, but the passengers, cabin crew and Fariq were enveloped in darkness, fogginess from rapid decompression and increasing cold. The quick right-left extremely banked turns threw those standing, including the cabin crew and Fariq, off their feet, many crashing into the passengers. The cabin filled with screams of confusion and terror.

Like all airliners, MH370 would have had portable oxygen bottles and masks stored in lockers for the cabin crew or pilots to use in the event of rapid decompression or fire. But it was too difficult for Fariq or the cabin crew, during the sharply banked turn of more than two minutes, to make their way in the darkness to the lockers to deploy them.

The young and agile Fariq somehow negotiated his way to the cockpit door in the difficult conditions, clamouring from one row to another taking the occasional breath of oxygen from masks fallen to vacant seats. At that stage he thought his duty was to assist his captain in dealing with a life-threatening calamity of some sort. Zaharie kept the door locked, and after a period Fariq banged on it, saying, 'Captain, please let me in, what's wrong?'

Seconds after that, Fariq passed out and collapsed at the foot of the cockpit door. The effects on humans of rapid decompression and hypoxia, or oxygen deprivation, at high altitude are well known. Most military pilots and many civilian ones go through simulations in decompression chambers. For those readers interested, there are some excellent YouTube videos showing them. The cabin quickly goes foggy as the moisture condenses out of the air, and the cold from outside starts to seep in. People who go through the process in simulation report different symptoms, but ironically, the most common is a sort of drunken sense of feeling good. That insidious process is well established throughout aviation history.

'One does not suffer in any way; on the contrary,' French scientist and experimental balloonist, Gaston Tissandier, wrote in 1875. 'One feels an inner joy, as if filled with a radiant flood of light . . . one becomes indifferent, one thinks neither of the perilous situation nor of any danger.' Tissandier wrote those words about hypoxia after he and two fellow adventurers, journalist Joseph Crocé-Spinelli, and naval officer Théodore Henri Sivel, attempted an altitude record in a balloon. They did well, reaching 28,000 feet, but Crocé-Spinelli and Henri Sivel died of hypoxia; Tissandier is said to have gone deaf as a result of the experience. He wrote that he wanted to reach the oxygen bags, but couldn't, and then didn't really care.

After the oxygen got sucked out of MH370 during rapid decompression, for the first 30 seconds or maybe a bit longer, passengers could have maintained what's called useful consciousness – the ability to know what's going on and perform basic functions like putting on an oxygen mask. But then all those who did not get an oxygen mask on within that short time would see their blood oxygen levels drop dramatically. Their fingertips would have started to tingle and they would have become lightheaded. But ironically, and catastrophically, those passengers who did not get their oxygen masks on in 30 seconds of total darkness and steep bank probably stopped worrying about that or anything else. If you have ever wondered why during the pre-flight passenger safety briefings on airliners the message is to put on your own oxygen mask first before helping others, that's why: if you spend more than 30 seconds or a bit longer trying to put the oxygen mask on your rambunctious child before putting your own mask on, you probably won't succeed, and pretty soon, you won't even care.

By the time Zaharie finished the steeply banked turns – more than two minutes – the period of useful consciousness would have expired for anyone who did not have an oxygen mask on. Within three or four minutes at most they would have passed out. While their hearts would likely have stayed beating for a while, after several minutes of unconsciousness they would have started to suffer brain damage. Some passengers would have become brain dead, others would have died.

For those who somehow did manage to find the drop-down masks in the darkness and sharp bank angle and got them on during the short period of useful consciousness, it would only be a temporary reprieve. The oxygen from the drop-down masks is designed purely to keep passengers alive long enough for the pilots to put the aircraft into a rapid descent to lower altitudes where there is enough oxygen for them to breathe, usually about 10,000 feet if the terrain allows it.

On the Boeing 777, the oxygen in the drop-down masks for the passengers does not come from oxygen bottles, the way it does for the pilots, but is chemically generated. How long it lasts depends on altitude. In a normal scenario of a rapid descent, the passenger oxygen would last 22 minutes, but if the aircraft stayed at 35,000 feet it would only last about 12 minutes.

That makes the timing of Zaharie's murderous plan ruthlessly effective. The elapsed time from the moment the aircraft made the turn at waypoint IGARI at 1:21am, until it appeared back over the east coast of the Malay Peninsula at 1:37am, was 16 minutes. The oxygen from the drop-down masks would have expired about four minutes earlier, and any passengers or crew who had them on would have lost useful consciousness or passed out altogether in those four minutes.

That would explain why there were no text messages or cell phone calls of alarm, distress or final words from any of the passengers or crew once the aircraft passed near or over built-up areas like Kota Bharu or Penang: they were all unconscious or dead. It has been established that had anyone been conscious when MH370 passed near Penang, they may have been able to make a mobile phone call. At 1:52am, first officer Fariq's phone made contact with the Penang mobile service; Malaysian authorities say it was just an automatic log-on, not an attempt to make a call or send a text message.

To be even more sure, Zaharie flew higher after the initial turn – the oxygen would have run out even faster and the hypoxia would have been more severe at 40,000 feet. The Malaysian safety investigation report quotes a publication *Basic Flight Pathology* as saying useful consciousness is between 30 seconds and one minute at 35,000 feet, but only 15 to 20 seconds at 40,000 feet.

Zaharie waited half an hour in all after depressurising the aircraft, to be sure the 238 passengers and crew in his charge were neutralised and he was flying an airliner of the unconscious, brain-dead and dead. Then he again reached up and pushed the pressurisation button to 'on', and within a few minutes the cabin was back to near ground level air pressure, and warm. In a leisurely fashion Zaharie took off his jacket, gloves, scarf and cap and comfortably settled back to proceed with the rest of his elaborate murder-suicide plan.

The aircraft tracked along the airspace border between Malaysia and Thailand – a deliberate ploy by Zaharie to further confuse authorities; Thai and Malaysian controllers might have thought the aircraft was the other's responsibility. This was indeed the case, it later emerged: Thai primary radar detected the aircraft, but Thai controllers did not alert Malaysian controllers because, Thai officials said, the Malaysians did not ask about it.

Malaysian military radar then tracked MH370 to Penang, a bustling island city on peninsular Malaysia's west coast. At 1:52am, the Malaysian safety investigation report says, the radar 'blip' was 'observed to be at 10 nautical miles south of Penang Island on a heading of 261 degrees.' It gave Zaharie a good look at the lights of the city where he was born and grew up – for him the slow, curving turn he made around it marked final salute to his happy boyhood memories.

After Penang, the playback of primary radar shows MH370 headed up the Straits of Malacca on Airway Route N571. Zaharie selected that segment of regular, normal commercial airliner flight because had the Malaysian or Thai military been actively watching MH370 on primary radar on that phase of the flight, it would have appeared unremarkable: an aircraft proceeding steadily in a north-westerly direction along a conventional air route, passing through waypoints, likely on its way to India or beyond.

The primary radar tracked MH370 passing through the waypoint VAMPI, then MEKAR, beyond the northern tip of Sumatra. At 10 nautical miles beyond MEKAR, and before it got to the next waypoint, NILAM, MH370 disappeared from primary radar; it had simply gone beyond the usual 250 kilometres radar range, at 2:22am.

Zaharie had planned this part of the flight as a ruse, knowing searchers would, in real time or on playback, consult the primary radar, and see MH370 flying on a straight north-westerly track and official airway until it dropped from radar coverage. Anyone trying to find the aircraft after it disappeared would therefore look on that track – and, at one point in the subsequent search and rescue mission, they did.

But that's not where MH370 actually went.

After flying about 15 minutes farther along the north-west N571 route just to be absolutely sure he had been out of primary radar range for a while, Zaharie turned the aircraft left on a track going almost due south, to the middle of nowhere in the southern Indian Ocean – just like the imaginary flight he had practised on his home computer flight simulator. Zaharie punched into the Flight Management System, or autopilot, a true heading for it to steer of 188 degrees, which would take him far to the south.

At that point, Zaharie thought he had achieved his complex plan of avoiding detection and interception, and could hide the aircraft and the 238 souls in his charge forever. But there was one thing he didn't know – hardly any commercial airline pilots did at that time since it is not used for navigation. Automatic satellite 'handshakes' are sent, in the case of MH370 roughly hourly, from the aircraft to a ground station via a satellite so as to transmit, in this case, engine performance data to aircraft maintenance engineers. Through some clever deduction, scientists were later able to use the satellite hand-shakes to establish the general direction the flight took south, but not the final resting place of the aircraft.

Over the next nearly six hours, Zaharie had little to do since the autopilot was taking the aircraft where he wanted it to. There was no-one on board to talk to – the passengers and crew he was responsible for were piled like rag dolls over one another in their seats in the cabin or lying sprawled out in the aisles. There was no mobile phone coverage, and he made no radio transmissions.

But Zaharie wanted to have a look at his deadly handiwork. One of the mysteries of the flight is that the automatic satellite signals stopped for a period, then started broadcasting again at 2:25am with a 'log-on request'.

As mentioned, Zaharie at the start of the hijack disabled the circuit which powered the cabin lights. But without realising it, he also switched off the automatic satellite communication system known as the satellite data unit or 'SATCOM'. To have a look back in the passenger cabin, he repowered the same circuit, turning the lights back on but also, again unwittingly, reconnected the satellite data unit.

There is a hint in the ATSB reports that this is what happened. It says the SATCOM went down somewhere between the last ACARS message at 1:07am, and an unsuccessful automatic attempt by the satellite ground station to re-establish contact with the aircraft occurred, about an hour later, at 2:03am. An interruption of the SATCOM, the ATSB said, could be due to engines flaming out, or 'intermittent technical failures'. But it could also be the result of pilot intervention, by changing the electrical routing system using switches located in the overhead panel in the cockpit, or via the circuit breakers in the electronic equipment bay being pulled and later reset.

The ATSB concludes the reason the satellite data unit went off in this phase of the flight and then came back on with a log-on request at 2:25am was likely due to a power interruption.

'As this power interruption was not due to engine flame-outs, it is possible that it was due to manual switching of the electrical system,' the ATSB said.

Of course, once Zaharie made the final turn and set the autopilot for the long track south, he knew he could have ended his involvement right there and then. He could have just again reached up and pressed the button turning off the pressurisation; he would know death by hypoxia is a fairly painless, even pleasant way to go in a manner of minutes.

But Zaharie had a very calculated, pre-planned and complex strategy from start to finish to make sure the aircraft would never be found. He wanted to finish the job: fly the aircraft to the end and ditch it in a controlled fashion to see it break up into only a few pieces and sink, rather than create a big debris field by crashing the plane in an uncontrolled dive and hitting the water at high speed. A debris field from an unpiloted crash would have been visible to searching aircraft, or on satellite photo playback.

Zaharie also wanted to run the aircraft out of fuel or very close to it, to avoid an oil slick which, like a debris field, could also give away its final resting place to search aircraft or satellites. Gliding an aircraft to a controlled ditching is entirely doable, especially if the question of whether the pilots, cabin crew and passengers survive is not a concern.

At a bit after 8:00am, having travelled for around seven-and-a-half hours since take-off, MH370 was close to running out of fuel. At that stage, having started in the northern hemisphere, Zaharie had taken the plane to about 38 degrees south, about the latitude of Bass Strait. Zaharie had set the fuel in 'cross feed' mode, in which fuel could flow from the fuller tank to the less full one, so the time taken for the second engine to flame out after the first died from fuel exhaustion was not long.

By that stage, at 40,000 feet, having flown all night, the sun was coming up in the east – not at ground level yet, but at the altitude MH370 was cruising. After both engines flamed out, Zaharie wanted to get the aircraft considerably lower for a variety of reasons.

Firstly, and very practically, with no engine power he would have to get the nose down quickly to maintain a safe airspeed and avoid an aerodynamic stall where he would fall out of the sky. Secondly, although he would again have donned his oxygen mask, without engine power the aircraft would again rapidly decompress, making the cockpit uncomfortably cold and foggy. Thirdly, while any ships below him would still be in darkness, at dawn MH370 would shine out brightly at 40,000 feet; better to again get below the sun and back into the cover of night. Zaharie took manual control of the aircraft and put it into a steep accelerating dive of 20 degrees, equal to an initial descent of 17,500 feet per minute, before converting the kinetic energy of the dive into a glide to take him about 90 nautical miles further before reaching the ocean surface.

Two things happened automatically when MH370 ran out of fuel. The ram air turbine, a fan-like device, deployed from the fuselage into the slipstream, generating just enough hydraulic power and electricity to operate the control surfaces and power the main instruments, but not enough to lower the flaps. But then, a minute or so later, the auxiliary power unit automatically powered up.

The auxiliary power unit is another, smaller jet engine, used not to propel the aircraft forward but to generate enough power to operate the aircraft's primary systems. Pilots have the option of firing it up on the ground before flight to run the plane's basic systems like air conditioning, without having to start the engines. On some aircraft, to start the main engines pilots have to first get the auxiliary power unit going. Importantly, with the auxiliary power unit running, the flaps can be lowered even when the engines have run out of fuel; it is designed to run for a period of some minutes after main engine fuel exhaustion. That enabled Zaharie to complete his plan.

Zaharie ordered the extra fuel and planned the flight precisely so that when he was gliding towards the surface of the ocean, the sun was just coming up at sea level. By the time Zaharie was in the last few thousand feet of his descent, it was not long after dawn but clear daylight.

The weather and sea conditions in that part of the southern Indian Ocean on the morning of 8 March 2014 are fairly well established from satellite reports. Zaharie turned the aircraft into the south-westerly wind. He saw the primary three- to four-metre swell radiating its usual direction northwards from the deep low-pressure weather systems far to the south. There is a well-established protocol professional pilots know when it comes to ditching an aircraft at sea, the aim being to give the aircraft the best chance of minimising damage and staying afloat long enough to get passengers off into life rafts. That involves trying to land the aircraft parallel with the direction of the swell, and on the back of a wave. Zaharie ditched at the top back side of the swell which was running at the time.

A ditching in this direction, with the receding swell on the aircraft's right, meant the right wing hit the swell first. Even with flaps lowered, which enables aircraft to land at lower speeds, the ditching speed was around 250 kilometres per hour, and first the right then the left engines were torn off as they dragged through the water. The right flaps and flaperons, having been fully lowered by Zaharie, progressively dragged along the surface of the water, eroding their trailing edges, before the pressure became too great and they too broke off altogether.

The fuselage broke wide at the weakest part – the forward wing junction – and separated. The aircraft sank with the fuselage in two main chunks. Zaharie was knocked out on impact, nearly dead, and quickly drowned, as he had expected.

And with that, at around 8:30am on 8 March 2014, Zaharie achieved exactly what he wanted to do when he first started modelling it on his home computer flight simulator: in an act of mass murder-suicide, he had made a jetliner, himself and the 238 innocent souls on board vanish without a trace in one of the world's deepest, wildest and most remote stretches of sea.

There have been many confirmed cases of pilot hijack/suicide on commercial airliners, and quite a few other suspected ones. The most infamous in recent years was the 2015 Germanwings Flight 9525, which left Barcelona on 24 March heading for Dusseldorf with 150 people on board. Co-pilot Andreas Lubitz waited until the captain left the cockpit for the toilet, then locked the door and flew the Airbus A320 into the French Alps, killing himself and everyone else.

Spookily, in the 10 minutes from the time Lubitz set the flight management system for 100 feet, until the aircraft crashed, the cockpit voice recorder revealed he did not say a word and his breathing remained normal. This was all while air traffic controllers repeatedly tried to engage with him and the captain banged on the cockpit and shouted. During the very last moment of the cockpit voice recording, passengers can be heard screaming.

The air crash investigation found the young Germanwings first officer had psychological issues that had not been picked up. He apparently feared he was losing his vision, but hid the fact from his employers. In such cases, there's often a big difference between the public persona and the demons that lurk within. Friends and neighbours who knew Lubitz described him as 'quiet' but 'fun', and said he loved flying – just like Zaharie loved flying.

Another prominent case was SilkAir Flight 185. The Boeing 737 took off from Jakarta bound for Singapore, and crashed almost vertically down into the Musi River in southern Sumatra on 19 December 1997, killing all 97 passengers and seven crew on board. In that case, attention focused on the captain, Tsu Way Ming. He had dropped more than $US1.2 million in losses in high-risk securities trading, and taken out a $US600,000 life insurance policy that took effect the day of the crash. His possible stressors were many. Six months earlier Tsu had faced disciplinary action by SilkAir, an airline majority-owned by the Singapore government, for turning off a cockpit voice recorder.

The 19th of December was also the anniversary of a tragedy still haunting Tsu. On that day in 1979, four of his Singapore Air Force colleagues had crashed into a mountain. The ace flyer Tsu had been due to lead the training exercise but pulled out when his Skyhawk developed a fault – the suggestion is that he blamed himself for not being with his colleagues.

The Indonesian government investigation found there was not enough evidence to determine the cause of the crash, but the US National Transportation Safety Board said it was most likely murder-suicide, committed by Tsu.

A similar disagreement between two investigating bodies occurred in EgyptAir Flight 990, flying from Los Angeles to Cairo via New York, on 31 October 1999. It crashed into the ocean off Nantucket Island. The black boxes were recovered, and they record first officer Gameel Al-Batouti repeatedly saying, 'I rely on God,' in Arabic as he pushed the control column forward and shut off the engines, while the captain repeatedly asked, 'What's happening?' The NTSB concluded Batouti deliberately crashed the plane for motives unknown, while the Egyptian investigation settled on elevator failure, something the NTSB said was not consistent with the facts.

This leads on to the big question which has to be asked in the case of MH370: is there anything in Zaharie's background to explain why he would have taken himself and 238 souls in his charge to a watery grave deep in the southern Indian Ocean?

The dominant, though certainly not unanimous, opinion in the international professional aviation community is that the disappearance of MH370 was most probably a case of pilot hijack by Zaharie.

The general view is that most other scenarios, such as terrorist hijack gone wrong, rapid decompression, and onboard fire, require an extraordinarily large number of individual and unlikely occurrences to happen in a certain sequence. Although the promoters of those theories all posit an explanation for why there was no distress call, that element is problematic in the eyes of many professional pilots and air crash investigators. By contrast, the 'pilot hijack' theory basically requires just one thing – for Zaharie to want to do it – and all the other known facts, including the lack of a distress call, fit neatly into place.

But this remains the biggest enigma: what would have motivated Zaharie to meticulously plan, then carry out, such a heinous crime?

There is no one clear answer, but a few tantalising clues.

While there was a lot of good journalistic work done by Malaysian and international reporters investigating Zaharie in the first days and weeks after 8 March 2014, it yielded more smoke than flame as to motive. He was said to have split from his wife, but she denied it, making it another murky case of 'he said/she said'.

An examination of his many social media posts showed Zaharie liked cooking, particularly noodle dishes, though not as much as he liked aviation: one post shows him with some mates playing with a model flying boat on a lake. There was nothing jihadist; he actually posted condolences to the victims of the Boston Marathon bombing in 2013. He seemed to have some interest in debates about atheism and rationalism. There was nothing coming even close to a smoking gun in terms of suicidal, political or terrorist motive. All the interviews with his friends and colleagues described him as a genial, easygoing, fun guy.

The most promising lead was the link with Anwar Ibrahim, the opposition figure and de facto leader of the People's Justice Party in Malaysia, and the fact that hours before the flight Anwar had been convicted of sodomy and sentenced to five years in jail in what was widely seen as a political trial. There were some reports Zaharie had attended the court hearing, but that was never conclusively established. Anwar, who was free in the days after the disappearance of MH370 pending appeal, was grilled by media outlets about the connections.

Anwar said Zaharie was certainly a supporter, as a member of his political party, and he recognised him from photos of party meetings. He said he had been unable to establish whether Zaharie had been in court on the day, but said friends had said the pilot had been upset and disgusted by the conviction. Finally, Anwar said he had determined Zaharie was a distant relative of his daughter-in-law. But Anwar said the suggestion Zaharie had taken 238 people to their deaths as a protest against his conviction was absurd and grossly unfair.

The Australian's South-east Asia correspondent, Amanda Hodge, spoke to Sivarasa Rasiah, a People's Justice Party MP and long-time lawyer for Anwar.

In a joint article, Hodge and I reported Sivarasa saying he had befriended Zaharie after he joined the party ahead of the 2013 elections, in which Anwar's party won the popular vote but lost the election. The two men bonded after belting out a particularly tortured karaoke duet of 'Hotel California' at a party fundraising effort in 2012 and Sivarasa says they just 'sort of took to each other'. The last time he remembers catching up with the amiable pilot was when Zaharie dropped in with a bottle of Chivas Regal for the Indian Malaysian MP during the Hindu festival of Deepavali.

'Pilot suicide is rubbish as far as I'm concerned. Absolutely no way,' Sivarasa told *The Australian*. 'I knew he had marital issues. Everyone in his circle knew.'

Sivarasa also dismissed the idea that his friend might have hijacked the plane in fury at Anwar's second sodomy conviction, handed down just five hours before MH370 took off. There would have been no time to plan for such an event from the time Anwar was convicted at 7:30pm to the time the Beijing-bound flight became airborne. Sivarasa said he was 'quite sure' Zaharie was not present in court on the day Anwar was convicted.

The other nagging problem with the theory that Zaharie hijacked the plane as a protest is that whoever was at the controls issued no public communication of any sort that this was a political statement.

Malaysian political scientist Wong Chin Huat told CNN at the time that while it was quite reasonable to query the motivations of everyone possibly involved, he thought any link with Malaysian domestic politics was 'a red herring'.

'Had the captain intended to cause this incident in protest, there should be clearly some clue. It's pointless to make a political statement in silence,' he said.

A mentionable fact in the mix is that among those Australian next-of-kin with whom I have spoken, there is no resolve to blame Zaharie. Danica Weeks said she was reluctant, in the absence of concrete evidence, to accept Zaharie took down MH370, and with it her husband Paul.

'I just think it's unfair to crucify someone without the proof,' she said.

Like Danica, Zaharie's wife had lost her husband. Danica said to further heap innuendo on the family by alleging pilot hijack would be unfair.

The next-of-kin have become hunters of their own for MH370. They have been studying aviation, the Boeing 777 and precedents, and following the theories. Danica favours another scenario canvassed later in the book, of onboard fire.

'I believe there was an incident on the plane, possibly exploding oxygen tanks, and the pilot tried to turn the plane back to Kuala Lumpur. Hypoxia set in and the plane flew on for seven hours,' Danica said. She said if the plane had been hijacked, Paul would have intervened. 'He's a big strong guy, he's from the army. He'd be there. He would have fought tooth and nail.'

Jeanette Maguire, whose sister Cathy Lawton disappeared on MH370, has similar inclinations.

As to Zaharie, she said, 'I can't lay blame. I feel for the families when there is no proof. It's unfair to blame someone who can't defend themselves.' Rather, Jeanette said, 'my first thought was fire. The ACARS has to be shut down if there's a fire. There was something which happened on board, they had to turn everything off to isolate this fire,' she said. 'I thought of a hijacking, but no-one was coming forward, and that sort of scenario would be harder to comprehend after 9/11.'

Jeanette said she spent a lot of time talking to ATSB officials and they were, she said, 'very good with my theories and understanding airplanes and how they work'.

'That's how I spent the first couple of years, investigating, trying to do my own type scenarios. I have done nothing but google airplanes since that day.'

One good practice in journalism is to, months or even years after the immediate circus of a massive international story with a mystery to it breaks, revisit it to see with the passage of time who will now talk, and what might now be found out.

In late 2018, multi award–winning journalist Paul Toohey, with whom I worked at *The Australian*, had another look at Zaharie's social media activity, particularly on Facebook. What he found and published in Sydney's *The Sunday Telegraph* suggested two of the characteristics already known about the pilot – that he intensely liked younger women and intensely disliked the Malaysian Prime Minister – were far more pronounced than had previously been made out.

'Zaharie was not merely politically active, as some have said,' Toohey wrote. 'He was virulent, at one point labelling then prime minister Najib Razak a "moron" on his Facebook page.'

More salaciously, Toohey revealed, in 2013 Zaharie had apparently developed an obsession with Penang-based model Qi Min Lan, also known as Jasmin Min, who had turned 18 that year.

Zaharie did not know the young woman personally – and she never responded to his posts – but he was 'fixated', Toohey wrote.

The pilot's posts on Facebook directed at the model included 'you're hot', 'tasty', and 'gorgeous'.

Toohey quoted psychologists who said the pattern of behaviour demonstrated obsessiveness and recklessness.

Two years earlier, *The Australian*'s Amanda Hodge had found a woman Zaharie did know personally, and was clearly deeply involved with in one way or other. Through good old-fashioned journalistic legwork, Hodge in September 2016 got the sensational break on Zaharie which opened up a new direction for the MH370 debate.

Hodge tracked down Fatima Pardi, a former kindergarten teacher and then a worker with the People's Justice Party. She told Hodge she met Zaharie when he joined the party and began attending political events. Pardi said Zaharie had become her mentor and a father figure for her children, one of whom suffers from severe cerebral palsy.

She insisted it was not a sexual affair.

'Of course there was gossip, people will always talk whether you're good or you're bad,' Pardi told Hodge. 'People think I am the "other woman". But we were close because the children loved him.'

The relationship ended a few months before the plane went missing, but Pardi claimed to have had a WhatsApp exchange with Zaharie two days before the flight.

'That last conversation was just between me and him. I don't want to talk about it,' Pardi told Hodge.

'I'm afraid what I say will be misunderstood,' she said. 'It was a personal matter, a private issue.'

She added that Zaharie had not seemed stressed.

Hodge's interview with Pardi was, literally, a world exclusive; the Malaysian woman had not spoken to the media before. Pardi told Hodge the only reason she did so was to dispel any thought Zaharie was the sort of man who would take 238 people to their deaths; she said he was fine and generous.

'We both wanted to make a change for our country. That's why we were involved in politics,' she said.

'We talked about family, we talked about interests and that's how he got close with me and my children.'

Zaharie himself had three grown-up children, in their 20s at the time of MH370's vanishing.

Zaharie's elder sister Sakinab Shah has described her brother — the eighth of nine children and the family favourite — as an enormously affectionate individual 'who loved life, loved fun'.

She acknowledged, in an interview with Hodge, that her brother and his wife, Faizah, had 'normal' marital problems, but said he wore his troubles lightly. Sakinab Shah confirmed Pardi had contacted her after MH370 went missing and that the two had met, but she was one of several of her brother's women friends she had met over the years.

'Honestly, I have met many, many other friends of his. A lot of times I gave him a telling-off about this. It was never anything serious,' she said. 'He was naughty, I admit that, but at the end of the day he always went home.'

So, when it comes to one clear, decisive, indisputable reason or motive for Zaharie to hijack his own aircraft and kill all on board, the professional investigators, the journalistic community and the international MH370 club addicts are still looking for one.

The thing about a lot of truly dreadful crimes, though, is that the driver may be hidden, even to the perpetrator. While modern society likes to find clear explanations, believes they must be there, and feels better when they are found, sometimes, experts say, they just aren't.

In a story looking at the Germanwings case, the BBC explored what motivates aviation mass murder-suicide. The broadcaster quoted Simon Wessely, president of the Royal College of Psychiatrists, saying sometimes it's just too hard to tell.

'It's possible something will emerge, but in most suicides people leave clues or a message. Incredibly extreme events like this are sometimes just inexplicable.'

The disappearance of Malaysia Airlines Flight MH370 remains baffling today, just as it was to Malaysian authorities in the early hours of 8 March 2014, and the days after that.

TWO

INTO THIN AIR

The night of Friday, 7 March 2014, was one of the rare times when Malaysia's civil aviation boss's mobile phone ran out of power.

Azharuddin Abdul Rahman, then chief of the Civil Aviation Department, had been to a family dinner: his niece was to be married at the weekend, and it had been a festive pre-wedding get together, so he was ready for sleep. He put his phone on charge, and went to bed without waiting for it to acquire enough power to start up again.

It was only after pre-dawn prayers next morning that he switched on his phone. A flood of messages started streaming in, and Azharuddin stared at the screen in disbelief as they appeared by the dozen. As he later related in the excellent 2018 British television documentary *MH370: Inside the Situation Room*: 'I straightaway told my wife, something is not right.'

That turned out to be the understatement of the year. At that point Azharuddin did not know Malaysia Airlines Flight MH370 had vanished into thin air. He also had no idea that MH370 would ultimately cost him his job, four years later.

Azharuddin made some calls and asked some of his senior officers to meet him at the Sama-Sama Hotel where the first press conference was to be held. In a 2018 interview with the *New Straits Times*, Azharuddin described his thoughts at the time.

'I said to myself: "My God, a Triple Seven . . . that's a big jet". Initially, I thought it was just another airplane that went off our radar scopes . . . but in this industry, we are trained to prepare for the worst-case scenario.'

The air traffic controllers under Azharuddin's authority should have been trained better for the worst-case scenario; when MH370 disappeared, disbelief, confusion and panic set in.

After advising MH370 to switch to Ho Chi Minh control, and hearing Zaharie acknowledge with 'Good night, Malaysian Three Seven Zero' at 1:19am, Kuala Lumpur controllers' interest in the flight had waned, as they assumed their Vietnamese counterparts were on the case. Their attention was jolted back pretty quickly when, at 1:39am, Ho Chi Minh air traffic controllers said MH370 had not contacted them and, even more alarming, secondary radar contact was lost at BITOD, a waypoint not far after IGARI. The segments below are from the official transcript of the air traffic control communications as published by the Malaysian safety investigation, verbatim except for the removal of some surperfluous pauses like 'eer' or 'ahhh'. The transcription may not have been perfect from the sometimes scratchy recordings, and the controllers and other officials were talking in the international language of aviation – English – which was not their native tongue. But the gist of the content and tenor are clear.

Ho Chi Minh air traffic control (HCM): Any information on
Malaysian Three Seven Zero, sir?
Kuala Lumpur air traffic control (KL): Malaysian Three Seven Zero
already transfer to you right?
HCM: Yeah, yeah, I know at time two zero. But we have

no . . . just about in contact . . . after BITOD we have no . . .
radar lost with him. The other one here to track identified on
my radar.

KL: Okay at what point?

HCM: And no contact right now.

KL: At what point?

HCM: Yeah.

KL: At what point?

HCM: Yeah.

KL: At what point you lost contact?

HCM: BITOD.

KL: BITOD, hah.

HCM: Yeah.

KL: BITOD. Okay. Call you back.

This communication was 19 minutes after Zaharie should have contacted Ho Chi Minh controllers and when they should have taken over responsibility for guiding the flight. The agreement governing air traffic control between the two countries specifies that 'the accepting unit shall notify the transferring unit if two-way communication is not established within five (5) minutes of the estimated time over the Transfer of Control Point'. That is, if the MH370 pilots had not radioed Ho Chi Minh control by 1:25am, five minutes after the transfer was to have taken place, those Vietnamese controllers should have contacted Kuala Lumpur to ask what was going on. Instead, they waited another 14 minutes. By this time, MH370 was flying back over Malaysia. The controllers in Ho Chi Minh and Kuala Lumpur could not have known that though and, with a disappeared airliner on their hands, they desperately tried to work out what had happened to it.

At 1:41am, Ho Chi Minh again asked for information on MH370, and the reply was that, after IGARI, MH370 did not return to the Kuala Lumpur frequency. Seconds later, a Kuala Lumpur controller made a 'blind transmission' to MH370. That's when there has been a break in communications, and the controller wants to contact an aircraft not with any specific navigational instruction but just to re-establish contact.

'Malaysia Three Seven Zero, do you read?' the controller asked.

There was no response. Five minutes after that, the Vietnamese controllers told their Malaysian counterparts they had tried to contact the aircraft numerous times over 20 minutes. Clearly alarmed, the controllers tried other things – making calls on other frequencies including emergency channels, and through other aircraft in the area, asking their pilots to try to reach MH370 by relay, with no result. The note of panic, and positioning of whose fault this looming crisis was, can be detected in the transcript.

At 1:58am, the following exchange took place:

HCM: Could you check back for your side?
KL: Okay we will do that, and the first, at IGARI did you ever in contact with the aircraft or not first place?
HCM: Negative sir, we have radar contact only, not verbal contact.
KL: But no, when aircraft passed IGARI did the aircraft call you?
HCM: Negative sir.
KL: Negative? Why you didn't tell me first within five minutes? You should have called me.
HCM: After BITOD seven minutes we have no radar contact, then ask you.

As 2:00am came round, it had been 40 minutes since the aircraft had, as far as the controllers could see, vanished from the face of the earth, but then red herrings started to further confuse the situation.

Kuala Lumpur controllers had been in discussions with Malaysia Airlines' operations centre, and relayed to the Vietnamese that they had been informed MH370 was in Cambodian airspace. But the Ho Chi Minh controllers queried that, saying they had been in touch with their counterparts in Phnom Penh who had no word on MH370 and were just as much in the dark – the flight plan did not call for the aircraft to transit Cambodia. Kuala Lumpur said they would check back with their supervisor.

The misinformation reflected a grievously wrong assumption at the Malaysia Airlines operations centre. The officers there were confident they knew where MH370 was because the aircraft was able to exchange signals with the Flight Explorer aircraft tracking website, or so they thought.

Communications between the Malaysian and Vietnamese controllers sometimes ran into difficulties, the Malaysian safety investigation report found. Kuala Lumpur asked whether Ho Chi Minh was taking 'radio failure action' but, the investigation report said, 'the query didn't seem to be understood by the personnel'.

Malaysia Airlines operations officers repeatedly expressed confidence they could track MH370 even if radio communications and satellite phone and fax contact was lost, and insisted it was still steadily moving on Flight Explorer. At 2:20am, the Ho Chi Minh controller said that was all very well, but from where they sat, MH370 had 'disappeared'. The Kuala Lumpur controller replied 'Disappeared, okay,' but a couple of minutes later added, 'Nah, I am not sure, but the company already sent a signal to the aircraft to contact the relevant air traffic control unit'. This refers to another element confusing the controllers – not only did Malaysia Airlines tell them MH370 was still flying and sending tracking signals to Flight Explorer, but that they had sent a signal to the aircraft which the equipment showed had been successfully transmitted, even if there was no reply.

The Kuala Lumpur controllers started to recognise this was more than a glitch, and in turn worried about whether Malaysia Airlines' operations officers fully appreciated the gravity of the situation.

They urged the pursuit of every possible means to contact the pilots, including by satellite phone and fax.

In an exchange at 2:34am, more than an hour after contact was lost, a controller contacted Malaysia Airlines (MAS) operations.

> KL: This is MAS Operations, is it?
> MAS: Ya ya.
> KL: Okay . . . regarding your Malaysian Three Seven Zero . . .
> MAS: Herha.
> KL: Ho Chi Minh said still negative contact.
> MAS: Haa.
> KL: And the no radar target at all.
> MAS: Okay.

As the night wore on, the Malaysians started using a uniquely Malaysian English quirk: ending sentences with 'la'. It has various uses, but most often is used for emphasis, to communicate that something is serious and you want to the listener to pay attention. It's used in a similar way to how in some English-speaking countries one might use the word 'man' – 'If you have your own best interests at heart, you'll do it, man!'

> KL: Can you, I mean is there . . . any possible for the aircraft to answer you?
> MAS: Eer . . .
> KL: Any way aircraft can answer you?
> MAS: Do know . . . you have to try the satcom, la, Sir.
> KL: Hmm.
> MAS: Will try the satcom and see.
> KL: Okay . . . see whether they can, I am sure, whether the position or whether they contact with anyone and the estimate for landing or anything.
> MAS: Okay.

KL: Okay and, okay, because, Ho Chi Minh still worry because
they have completely no contact at all, either radio or radar.

At 2:36am, when the aircraft had been out of contact for an hour and 15 minutes, Malaysia Airlines operations said MH370 was 'somewhere in Vietnam' and gave coordinates based on Flight Explorer to Kuala Lumpur controllers, who in turn relayed them to Ho Chi Minh.

Fuad Sharuji, Malaysia Airlines' crisis director, got a call at about 2:30am. Being woken up to deal with one problem or another was a regular part of the job, but being told a Boeing 777 had disappeared altogether was not.

Sharuji opened up his laptop, accessed the flight systems, saw there were four other aircraft that were in the vicinity of where MH370 was supposed to be, and to his shock and amazement, found MH370 just wasn't there at all.

At 2:40am, Malaysia Airlines operations made a satellite telephone call to the pilots – it went unanswered. Malaysia Airlines was starting to realise it had a serious problem – it just didn't know what.

Just before 3am, 30 minutes after that first phone call, Sharuji declared a code red emergency.

'You really need three people to agree to declare code red because that is the most serious crisis for us. But because my CEO was not available and the director of operations was not immediately contactable, I had to make the big decision by myself,' Sharuji told *StrategicRISK Asia-Pacific* in 2016.

With the airline's crisis procedure protocol put into action, within an hour most of its top officers had arrived to set up shop in its Emergency Operations Centre in Kuala Lumpur. They looked at the aircraft maintenance log, and it recorded no known technical problems. They checked whether MH370 was carrying any dangerous goods – that too came up blank.

What flummoxed the Malaysia Airlines officials was that Flight

Explorer kept showing the aircraft blithely tracking on its planned course towards Beijing.

Then the penny dropped.

Perhaps a senior Malaysia Airlines officer, woken up and called in during the middle of the night, was told by his subordinates something like, 'It's all right, sir, Flight Explorer shows MH370 is on course', to which the senior officer might have replied, 'You bloody idiots . . .'

In any event, at 3:30am, the Malaysian safety investigation report says, the operations officers at Malaysia Airlines told the Kuala Lumpur control shift supervisor they now realised 'the flight tracker information was based on flight projection and was not reliable for aircraft positioning'.

In other words, Flight Explorer was not tracking where MH370 actually was in real time at all, but rather where it should be if the flight had proceeded normally.

And it had not proceeded normally for some time. By this stage, MH370 had flown back across the Malay Peninsula to Penang, turned north-west up the Straits of Malacca, gone out of radar range, and at some point turned south on a track to the southern Indian Ocean.

There were other communications among Malaysian and Vietnamese controllers, Malaysia Airlines and controllers in other countries over the next couple of hours. Kuala Lumpur asked Ho Chi Minh, have you contacted Hainan, the next air traffic control sector? Had Hong Kong or Beijing heard anything? Singapore air traffic control, on behalf of Hong Kong, asked if there had been any news of MH370.

At 5:20am, four hours after the aircraft's disappearance, the Malaysian safety investigation report says when a senior Malaysia airlines captain asked for information on MH370, he opined that based on known information, 'MH370 never left Malaysian airspace'.

It was in some respects the most sensible, logical observation of the night, and it may be what finally prompted Malaysian controllers to belatedly accept the obvious and act on it. Ten minutes later, the Malaysian control watch supervisor contacted the Kuala Lumpur Aeronautical Rescue Coordination Centre to say Malaysia Airlines Flight MH370 was missing. Azharuddin later said the four-hour delay in sounding the alarm was primarily the fault of Vietnamese controllers, who were responsible for the aircraft after the planned handover at IGARI.

The scheduled arrival time for MH370 in Beijing was 6:30am, and Malaysian authorities were still hoping that, by some miracle, it might just land safely and report some malfunctions in the communications systems. Ahmad Jauhari said in *MH370: Inside the Situation Room*:

'Six-thirty was the time the aircraft was supposed to land at Beijing, we are still hoping the aircraft will appear. But 6:30 came, and there's no aircraft. You know, we felt terrible – sick, really.'

Two minutes later, at 6:32am, the Rescue Coordination Centre issued what's known as a DETRESFA message, shown below.

FIGURE 2: DETRESFA MESSAGE

```
KLA637 072232
SS WMKKZQZX WMKKZRZX
072232 WMFCZQZX
(ALR-DESTRESFA/WMFCZQZX/MISSING
-FPL-MAS370-IS
-B772/H-SDFGHIJ3J5M1RWXY/LB1D1
-WMKK1635
-N0470F290 DCT PIBOS R208 IKUKO/M081F330 R208 IGARI M765
 BITOD/N0480F330 L637 TSN/N0480F350 W1 BMT W12 PCA G221
 BUNTA/N0480F370 A1 IKELA/N0480F370 P901 IDOSI/N0480F390 DCT CH
 DCT BEKOL/K0900S1160 A461 YIN/K0890S1130 A461 VYK
-ZBAA0534 ZBTJ ZBSJ
-PBN/A1B1C1D1L1O1S2 DOF/140307 REG/9MMRO EET/WSJC0032 VVTS0042
 ZJSA0210 VHHK0233 ZGZU0304 ZHWH0356 ZPE0450 SEL/QRCS
 RMK/ACASII EQUIPPED
-E/0710 P/TBN R/UVE S/M J/LF D/8 290 GREY A/WHITE WITH RED AND
 BLUE STRIPE C/TBN)
```

DETRESFA is the code word used to designate a 'distress phase' in aviation. It's defined under ICAO protocols as 'a situation wherein there is a reasonable certainty that an aircraft and its occupants are threatened by grave and imminent danger and require immediate assistance.' It takes the form of an international coded message – almost impossible for a layman to decipher – with a set of information according to an established protocol. In the MH370 DETRESFA message, the key word is 'MISSING'. It listed the type of aircraft, the airline and flight number, the aircraft's registration number 9M-MRO, the last contact at IGARI, and finished off with a brief description of the plane's livery: 'GREY A/WHITE WITH RED AND BLUE STRIPE'. The DETRESFA signal went out nearly six hours after MH370 took off, and more than five hours after it disappeared from radar screens around South-east Asia, and from radio and ACARS communications.

At 7:14am, when MH370 would have had only about an hour's fuel left, Malaysia Airlines operations tried another satellite telephone call to the pilots – it too went unanswered. MH370 had covered most of its track to its end point in the southern Indian Ocean. If, in the Theory One 'Rogue Pilot to the End' scenario, Zaharie was still flying the plane, he would no doubt have been thinking 'it worked . . . I've done it . . . they don't know where I am.'

The Malaysian Air Force hadn't shown up, the radio transmissions asking him to respond, including from Ho Chi Minh controllers and aircraft flying in the general area where he should have been but was not, showed the authorities were clueless about where he really was and what he was doing.

If he had hijacked the plane, Zaharie must have thought he'd got away with it.

THREE
THOUGHTS AND PRAYERS

The situation of a big airliner with more than 200 people on board not showing up at its destination on time is not, of itself, unusual. But if an aircraft does not show up on time, and the airline cannot tell those waiting at the airport for loved ones when or even if it will arrive, that is highly unusual.

At Beijing's Capital International Airport on Saturday, 8 March 2014, at the top of the big 'arrivals' board all morning, a line of red text read: 'Flight MH370, from Kuala Lumpur, STA 6:30. Delayed.'

People started gathering below the board – friends and relatives of those waiting for those on MH370 to arrive, journalists who had heard whispers and then shouts the aircraft was missing, and policemen keen, in the Chinese communist way, to keep order.

'I'm very, very worried now,' Zhai Le, who was to meet a group of friends off MH370 and then set off on holidays with them, told reporters at the scene.

Some relatives started becoming hysterical when no-one could tell them what was going on. A cameraman was reported punched by one of them.

Chinese authorities don't like such scenes, and got buses to load up relatives and take them to a hotel about 15 kilometres away, to be out of sight and briefed if and when new information arrived.

Just after 1:00pm, the line of red text saying MH370 was 'Delayed' just disappeared without explanation.

It was clear to Malaysian authorities they had to say something official. Late morning, Malaysia Airlines issued a statement saying the aircraft was missing, and that it would hold a news conference soon. Like other major media groups, CNN didn't wait for the press conference – they went straight to air.

'This is Piers Morgan live. Breaking news tonight, a Malaysia Airlines plane carrying 239 people, bound for Beijing, is missing,' the bulletin started. 'According to a statement from the airline, air traffic control lost contact with Flight MH370, from Kuala Lumpur at 2:40am, about two hours after take-off. We are awaiting a press briefing from the airline, which of course we will bring you live when it happens.'

It was the chief executive of Malaysia Airlines, Ahmad Jauhari Yahya, who had the horrifying task of fronting up and officially breaking the extraordinary news at the press conference.

'We are deeply saddened this morning,' Ahmad Jauhari told journalists.

He outlined details of the flight and who in general terms was known to be on it, who the captain and first officer were, and said the focus was to work with the emergency response.

'Our thoughts and prayers are with all affected passengers and crew and their family members.'

It was an extraordinary story: a big airliner, 239 people, and the operative words 'missing' or 'disappeared'.

'An international search and rescue operation is underway after a passenger jet disappeared over the South China Sea early this morning,' was how one British presenter broke the news to her television audience.

But not everyone is glued to television or radio news, or internet news sites. For some of those whose husbands, wives, sisters, brothers, and in a few cases children, came to disappear on a regular scheduled flight, the horror of what had happened came in ways they still break down in telling.

For Danica and Paul Weeks, 7 March 2014 was the day all their luck seemed to be going the right way.

'Everything was great,' Danica told me in an interview near her home on Queensland's Sunshine Coast. 'We had two little boys, I had a beautiful husband, he had this great job.'

The couple lived in Perth, and Paul was headed to Beijing for induction to a big assignment for a major mining project in Mongolia. It was his big break as an engineer.

Danica and Paul had been together for 14 years. They first hooked up when they were both young, expatriate Antipodeans, doing the usual 'grand tour' of living in Britain on two-year working visas and seeing Europe.

'We met at the Munich Beer Fest,' Danica said of how she first found her husband. With a bit of a smirk, she added, 'I moved in with him two weeks later.' That lovenest was in Turnpike Lane, London, N8 0DU, in the year 2000.

Paul had grown up in Christchurch, and been a mechanic in the New Zealand army. After the sojourn in Europe, he wanted to go home and enrol in university to study mechanical engineering. Though her family had moved to Queensland's Sunshine Coast when she was 10, Danica was also originally a New Zealander, having been born in the North Island town of Napier, so the move to Christchurch was to familiar territory.

The couple lived in Christchurch for 10 years, with Danica, a chartered professional accountant, putting Paul through university, after which he made a good living doing energy audits on buildings. Then the family's first external calamity arose.

'I had Lincoln during the first earthquake,' Danica explained. 'After that they didn't need energy audits on buildings because the buildings were collapsing.'

So, the couple moved to Perth, just as the mining boom started to get into gear. After working in the sector for some years, Paul was made an extraordinary offer. A contact at Rio Tinto was heading to Mongolia to work on the Oyu Tolgoi copper and gold mine in the Gobi Desert. He invited Paul to come to Oyu Tolgoi to work as a supervisor, Danica said, as the company was having challenges on the site.

'He wanted Paul to come and sort it out,' Danica said. 'He was really excited, it was his dream job.'

The deal was that Paul would work 28 days on, 14 days off. Given how hard he worked in Western Australia, Danica said, though the absences would be long, the fortnight of concentrated family time sounded good.

For the Weeks family, it looked like the start of a dream run. Danica drove Paul to the airport, with her sons Lincoln, aged three and a half at the time, and Jack, 11 months, in the back getting ready to head on to Lincoln's soccer training.

'I dropped him off, we told each other we loved each other,' Danica recounted. 'I remember crying, because it was a change for us – he was going for 28 days. I bawled my eyes out.' Danica observed that all couples have their own sayings – some trite, some schmalzy. Theirs was 'the cream always rises to the top', and they said it to each other before Paul headed onto the flight to Kuala Lumpur. Danica says she stills sees Paul's departure in her mind's eye.

'He just walks out that door, and that's that.'

THE HUNT FOR MH370

'To me, March 8, 2014 was like yesterday,' Danica said.

The television in the kitchen wasn't working, so while she might have kept an eye on it otherwise, she was just pottering around with household chores and having coffee with her mum as she did most Saturdays at the local shopping centre.

Later that afternoon the phone rang. A woman on the other end of the line asked after Paul. When Danica said he wasn't there and she hadn't spoken with him, the woman on the phone – a reporter from the *New Zealand Herald* – then asked: 'You haven't heard there has been an incident with the plane?'

'I just dropped the phone, I went into hysterics, I just ran out the door and fell on the grass,' Danica related. 'I thought it had crashed.' Paul's mother was living just down the road and heard the shrieks, recognised Danica's voice, and rushed over. Danica tried to get a grip.

'The plane's missing. I thought, okay, it's just missing. Gather yourself.'

Paul's brother Peter was staying with their mother down the road, and was assigned to check that the flight in question, Malaysia Airlines Flight MH370, was indeed Paul's flight.

'He just came back and said yes, it's his plane.'

Fortunately, Danica's mother and stepdad were living in their caravan in Perth at the time, as part of their five-year travels around Australia.

'She's the only one who got me through all this,' Danica said. 'Mum and I just sat on the couch crying and screaming.'

Danica said later in the day Lincoln came into the bathroom while she was in the shower and asked, 'What's wrong?'

'I said "Daddy is missing darling". He said "don't worry, Mum, I find him".'

Still hysterical and in a daze, it was then Danica called Lincoln's best friend's mother and asked if she could have Lincoln over to stay for a few nights as she feared the emotional toll it would take on her young son as the whirlwind of reporters descended on her house.

Danica debated what to do about the journalists camped outside – there were not, all up, that many Australian next-of-kin whose family members had disappeared on MH370, making those who were, prime targets for media interviews.

Danica said she sought counsel from friends from her London days who were in Perth as to whether she should speak to the media, and they put to her, 'if you are up to doing it, I think you should'.

Danica went out to talk to the media scrum, saying to herself, 'I am doing it for Pauly, I want him found. I think this is the way to do it.'

She says it was one of the best moves she made, empowering her both immediately and over the coming years.

Danica described the media as 'totally respectful' and 'amazing with me'.

'Here I am a housewife, working part time,' she said. 'I didn't have a voice to talk, the media gave that to me.'

It helped a bit in dealing with the extraordinary circumstances of having sent her husband off on a trip on a major airline one day, and learning a day later he had disappeared on a big modern airliner which just vanished without explanation.

'Everything since then is like a blur, and there is nothing more I know from that day.'

'I made Mum sleep in my bed for four months afterwards.'

For Brisbane couples Cathy and Bob Lawton, and Mary and Rodney Burrows, it was to be the ultimate break: a five-week overseas trip in which each of the four of them got to tick off at least one item on their 'bucket list' of places they wanted to see in their lifetimes.

The Lawton and Burrows families had become deeply intertwined over many years; the link began when the Lawtons' second of three daughters, Amanda, became friends at school with the Burrows' eldest son, Jayden. The itinerary of the trip the two middle-aged couples planned to take together reflected an aggregate of circumstances, special longings and cost considerations.

'Originally Cathy really wanted to go to Alaska, and it was the money that put her off such an expensive trip,' Cathy Lawton's sister Jeanette Maguire said in an interview at her home in the Brisbane western suburb of Forest Lake where she lives with her husband Shaun and their children.

Cathy and Jeanette's nephew had married a Vietnamese girl and they lived in Vietnam. Cathy had really wanted to go to the wedding, but couldn't make it.

'She decided, "I never got to visit Vietnam then, so let's go",' Jeanette said.

The plan was to fly to Beijing, travel to Hong Kong, and take a 'celebrity millennium cruise' to Vietnam.

'That was a last-minute decision to go to China; Cathy wanted to see the Great Wall, and the Burrows said sure, we'll go there as well,' Jeanette said.

Kuala Lumpur was then tacked on because Bob's cousin lived there. All up, it had the lot.

'They were so excited,' Jeanette said of her sister and brother-in-law's anticipation. 'They had been talking about it constantly. They were coming up to their twenty-fifth wedding anniversary.'

It had been an at times hard road for the couple, who married as childhood sweethearts when Cathy was 19. Bob worked for a plywood company, and Cathy as a commercial artist – until some tragic quirks of health stopped her.

'Cathy was born blind with glaucoma,' Jeanette said. 'They operated on her when she was a baby, and she gained full sight in one eye. They scarred the other eye.' Cathy grew up very visually impaired. She had to wear glasses, and she struggled in the classroom.

Over the course of her life, Cathy's eye colour changed slightly, three times: she had to have three cornea transplants, and the matches to the original were the best available but naturally a bit different.

'Her glaucoma was under control until it came back when she fell pregnant with their first child,' Jeanette said. 'That was the horrific part. She couldn't go back to work after she had Glenda. She couldn't see well enough, although she used a big magnifying glass.'

'She never had any self-pity . . . She was always clear on what she wanted and how to get there.'

The last time Jeanette saw her sister was on the Sunday before MH370 disappeared.

'We celebrated her birthday. Went out for lunch,' Jeanette said.

The following Saturday, Jeanette was preparing to attend her children's first soccer game of the season. 'The phone rang, it was my niece Glenda, and she said, "Mum and Dad's plane has gone missing."

'I said, "How do you know?"

'She said, "Mum and Dad's close friend was working and saw a live post come up. They knew the itinerary."

'I said, "Shaun, turn the TV on, turn the TV on."'

Jeanette asked if her mother – Glenda's grandmother – had been told. Then she instructed Glenda to gather everyone together at her grandmother's house. 'Shaun was asking me what was going on, and I couldn't get the words out,' Jeanette said. She checked the itinerary to make sure they had the right flight. 'Then I lost it. It was tough.'

Jeanette was determined to keep life normal for her family until more was known, and insisted Shaun take the boys to soccer.

Cathy and Jeanette's elder sister Eileen was on a family day trip to Mount Tambourine, and she asked them to pick her up on their way back through.

'I couldn't drive, I think I had gone into a state of shock. I was just falling apart, minute by minute.'

Jeanette and Shaun Maguire had a particularly good set of neighbours.

'We knocked on the door and I couldn't speak. I felt like I'd been drugged.'

One neighbour made calls on Jeanette's behalf, including to the Department of Foreign Affairs. Then Eileen arrived with her family, and took Jeanette to their mother's house.

'Cathy's face came up on the TV – they had hacked her Facebook page, it was devastating.'

Jeanette spent the first four days at her parents' house, ringing Malaysia Airlines and asking if Cathy had boarded the plane.

'They told us they couldn't tell us anything.'

One evening, while sitting in recliners and watching the initial stages of the search on TV, Jeanette said, 'I don't know why they are searching there, the plane's gone left. I don't know, I just felt it.'

FOUR

'STILL, THERE WAS NOTHING. TOTALLY NOTHING'

When Malaysian Prime Minister Najib Razak ordered authorities to launch a full-on search and rescue mission to find MH370 and the 239 souls aboard, the question was where to look.

The authorities did not have a lot to go on. They did not know what had happened to the aircraft – no distress call had been issued advising of any onboard problems. They did not know where it was – it disappeared over water in the middle of the night, and there were no eyewitness accounts of an aircraft coming down. And they did not know whether or not some or all of those on the flight might still be alive.

What they did know was that at 1:19am, Zaharie had transmitted his final words, 'Good night, Malaysian Three Seven Zero', and then the aircraft had passed through waypoint IGARI in the South China Sea. And they knew that moments thereafter, MH370 disappeared from controllers' screens, meaning its secondary radar transponder must in some way have been disabled. With so little information to hand, the Malaysian authorities decided there was no other logical course of action than to start looking in the last place the aircraft was heard from by radio and secondary radar: the South China Sea around IGARI.

Malaysia's defence minister and acting transport minister at the time, Hishammuddin Hussein, thought that while the disappearance of MH370 was tragic, finding it or its remains would be relatively straightforward.

'I wasn't too worried because you have got fishermen, you have liners,' he said in *MH370: Inside the Situation Room*. 'This is an area that is reasonably easy to identify where, if the plane did go down, where it went down.' Hishammuddin's thought process was entirely logical, but as with everything else that followed, logic was overturned several times when it came to MH370.

The international search effort geared up big and fast, with aircraft and ships from Malaysia and its regional neighbours weighing in, along with the US and Australia.

Australia sent two RAAF AP-3C Orion maritime patrol aircraft to join the search.

'This is a tragic mystery as things stand but Australia will do what it can to help get to the bottom of this,' Prime Minister Tony Abbott said.

China deployed two well-equipped warships, *Jinggangshan* and *Mianyang*, adjusted its satellites to help focus in on the search area, and sent more ships.

Vietnam sent surveillance aircraft and ships and, in a move reflecting the cooperative international quality of the effort, allowed China, an on-off enemy, to sail its ships into Vietnamese waters.

The Philippine Navy sent *Gregorio del Pilar*, *Emilio Jacinto*, *Apolinario Mabini* and search and rescue aircraft.

Indonesia announced that it would send five ships, while launching fast patrol vessels straight away.

Singapore's Air Force got a C-130 Hercules in the air, and two more C-130s on Sunday, and the government dispatched several ships.

The US Seventh Fleet deployed a P-3C Orion craft from Kadena Base in Okinawa, two destroyers with helicopters on board, and a support vessel.

The immediate search area was a 50 nautical mile radius around the last point of contact at IGARI.

It was a massive international search effort, but all it turned up was a series of false alarms.

An oil slick was spotted, a ship was deployed to take samples, but it tested as not being aviation fuel. What looked from the air to possibly be the tail of a Boeing 777 turned out to be a big piece of white canvass happily drifting around.

The crew from a Vietnamese jet reported seeing a 'possible life raft' floating in the sea around 400 kilometres off the country's southern coast, and when helicopters were deployed for a closer look, it was found to be just 'a moss-covered cap of cable reel'.

The international media rapidly descended on Kuala Lumpur, and Najib decided he himself should head the panel of officials at the press conference they were clamouring for. Scenes in television shows and movies of press conferences with a pack of journalists chaotically jostling to shout out questions above each other are usually over-egged, but this one was exactly that. Already, there had been scores of rumours about what might have happened to MH370, and journalists' demands for clarification of the facts were insatiable. It was a rare case where the phrase 'media circus' was entirely apt.

'What is the most likely theory?' a journalist asked.

'No, that's too speculative,' Najib responded. 'We cannot indulge in speculation at this stage.'

Another journalist wanted to confirm that there was no wreckage, to which Azharuddin responded, 'We have not found any.'

'Is there a possibility of terrorism?' another journalist asked.

'We are looking at all possibilities, but it is too early to make any conclusive remarks,' Najib replied.

The international media pack were frustrated – how were they going to file informative stories if the Malaysian officials produced no answers?

Some of the best insights into the thought processes of the government and airline leaders who dealt with the MH370 crisis came in the aforementioned 2018 television documentary *MH370: Inside the Situation Room*, produced by independent British film group Knickerbockerglory. The filmmakers spent a considerable amount of effort securing access to the key players, including Najib. In the documentary, Najib explained the dilemma for his government.

'People were hungry for information, but at the same time, as the government, we have to be responsible, and I decided we would only be issuing statements that were verified and corroborated.'

March 8 had been a torrid, difficult day for all concerned, but behind the scenes, different sets of experts were looking at every available piece of data, and as the day moved into night, they were stunned by what they found. Ahmad Jauhari, the Malaysia Airlines chief executive, got a bizarre call from the company's engineering department.

As mentioned in Chapter One, a fact known to very few people including airline pilots – at least before MH370 disappeared – is as follows. Aside from the communications systems available to the pilots – radio, satellite telephone and fax, ACARS, the secondary radar transponder – airliners are separately equipped with various types of automatic communications transmission systems via satellite. These systems are usually designed to enable aviation engineers and logistics experts to keep track of the status and performance of individual aircraft and their major components. Jet engine manufacturers and the airline engineers who maintain them, for example, like to get data from the engines they may have to service or replace directly, as it can help speed up their processes.

What his engineers told Ahmad Jauhari left him gobsmacked, but with renewed hope. While the last radar transponder signal had been received at 1:21am, the automatic satellite signals from another transmitter on MH370 were received until well after 8:00am – another seven hours.

What could it possibly mean? Could MH370 have flown on after it disappeared and landed somewhere safely? That time frame was close to when the aircraft would have reached fuel exhaustion – could that mean it simply flew until the tanks ran dry?

Because of the uncertainty of the implications, this was one piece of information the Malaysian leadership decided to not immediately make public; the fear again was that it could create false hopes among the families. The automatic satellite signals work roughly like this: a transmitter on the aircraft – in this case the Rolls Royce engines – sends an electronic 'handshake' to a satellite, and that signal is relayed to a ground station and in turn to the client seeking the data.

FIGURE 3: BASIC SATELLITE COMMUNICATION

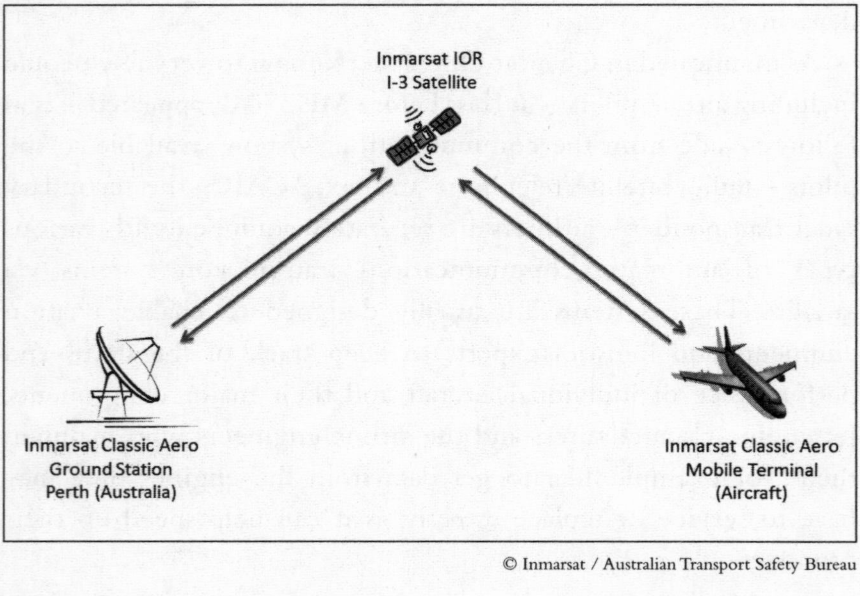

Inmarsat IOR
I-3 Satellite

Inmarsat Classic Aero
Ground Station
Perth (Australia)

Inmarsat Classic Aero
Mobile Terminal
(Aircraft)

© Inmarsat / Australian Transport Safety Bureau

The electronic satellite 'handshakes' from MH370 were roughly hourly. In this case, the satellite relaying the data on the day in question was one positioned in geostationary orbit pretty much plumb bang over the middle of the Indian Ocean. That satellite belonged to the British company Inmarsat. What the Malaysians then asked Inmarsat to do was nigh impossible: use the satellite data to find MH370.

Inmarsat told the Malaysians it was not going to be easy – the satellite was not designed to track anything, just relay communications – but they would give it their best shot.

As this was going on, another astounding discovery was unfolding. As discussed in Chapter One, there are two main types of radar for the purposes of tracking aircraft: secondary (transponder), and primary. While MH370's secondary transponder stopped broadcasting at 1:21am, primary radar systems in Malaysia and its neighbours were operating constantly. They can't tell which aircraft is which – sometimes they can't even know for sure if the bounce-back 'blip' on the screen is actually an aircraft or an anomaly. But primary radar can detect something in the air, and in modern systems, the reports are automatically recorded and can be played back.

The Malaysian military had been going over those recordings from its radar installations. General Rodzali Daud, Malaysia's Chief of Air Force at the time, got an astounding message from the operational commander, saying a strange track had shown up. The track started where and when MH370 had disappeared at IGARI, then headed back over the Malay Peninsula towards Penang, and then north-west up the Straits of Malacca.

If the aircraft making that track had been MH370, the implications were enormous. Could MH370 have experienced some technical problems and turned back, having suffered some serious malfunction which damaged its communications systems? In that case, why did it not land at Kota Bharu or Penang? Or could it be a coincidence – was the track that of some private jet aircraft with a flight plan filed but yet to be matched? Or could it just be what are known in the radar profession as 'ghosts' – false readings that can be produced by anomalies such as reflections off clouds? But if the mysterious track had indeed been made by MH370, it meant it had not come down in the South China Sea – it was more likely on the other side of the Malay Peninsula, possibly in the Straits of Malacca or farther north.

It was a huge conundrum for the Malaysian authorities. What to do: take the military radar track to be that of MH370 and drop the search in the South China Sea and move it to the Straits of Malacca? Stick with the current search zone and wait until there was more certainty about what the military radar really did show? How long could that take?

The government concluded there was only one responsible way forward.

'There was no textbook to say what was the correct thing to do, but I wanted to find the plane at all costs, so I immediately instructed for an additional search and rescue to be done on the western side,' Najib said in *MH370: Inside the Situation Room*. 'But because they were not sure it was MH370, we had to continue the search in the South China Sea.'

The result was that what was already an extraordinary international effort to find a missing aircraft became even more ambitious. At its height, 42 ships and 39 aircraft from 12 countries were scouring huge tracks of the Straits of Malacca to the west, and the South China Sea to the east. As the search zones were divided up and assigned to the ships and aircraft of different participating countries, highly sophisticated new aircraft like the US Air Force Poseidon P-8 were looking in one sector, while ageing Soviet-era Vietnamese Air Force aircraft were looking in others.

But there was no sign of MH370, not a skerrick.

After a few days of searching both areas, Hishammuddin and other officials fronted an increasingly hostile international media.

It was a tough performance to pull off given the inherent nature of the script.

'Where is the focus of your search, can you confirm if the plane has turned back?' a journalist asked.

'We are focusing both in the South China Sea, and in the Straits of Malacca,' Hishammuddin replied.

Another journalist put to Hishammuddin, 'You're searching east, you're searching west, you don't seem to know what you have seen on radar, and it has taken you now, five days later . . . this is utter confusion now, isn't it?'

'I don't think so,' Hishammuddin replied. 'I think it is far from it. It is only confusion if you want it to be seen to be confusion. We have made it very clear that we have been very consistent in our approach . . . we are still not sure it is the same aircraft, that is why we are searching in two areas.'

One question was: 'Why is it that Malaysia lacks the transparency and are very stingy with information?'

Hishammuddin came up with a rather elegant response to that one: 'Because the information is far between.'

The media contingent was obviously doubtful the full story was being told. A journalist who sounded American asked, 'Why not release the raw radar data? Are there any plans to do that?'

There weren't. It's a controversy to this day, with associations representing the MH370 families and international aviation professionals demanding the release of all the available primary information.

Hishammuddin told the filmmakers of *MH370: Inside the Situation Room*: 'Behind the scenes there were massive discussions between me and my military generals and the security experts to discuss what we are able to reveal . . . Military radar will never be released. Try and get that from the Pentagon.'

The search planes kept flying out to the east, and flying out to the west, the search ships kept sailing around looking for anything to do with MH370, and no-one found anything.

Najib could not believe it.

'I was completely flabbergasted,' he said in *MH370: Inside the Situation Room.* 'I had countless sleepless nights, thinking, where on earth is the plane? We had the best minds to advise us and still, there was nothing. Totally nothing.'

The search effort was in desperate need of a new lead, and it came a couple of days later from Inmarsat, and took the whole story into another new, extraordinary direction. Azharuddin got a call from the London-based British satellite company, which had been poring over the raw data from the satellite transmissions.

The Inmarsat official had some stunning news: they might be able to provide some guidance on where MH370 went. Azharuddin asked if a delegation from Inmarsat could come to Kuala Lumpur on the next available flight, and they were picked up by his officers and brought straight to the Sama-Sama Hotel where he was staying.

The Inmarsat officer talked about all sorts of strange things like burst frequency offset, burst timing offset, and the first, second, third, right up to Seventh Arc. Even to aviation experts such as Azharuddin, it was esoteric to the point of being alien, but once explained, the implication was huge. By analysing the seven roughly hourly electronic satellite 'handshakes' from MH370, and looking at how long they took to go out and come back between the aircraft and the satellite, Inmarsat had been able to establish seven rings around the Asia-Indian Ocean region upon which the aircraft would have been at the time of each of the seven handshakes.

So it was not the actual location of the aircraft that Inmarsat could provide – the satellite was not tracking MH370 per se. Nor were the rings even the actual flightpath of the aircraft; they were the arcs of distance somewhere along which the aircraft would have been from the satellite at the hourly handshakes.

FIGURE 4: POSITION RING DEFINED BY BURST TIMING OFFSET MEASUREMENT

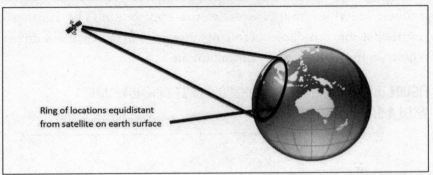

Ring of locations equidistant
from satellite on earth surface

© Inmarsat / Australian Transport Safety Bureau

It was all rather confusing, but the takeaway message was huge. Working with the British government's Air Accident Investigation Branch, Inmarsat had plotted the maximum endurance distance the aircraft could have travelled from its last known position either way along the arc indicated by the seventh and last satellite hand-shake – what would come to be known as 'the Seventh Arc'. From that it was possible to size down MH370's possible resting place to two bands, one curving north–west and one south–west.

The first problem was that Inmarsat could not say which way along the Seventh Arc MH370 flew – north to central Asia, or south to the southern Indian Ocean. The second problem was that both bands were massive – the one to the north–west extended all the way across central Asia to the Caspian Sea; the one to the south–west a good part of the way towards Antarctica.

It was, like the military radar tracking, a difficult one to explain convincingly to the media and the families. On 15 March, a week after MH370 disappeared, Najib again took it upon himself to drop the bombshell to the media.

'Today we can confirm MH370 did indeed turn back consistent with deliberate action by someone on the plane,' the PM said. 'We are unable to confirm the precise location of the plane; however, the aviation authorities have determined the plane's last communication with the satellite was in one of two possible corridors.'

The 'corridors' were, in fact, huge swathes of the globe. The southern corridor just covered vast, empty ocean. The northern corridor spanned millions of square kilometres of land across a dozen countries from Vietnam to Turkmenistan.

FIGURE 5: THE CORRIDORS OF MH370'S LAST COMMUNICATION WITH A SATELLITE

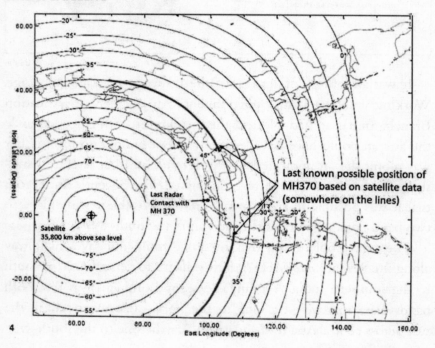

© Ministry of Transport Malaysia

There was no way one could possibly even think of mounting a search and rescue operation systematically across such huge areas. The only way forward would be via a process of elimination, and a doable exercise would be to see if any of the countries in the northern corridor had picked up MH370 flying through their territory. Najib contacted national heads of government along the northern corridor to ask them to check to see if an aircraft matching MH370's description had been detected moving through their territory.

Along the southern corridor, there was nothing but ocean, and the closest country to it was Australia. On 18 March, the Australian government agreed to start looking at an enormous stretch, based in only very loose terms in the early days on where the satellite data indicated MH370 might be.

The Australian Maritime Safety Authority (AMSA) said the search zone would cover 600,000 square kilometres of ocean in an area 3000 kilometres south-west of Perth. Initially, it was just a needle-in-haystack token operation: one RAAF Orion began searching the Indian Ocean to the north and west of the Cocos Islands, while another Orion continued to search west of Malaysia.

As part of the switch in the search strategy, the hunt in the South China Sea was called off – whatever else it did, MH370 was now fully confirmed as having turned back over Malaysia.

Since it was clear that whichever way MH370 had gone, it was at least for the first couple of hours under the control of a pilot, attention again came back to the possibility of a hijacking. The Royal Malaysian Police investigated what was known about both the passengers and crew, with assistance from Interpol. No-one suspicious emerged. The two Iranians travelling on stolen passports were looked at particularly carefully, but were also cleared of any known terrorist links; their sole motive seemed to be illegal immigration to Europe by a roundabout route.

The next piece of the MH370 jigsaw again came from Inmarsat, just over two weeks after MH370 disappeared. The tech-heads at the British satellite company had kept grinding down the data and working out new ways to unlock its meaning. They posed the question: what do the automatic satellite handshakes from similar flights going roughly along the northern and southern corridors – or as close to them as can be reasonably compared – indicate might be different between them?

Inmarsat's conclusion was, if correct, effectively the final death knell for the 239 people on board MH370: the analysis indicated the aircraft had flown not north–west over land, but south to the middle of nowhere in the southern Indian Ocean where it could only have run out of fuel.

Najib was shocked, saw the implications immediately, and knew an appalling decision and announcement lay before him.

On 24 March, Najib again confronted the international media pack.

'This evening, I was briefed by the representatives from the UK Air Accidents Investigation Branch. They have been able to shed more light on MH370's flight path. Inmarsat and the AAIB have concluded that its last position was in the middle of the Indian Ocean west of Perth.'

Then, Najib delivered the coup-de-grâce.

'This is a remote location far from any possible landing site.'

Some family members at the venue had to be taken out on stretchers.

Relatives of those on board received the news in a Malaysia Airlines SMS message which said: 'We have to assume beyond all reasonable doubt that MH370 has been lost and none of those on board survived.'

Despite the fact the Malaysian leaders knew how dim the chances were of finding any floating wreckage – let alone survivors – in the tumultuous seas of the southern Indian Ocean more than two weeks after the aircraft disappeared, the search had to be moved there exclusively, with the hunt anywhere else now concluded to be pointless. The Malaysians formally asked the Australian government if it would take over the major responsibility of leading such a search, and Tony Abbott agreed.

Although the Malaysian government's involvement in the hunt for MH370 went on for another four years and notionally continues to this day, this point marked the end of the first chapter in the saga where it had made every call on its own. In *MH370: Inside the Situation Room*, Hishammuddin said, 'Tell me one government that would not be confused.' It would be hard to argue against Hishammuddin's assessment: the bizarre initial disappearance of MH370 over the South China Sea, the primary radar tracking showing it turned back over Malaysia, the satellite data showing it turned again, south, and kept flying for hours without any communication to oblivion in the southern Indian Ocean – it was all completely inexplicable and confusing.

Hishammuddin said, 'We know that we have tried our best, that is all that we can say. We have done our best, and we will continue to do our best.'

Next, it was up to the Australians to try.

THEORY TWO:
ELOPE BY PARACHUTE

Zaharie Ahmad Shah had enjoyed several mistresses over the years, but none, he found, came close to Rina. She had long, lustrous hair, a sensuous figure, and looked even younger than her 28 years. Rina came from a family of fishermen on the coast who had done very well and now owned a number of vessels; she had just come into a handsome inheritance. In the meantime, to enjoy life in the big smoke, she had moved to Kuala Lumpur and found work running one of the security scanners at the airport. There she met the dashing airman Zaharie, and fell in love.

The love tryst couple decided on an elaborate plan to elope, and secretly establish a new life in another, obscure but pleasant, Asian country. Zaharie used a criminal connection to acquire two stolen passports — not that hard; as mentioned earlier, two Iranian would-be illegal migrants to Europe had done just that in order to get on MH370.

On the evening of 7 March 2014, Zaharie packed his flight crew kit with some extra warm clothing, a very bright waterproof torch, a referee's whistle and his paraglider parachute. If anyone at security asked he'd say — truthfully — that skydiving was his recreational pastime, and he'd heard of a great venue for it, the China GreatSky Skydiving Club at Beijing's Shahe Airport.

In this scenario, as in the one outlined in Theory One, 40 minutes into the flight, having sent his co-pilot Fariq Abdul Hamid back to get him a cup of coffee, Zaharie did a number of things in quick succession. He put on the warm clothing, turned off the ACARS system and the secondary radar transponder, tripped the circuit for the lights in the passenger cabin, put his oxygen mask on, depressurised the aircraft, and made a quick right-hand turn, immediately followed by a sharp and long highly-banked turn to the left.

Zaharie flew the Boeing 777 back over the Malay Peninsula, made a slow right turn just south of Penang, and set the autopilot on a course on Airway N571 up the Straits of Malacca. By this time all the passengers and crew had fallen comatose from hypoxia, or were dead. He turned the cabin lights circuit back on, opened the cockpit door, and stepped over the body of Fariq, into the passenger cabin. Zaharie then systematically but quickly went through the passengers' and crew members' wallets and purses and emptied cash into a waterproof container then into a haversack he'd brought for the purpose – notwithstanding Rina's inheritance, he'd like to do the right thing and contribute financially to their joint future together. At about 2:30am, when he knew he was out of primary radar range, Zaharie returned to the cockpit, took the plane down to 3000 feet and reduced speed. Seeing the lights of the fishing boat he was expecting, just as planned at the precise agreed coordinates, Zaharie made a pass over it, turned a couple of times and lined up for a second pass heading south, setting the autopilot to head for an imaginary waypoint far away in the southern Indian Ocean.

Zaharie put a deflated life jacket on along with his parachute, and slung the haversack with the cash, torch and whistle over his head. He returned to the passenger cabin, and opened one of exit doors just behind the wings, after pushing a lifeless flight attendant who had collapsed there out of the way. He waited until he again saw the lights of the fishing boat approaching, and bailed out.

At the helm of one of her family's fishing boats, Rina had watched the Boeing 777 pass overhead, kept an eye on the strong beam from Zaharie's torch as he descended, and set a heading for it. She saw the beam as Zaharie waved the torch in the water, and heard the whistle. Within 15 minutes the love of her life was safely aboard and in her arms, ready to secretly elope overseas to start a new life, the cash from the inheritance secure in the hold.

As the months and years passed, and in the absence of finding MH370 or any more new fundamental information, the international MH370 club of fascinated addicts of the mystery began a new round of debate about what happened on the aircraft. Some scenarios were pretty wild, some reasonably credible. Some were put forward by people with serious aviation knowledge and experience. When I first started writing about MH370, I received, unsolicited, a number of theories.

All but the first of them, 'Rogue Pilot to the End', outlined after Chapter One, do, in fact, produce the final outcome relied upon by the ATSB for its search strategy: that MH370 finished up as an unpiloted ghost flight, crashing down after fuel exhaustion after flying on autopilot.

Theory Two 'Elope by Parachute', came from a very authoritative source, Qantas's former manager of flight training, veteran airline captain David Shrubb, who is also a past president of the Australian Federation of Air Pilots and a former board member of Airservices Australia. There is, in fact, a precedent in aviation history for every key element required to make Shrubb's theory seem plausible. First, the bail out.

There is only one unsolved case of air piracy in US history, what's known as the D. B. Cooper hijacking. In Portland, Oregon, on the afternoon of 24 November 1971, a man calling himself Dan Cooper used cash to buy a one-way ticket on Northwest Orient Airlines Flight 305, bound for Seattle, Washington. Cooper was the quiet, unassuming type, looking like your average mid-40s insurance agent, wearing a business suit with a black tie and white shirt. Once on board, he ordered a civilised drink – a bourbon and soda. A bit after 3:00pm, he handed the stewardess a note indicating he had a bomb in his briefcase and wanted her to sit with him.

Cooper showed her what was in the briefcase: a collection of wires, switches, red-coloured sticks, and other objects. He threatened to blow up the aircraft if he did not get four parachutes and a

$US200,000 ransom – a huge amount of money back then. When the plane landed in Seattle, the man let the passengers and two of the flight attendants off the plane, and officials handed over the money in $US20 bills plus the parachutes. Once the aircraft took off again, Cooper told the pilots to 'fly to Mexico' – real slow and real low.

At some point thereafter, at night, Cooper lowered the rear stairway of the Boeing 727 – one of the few aircraft which had such a feature, which enabled the crew to independently embark or disembark the passengers from the rear. Then Cooper bailed out into the darkness, having left behind in the cabin, neatly on a seat, his clip-on tie – like a calling card. He remains missing to this day, despite an extensive manhunt which the FBI only gave up in 2016. The FBI never conclusively established his identity – it's not even known if Dan Cooper was in fact his real name – but the media dubbed him D. B. Cooper, and both the name and legend stuck.

Other elements of the elopement theory also have precedents. At lower altitudes and speeds, the passenger cabin doors of big airliners can be opened, usually for the purpose of clearing smoke and getting fresh air in case of fire. This is exactly what the flight attendants did on South African Airways Flight 295 in November 1987. The Boeing 747 Combi – a special design in which space normally used to carry passengers is sectioned off to carry freight – began the flight in Taipei, Taiwan, bound for Johannesburg via Mauritius. A catastrophic fire broke out in the cargo section, and while the flight attendants fought it, the smoke, through a flawed design in the air circulation system, entered the passenger cabin. Towards the end of the flight, the air traffic control transcript records a pilot telling a controller at the airport in Plaisance, Mauritius:

'Eh, Plaisance, Springbok 295, we've opened the door(s) to see if we (can?) . . . we should be OK.'

They weren't okay. The pilots tried to make Mauritius, but the plane went down, killing all 159 people on board. The wreckage was found, at a depth of nearly 5000 metres, after a long search using side-scan sonar.

And when it comes to finding someone in the water in the dark, even a small torch can make all the difference. In the middle of the night of 18 November 2009, pilot Dominic James had to ditch his Westwind twin-engine jet off Norfolk Island because appalling weather made it impossible to find the airport and he was running out of fuel; once in the water, he got his pocket penlight out and shone it into the darkness. Incredibly, a fireman saw the light from shore, and was able to relay directions to a rescue boat, which picked up all six souls from the medical evacuation flight.

Shrubb's 'elope by parachute' theory includes a motive for why Zaharie would have attempted such a feat. 'He wanted to leave his wife – quite a big deal for a Muslim,' Shrubb told me.

He also posited a motive for why the aircraft was directed to one of the most remote and deep corners of the seven seas, the southern Indian Ocean – it was essential to Zaharie's plan that it never be found.

'If ever found, it would show no captain on board and a door open,' Shrubb said.

That, of course, would have been a problem for the secret elopement.

Like just about every aviation professional around the world, Shrubb wants the international community to continue to hunt for MH370.

'When it is found we should look immediately to see if the captain is strapped in his seat,' Shrubb said. 'If he isn't, start an Interpol search to find him!'

FIVE
A PING FROM THE DEEP

It was 24 September 1979, and Flight-Lieutenant Angus Houston was on standby as an RAAF search and rescue helicopter pilot.

He was flying Iroquois from Amberley air force base in Queensland, and down south off the NSW coast it was blowing a gale.

'We were called out because there had been a Mayday call close to a place called Evans Head, which had a bombing range,' Houston told me in an extensive interview in Canberra.

'The winds were so strong that we had a very low ground speed to get down there. We deployed down to Evans Head and waited for a C130 to get there.'

The distress call had come from a cabin cruiser, *Nocturne II*, with five people on board. It had been hit by a large wave and sunk, and those on board had taken to the water. In the afternoon a RAAF P3 Orion came in to join the search.

'Miraculously, they had found them,' Houston said.

The Orion crew dropped equipment to the people in the water, and Houston and his Iroquois crew flew out to try to winch up the survivors.

'Because there was so much spray, visibility wasn't the best,' Houston said. 'In order to get to the search area, we were given radar vectors. We said yeah, we got through, we can see the smoke flare. It was extraordinarily difficult to pick up people in the water. We saw them, and one by one we picked them up. There were three survivors, and we picked them up from very heavy seas.'

Once on board, Houston, knowing there were supposed to be five people on board, asked after the other two. It turned out they had got into a small lifeboat and, the survivors told Houston, 'we saw them disappearing off very fast downwind'.

Houston flew a squared 'S' shaped search pattern downwind to try to find the remaining survivors.

'I couldn't find them. It was getting close to sunset and unfortunately we had to return and refuel.'

The two who took to the boat were found washed up on a beach a couple of days later. They were dead.

In 1980 Houston was awarded the Air Force Cross for his role in the rescue. The citation said of Houston:

'His display of outstanding skill, resolution and leadership undoubtably provided inspiration for his crew in effecting this most difficult rescue.'

Houston is one of those classic, old-style Australian gentlemen; a military officer of great competence, decency and devotion to traditional values like honesty, transparency and duty. In 2015, when Prime Minister Tony Abbott reintroduced knighthoods to modern Australia and honoured Queen Elizabeth's husband, Prince Philip, there was an uproar; but at the same time, he also knighted Houston, and there was not a word of complaint.

Born in Scotland, Houston emigrated to Australia aged 21, and worked as a jackaroo on a sheep and wheat property in Western Australia before joining the RAAF as a trainee pilot.

Houston moved steadily up the ranks having flown, and instructed, on a wide range of helicopters and fixed wing aircraft.

He flew long range maritime search and rescue missions, and as a senior officer, he helped plan Australia's military contribution in the first Gulf War.

Houston served as Chief of Air Force from 2001 and then as the Chief of the Defence Force from 2005. He retired from the military in July 2011.

For many years Houston was chairman of Airservices Australia which is the federal government authority which runs the country's air traffic control and airport fire and rescue services.

I caught up with Houston on a frosty Canberra morning in the winter of 2018 in a small meeting room at the Department of Veterans Affairs. At the age of 71, Houston still serves – he has a role in that department which, one gets the impression, he wants to do but keep low-key. His tall, lanky frame strode in, as usual conservatively dressed in a blue suit, to join me and his media adviser.

I had had some considerable run-ins with Houston some years earlier when he was Airservices Australia chairman and I was investigating that organisation over, among other things, how the executives (not Houston as chairman) seemed to be paying themselves huge bonuses when financial performance was declining. But Houston felt those encounters were surpassed by a duty to have the history of the search for MH370 most accurately recorded, and that the correct thing to do, on my request for an interview, was to grant a full hour of his time.

'You are writing a book . . . I felt it was important,' he told me.

Houston did not want to canvass his views of the different theories of what happened to MH370 – he said that once after giving a public address he had been approached by six individuals who each put a different theory to him. But he was prepared to talk about the maritime, air and underwater search he had coordinated, and that's what I wanted to hear about from him.

On Saturday, 29 March 2014, Angus Houston was driving down to Melbourne to deliver a car to his son, when he got a call from Transport Minister Warren Truss. Would he be willing to head up a new federal government coordinating body to find MH370? Houston said yes, he would.

Houston had had some inkling this might be coming. 'I got a sense late in March that the government was looking for somebody to coordinate the search,' he said. 'On a Friday afternoon I had a bit of a chat with some bureaucrats.'

The day after the approach from Truss, Sunday, 30 March, Houston joined Prime Minister Abbott, who had been attending to duties in Melbourne, on the prime ministerial plane to Perth, where the new organisation was to be established.

The transfer of responsibility for the search and rescue operation had shifted to the Australian Maritime Safety Authority almost as soon as the Malaysian government made the request.

The world's oceans are divided up under an international protocol into zones for which different countries with coastlines have responsibility for search and rescue. Australia's is enormous, and it covers that part of the southern Indian Ocean where MH370 was thought to have come down. At a press conference announcing Houston's appointment to the search coordination role, Abbott said Australia would bear the cost.

'It's an act of international citizenship on Australia's part,' he said.

Long range Australian patrol aircraft had started flying missions almost immediately, and Royal Australian Navy ships were deployed to the search area. But the feeling in the federal government was that there were so many moving parts building up – military, civilian, state and federal, and international – that a coordinating body was required to orchestrate the effort.

So it set up the Joint Agency Coordination Centre, and put Houston at the head of it as chief coordinator. Houston and his team got straight to work when he arrived in Perth – the first job was to set up shop. The best location turned out to be a floor on top of the Western Australian Premier's department, in the Dumas building. The top floor had been set aside by the state government to be available as an emergency situation room.

'What we did when we got in there is that we configured that big open space. We had desks put in and stationed the communications agencies and liaison officers,' Houston said. 'Malaysia had two officers from the Department of Transport. There was a Chinese individual who was a delightful fellow.'

There were officers from AMSA, the ATSB, the Australian Defence Force, the US Navy and the Western Australian government.

'They were all in a room – that was the means by which we effected coordination,' Houston said. 'I was there to coordinate over the top of the whole thing.'

Houston said the then premier, Colin Barnett, was particularly helpful.

'Barnett said, "whatever you need, if you can't get it through normal channels, contact me and I'll take care of it".

'A key role for the state government would have been if we found the aircraft, accommodating all of the relatives of those lost. Chinese culture is such that the relatives come to the nearest place where the aircraft crashed. They need to be there because this is their way of gaining closure.'

The aerial and sea surface search was hugely difficult. The search zone was so far away from Perth – between about 1500 and 3500 kilometres – that aircraft spent hours flying to it and flying back, leaving little time on station actually searching.

Speaking to reporters in Tokyo, Abbott described the hunt as the most difficult in human history. 'While we certainly are throwing everything we have at it, and while the best brains and the best technology in the world will be deployed, we need to be very careful about coming to hard and fast conclusions too soon.'

The assets for the search quickly mounted up.

On 31 March, the day after the JACC officially opened its doors, it issued a press release about the plan for the search that day.

'The Australian Maritime Safety Authority has determined a search area of about 120,000 square kilometres, west of Perth,' the press release said. 'Ten military planes – two Royal Australian Air Force P3 Orions, two Malaysian C-130s, a Chinese Ilyushin IL-76, a United States Navy P8 Poseidon, a Japanese Gulfstream jet, a Republic of Korea P3 Orion, a Royal New Zealand Air Force P3, a Japanese P3 Orion – will assist in the search, with a civil jet providing a communications relay.

'Nine ships have been tasked to search in four separate areas. Australian Defence Vessel *Ocean Shield* departed HMAS *Stirling* on Monday night.'

The next day, April Fools' Day, Danica Weeks decided to have a sticky beak.

She was working at an office just up the road from RAAF Pearce, and her route took her past the air base.

'I said to myself, you know what, I want to go in there and see what they are doing,' Danica told me.

In the three weeks since she put her husband on the plane towards Mongolia only to see him vanish, Danica had continued to try to get a grip on her life and pull it out of the blur.

She had sent Lincoln to stay with the mother of one of his friends; for days she grappled with how to bring him home and explain what had happened.

'Mum and I, we were just lost,' Danica said. 'I needed to bring Lincoln home, but what do I tell him?'

Apart from a phone call from a volunteer, who had no information, she had no real support from Malaysia Airlines, and only five days later did an airline representative show up on her door, who was sympathetic but not of much help. In the end, Danica hired her own counsellor to help guide her through the next moves.

At that point, she was employed part time, and after a brief respite she was 'showing up; when I was supposed to' even though, she said, she was 'not really there'.

'Pauly used to come out and have lunches with me . . . it was so surreal, it wasn't happening any more.'

Seeing the Pearce air base that April Fool's Day, Danica decided here was one thing she could practically do – seek more information from those conducting the search.

After talking her way in, Danica got to one of the top Australian military officers guiding the search, Group Captain Craig Heap, who spent the next two hours answering her questions as best he could.

'In the middle of it I just broke down and I hugged him, and I just said, "I'm just so glad that you are looking for Pauly",' Danica said.

That party-crash had the unintended, but delightful, consequence of hijacking the end of a press conference Houston was holding that day. A reporter said Danica had said 'the families weren't being told enough'.

Houston replied: 'Well, that's one of the principal reasons for setting up the Joint Agency Coordination Centre. I heard this morning, I got a call from Group Captain Heap, who's running the operation out at Pearce that Mrs Weeks had turned up at the gate. He is taking care of her at the moment, and I have told him to give her my phone number and also to give her assistance to get her down to us so that we can fully brief her on what we're up to and what's happening.'

Officially, the operation was a search and recovery mission, looking for wreckage from MH370 and bodies. With the passage of time, Houston observed, it would have been an extraordinary miracle to find anyone still alive and, presumably, clinging to life rafts.

'I don't think there was any hope for survivors at that stage,' Houston said.

As mentioned earlier, the search area had been defined based on the Inmarsat satellite data analysis showing MH370 came down somewhere along the Seventh Arc of automatic electronic handshakes, in the southern Indian Ocean in a band running roughly 1250 to 2000 kilometres west of the coastline of Western Australia. The section of the band to be searched was initially determined by a calculation of several variables indicating when MH370 would have run out of fuel and come down. Those calculations changed over time as new information and analyses came to light, and the target area moved up and down the arc. It was a long band, going from well into the tropics down to south of Perth.

While AMSA was in charge of the day-to-day direction of the search, and Houston's JACC responsible for overall coordination, the science guiding where to look was developed by an international collaborative group designated the Joint Investigation Team, based in Kuala Lumpur but including US and UK investigation agencies and their technical advisers, with representatives from China and France. The strategists brought a couple of intriguing elements into the equation, including one which your average individual would probably be unlikely to know even existed. It turns out that there is an international hydrophone system which listens to sounds underwater around the world, including the Indian Ocean, established as part of the United Nations Comprehensive Nuclear Test Ban Treaty Organisation or the Integrated Marine Observing System. The hunters sought and obtained recordings of low-frequency underwater acoustic signals from data loggers and hydrophones off the Western Australian coast.

Experts at Curtin University's Centre for Marine Science and Technology and at the Defence Science and Technology Organisation were asked by the ATSB to try to 'detect and localise underwater sounds that could be associated with the impact of the aircraft on the water or with the implosion of wreckage as the aircraft sank'.

Incredibly, something did come up.

'One acoustic event of interest was identified that occurred at a time that may have potentially linked it to MH370,' an ATSB report said. 'A detailed analysis of these signals has resulted in an approximate localisation for the source that was compatible with the time of the last satellite handshake with the aircraft, but incompatible with the satellite to aircraft range derived from this handshake.'

So, that novel avenue of inquiry did not yield the resting place of MH370: the signals matched the established time but not the established search zone. AMSA's search and rescue manager Alan Lloyd later said of the mysterious sonic event: 'That turned out to be a landslide in Mauritius.'

Lloyd, speaking at a small Institute of Public Administration seminar in Canberra in 2017 where he and other senior officials involved in the search reflected on the experience, added: 'It just shows you the level of new technology that was being utilised to try and define which of the routes was most credible.'

The investigators also considered a few airway routes which intersected with the Seventh Arc in the target zone in the southern Indian Ocean. One airway route, M641, crossed the Seventh Arc quite far north, at about latitude 21 degrees south, above the Tropic of Capricorn. While still no-one knew what happened on MH370, one conceivable scenario was that whoever was flying the plane set the autopilot on a track to Perth on an airway, and M641, which runs from Colombo in Sri Lanka to the Western Australian capital, might just have been it.

The target area was divided up into sectors, and some sectors subdivided with different colours indicating priorities. It was in the part of the defined priority 'red zone' at 21 degrees south that the search was thought best to start. This came from the convergence of the most likely routes MH370 might have flown based on different assumptions of speed, when the aircraft made the final turn south and so on, and where route M641 passed over the Seventh Arc.

From the start, there were two fundamentally separate elements to the hunt: the surface search for debris and bodies by aircraft and ships, and the below surface hunt for the underwater locator beacons attached to MH370's 'black box' flight recorders.

The two 'black boxes' are the key element of the grail quest to work out what happened to Malaysia Airlines Flight MH370. The flight data recorder monitors and stores data of hundreds of parameters of the flight, from speed, altitude, direction, and aircraft attitude to movement of the control surfaces, throttles and instruments by the pilots. The cockpit voice recorder uses microphones to record every sound in the cockpit, whether it be voices of the crew, warning alarms, or in a radical case, an explosion or gunshot.

Each black box has attached to it an underwater locator beacon or 'pinger' which emits an automatic acoustic signal or 'ping' at a certain frequency which can be picked up by acoustic listening devices operated by ships looking for it.

The search strategy for the underwater locator beacons was, in some respects, relatively straightforward: they would be in a debris field where the aircraft came down around the Seventh Arc. But the surface search for bodies or debris had to contend with a major problem related to the passage of time since MH370 went down. That search band along the Seventh Arc was, of itself, relatively narrow. It would have been contained and realistically locatable for a fairly fast and thorough visual search by aircraft and ships had it started on the day MH370 went down, or a day or so after that.

The problem for Houston was that three weeks had passed. By the time the JACC was established, the winds and ocean currents would have taken what was left of MH370 considerable distances from the crash site, and in not fully predictable directions.

The planners 'drifted' each proposed section of the search – they used three different computer models with sea current and wind algorithms to calculate an expanded area to look, fanning out from where the aircraft might have come down along the Seventh Arc. The longer the search went on, the farther debris could have drifted, and so the 'drifting' models took that into account and the target area kept expanding.

The currents and winds were moving whatever floating debris

there was between 0.5 to 2 knots per hour, so the search area was constantly growing exponentially. One technique to keep track of the search zone was to drop 31 self-locating data marker buoys throughout the Indian Ocean, which transmitted their position using satellite technology. This would tell the hunters where the water was physically going.

The total target area for the aircraft and ships over the 42 days from the day the Australians assumed the surface search for MH370 until it was eventually called off came to 4.7 million square kilometres, equivalent to about half the size of Australia or the continental United States, and all of western Europe.

Lloyd said AMSA's liaison with Defence was an example of how it's best not to overthink things.

'Basically, we said we need 10 aircraft a day for 30 days searching the middle of the Indian Ocean, go do it.'

But as the drift models continued to move north-west with the currents, Lloyd told the IPA gathering, so the logistics of the aerial search became ever more challenging.

'Even with basically the best military aircraft in the world, we were flying four hours, two hours on scene, and four hours back,' Lloyd said. 'I think we actually nearly had Western Australia run out of aviation fuel at one point, but of course Defence took care of that.'

The surface search was carried out seriously and meticulously – whenever a review of satellite imagery or aerial reconnaissance showed what looked like possible MH370 debris, it was investigated.

'All of them were checked out, and they were rubbish from fishing boats and the like,' Houston explained. 'The ocean was not as pristine as we thought it might be. None gave a lead.'

The surface search just kept getting bigger, with more and more search plane sorties, as such aerial missions are known, and ship patrols. On 8 April, the JACC issued its morning bulletin saying 'up to eleven military planes, three civil planes and 14 ships will assist in today's search for missing Malaysia Airlines Flight MH370.'

RAAF Pearce, 35 kilometres north of Perth, was where the main aerial search was launched from and a swarm of activity. The number and range of people involved was several hundred including military men and women, civilian pilots and support crews, AMSA staff, but also many volunteers. On 4 April, 26 State Emergency Service volunteers from Western Australia, New South Wales and Victoria flew as air observers on three of the civil aircraft.

It was at RAAF Pearce that Najib and Abbott made a joint show of force on 3 April to encourage the international search effort and thank those involved.

'I know it is a daunting task to go out there in very inclement weather, in very challenging circumstances,' the Malaysian Prime Minister said. 'Malaysia is indeed grateful for your courage and for your commitment.'

Najib also announced an initiative which was to have quite significant implications down the track: Australia had accepted Malaysia's invitation to participate as an accredited representative in the air crash investigation and would continue to work with Malaysia to draw up a comprehensive agreement on the search.

The countries of the world have an agreement under the International Civil Aviation Organisation known as Annex 13, which provides a protocol for how major air crash investigations are to be conducted. Under the agreement, the country of registration of the aircraft concerned – in this case Malaysia, where 9M-MRO was registered – has responsibility for the overall investigation. But that country can invite 'accredited representatives' from other nations – usually members of their respective countries' air accident investigation agencies – to be members of an international panel participating in the inquiry. Those can be nations which have an interest because they had a significant number of their citizens on the aircraft or the accident occurred in their territory, or because their investigation agencies have particular expertise.

With an accredited representative on the investigation panel, this meant the Australian government, and more specifically the ATSB, had a share of the responsibility for the process and outcome of the Malaysian-led investigation into the loss of MH370.

Contrary to some of the more sceptical interpretations, Houston insists the Malaysian government was absolutely committed to solving the mystery of MH370. He said Najib periodically sought briefings direct from him on how the search was progressing, as did Hishammuddin.

'They wanted to find it. I would say the Prime Minister was quite down because of what had happened,' Houston said.

At one point when he was meeting with Najib, Houston recounted, who should pop up with the Malaysian Prime Minister but the dashing Jean-Paul Troadec, the French celebrity air crash investigator. Troadec came to international fame as the highly visible president of the French Bureau of Inquiry and Analysis in Civil Aviation Security, whose acronym is the BEA, during the hunt for Air France Flight 447, a maritime search which bore some similarities with that for MH370, but also a lot of differences.

It turned out that Troadec, an aerospace engineer, pilot and one-time military parachutist, had been engaged by the Malaysian government as a consultant to advise on the search for MH370.

'He's a fairly charismatic sort of person,' Houston said of Troadec.

At a press conference later on, Hishammuddin mentioned that Troadec had been brought on board, proudly saying, 'We've got the man himself advising us.'

Houston, who had himself been a pilot in dozens of search and rescue missions, threw himself into the complex task of coordinating the aerial and surface search for MH370, but he revealed to me he did not have huge hopes that this part of it would yield results. The Malaysians and the JACC had had a good look at the case of AF447, which was likely one of the reasons Troadec's advice was sought.

The brand new Airbus A330–203 crashed into the Atlantic Ocean on a flight from Rio de Janeiro to Paris on 1 June 2009. The investigation determined the aircraft's pitot tubes, which measure airspeed, became blocked by ice crystals during a tropical storm, causing the autopilot to disengage. The pilots took control but reacted badly, over-correcting and pointing the nose too high, and the aircraft stalled and pancaked into the ocean with the loss of all 228 people on board.

The black boxes yielded some chilling details of the last few minutes of the flight, some of which had a very French flavour. Just minutes before the crisis, the captain, 58-year-old Marc Dubois, had told the two co-pilots he had not got much sleep the night before because he had been out on the town in Rio with his girlfriend, off-duty Air France flight attendant and occasional stage singer Veronique Gaignard, who was on board the flight. He had gone to the two-berth rest compartment behind the cockpit for a doze – he was required under Air France regulations to rest for a portion of the long-distance flight. Reports said it took a minute or so for Dubois, after being summoned by the alarmed and comparatively inexperienced co-pilots, to return to the cockpit. Once there, he encountered a scene of panic and confusion as the co-pilots struggled to save the aircraft: he immediately ordered them to get the nose down, but one pushed his stick forward and the other pulled his up, cancelling each other out, and then it was too late. The terrain proximity warning sounded, and one of the co-pilots said:

'F*** we're dead!'

Troadec told *ABC News* Gaignard was not part of the investigation. The agency was 'not interested' in the 'private life of the pilot', Troadec told the news network.

The reason the dramatic full story of the crash of AF447, and the detailed series of events which caused it, became known was because the aircraft's black boxes were recovered. The flight data recorder told everything about the pilots' control inputs, the attitude and speed of the aircraft, and so on, enabling investigators to reconstruct with great precision the 'pancake' stall and how it happened. The cockpit voice recorder revealed the conversations of the flight crew and the warning alarms, right down to the end where the terrain proximity warning alarm went off.

In the case of AF447, the searchers were able to get a fair fix on where the aircraft might be because its route was known and automatic ACARS signals gave its position about every 10 minutes. The wreckage and an oil slick were spotted the day after the accident.

'With Air France 447 they found a lot of bodies and wreckage,' said Houston. 'After a while they found nothing more. They only found stuff in the water early on, and, by Day 16, there was nothing more that they found.'

By the time the JACC was established, Houston noted, it was Day 22 since the loss of MH370.

'Here we are, the JACC, set up 30th of March,' he said. 'It was well past the optimum time to be looking for surface debris. We ended up in a situation where the best time for the visual search was lost.'

Recovery of debris would be useful in the air crash investigation, and recovery of any bodies would be macabre but would nonetheless provide some closure for the families involved and possibly reveal further clues to what happened. But given the passage of time, the amount of drift would provide some, but probably not a lot, of real guidance to the precise location of MH370 on the seabed.

Incredibly, while in the case of Air France 447 some floating debris had been recovered within days, it took nearly two more years for underwater searches to find the main aircraft wreckage and black boxes. So the best hope for finding MH370, Houston said, was to track down the 'pingers', the underwater locator beacons attached to the black boxes.

The flight data recorder and cockpit voice recorders fitted to MH370 were equipped with Dukane DK100 underwater acoustic locator beacons that activate on immersion in salt or fresh water. They 'ping' at the rate of one pulse per second and at the operating signal frequency of 37.5 kilohertz.

The critical element in the equation was this: the beacons were equipped with batteries designed to operate for a minimum of 30 days after immersion. So Houston and his colleagues faced a race against time.

'What were we looking for? The prime focus was trying to locate the locator beacon,' Houston said. 'The big priority was to try to pick up the flight data recorder, and that would be a ping from the deep.'

Houston knew a lot about locator beacons – he'd gone hunting for them flying helicopter search and rescue missions in the wilds of Papua New Guinea, looking for downed aircraft.

'It's unmistakable,' Houston said. 'The closer you get the louder it gets.' So, find the 'ping from the deep', and you find MH370 – it sounded straightforward. But it turned out to be an extraordinarily frustrating, tricky, confusing and ultimately soul-destroying exercise.

There were, in fact, four vessels and several aircraft deployed in the bid to find MH370's locator beacon.

Ocean Shield had one version of the technology – a yellow device on loan from the US Navy, looking a bit like a delta wing model airplane that was towed deep behind the ship to listen for the pings from the underwater locator beacons.

The crew of the Chinese Maritime Safety Administration vessel MV *Haixun 01* were operating Benthos pinger detector equipment – another brand of acoustic devices which pick up the pulses from the black boxes – from a rescue boat.

The British Royal Navy's hydrographic vessel HMS *Echo* had a sophisticated made-for-purpose hull-based detection device.

Then there was an unexpected and extremely welcome volunteer: the British Royal Navy's Trafalgar Class nuclear submarine

HMS *Tireless* which, because of the very nature of undersea warfare technology, had some of the most advanced acoustic detection equipment in the trade.

'The British submarine had been patrolling in South-east Asia, and offered to help,' Houston said.

Just how much the British told the Australians about exactly what *Tireless* was doing is a moot point, Houston hinted, but he expected 'the senior officer would have had some idea where the nuclear submarine was'.

Then the Australian Defence Force and the defence industry worked on something else: developing the capacity of sonar buoys, or sonobuoys. The sonar buoys were, presumably, designed for anti-submarine warfare, but the defence and industry tech heads managed to adapt them to pick up the frequency of the underwater locator beacons. It looked promising; the concept was to deploy AP-3C Orion aircraft to drop sonobuoys at a depth of 300 metres beneath the ocean surface. One sortie was capable of covering an area of approximately 3000 square kilometres.

Unlike the surface search which had to account for drift, the acoustic signal hunt could be restricted to the relatively narrow band around the Seventh Arc – the assumption was that the aircraft would have come down after fuel exhaustion and the main, heavy metal parts of the fuselage and the engines would have sunk quickly and pretty much straight down.

But time was running heavily against Houston and his colleagues. MH370 disappeared on 8 March; the batteries in the Dukane underwater locator beacons were required to keep emitting pings for 30 days, and the manufacturer said at best they could go for 40 days. By the time *Ocean Shield* and *Echo* got on station it was early April – if the 30-day minimum limit expired on time that left only until 7 April to find the signal. If luck was with the searchers and the underwater locator beacons' batteries held out to the maximum, the window extended to 17 April, but that could not be counted upon.

It was nuanced from the start; while the locator beacon signal can usually be detected two kilometres or three kilometres away, sometimes even up to four kilometres, in one report the ATSB cautioned:

'Many conditions influence the actual detection range, environmental noise, the ability of the water to conduct the acoustic signal, and the sensitivity of the equipment used to make the detection. In reality for a robust search a maximum range to target area of approximately 1 km is used.'

But almost as soon as each surface vessel got on station, Houston told the author, 'we got the ping from the deep'.

The first was heard by the British ship *Echo*, on 2 April. The excitement at the JACC was enormous, but this signal was quickly discounted. 'False alerts may be experienced from biological sources such as whales, or interference from shipping noise,' the JACC said the next day.

In this case, it was later established, the ship was pinging itself: the ATSB reported that, following tests, 'this detection was discounted as being an artefact of the ship's sonar equipment'.

Then things became more serious.

On 4 April, *Ocean Shield* and *Echo* mounted a sweep of a single 240-kilometre track along the Seventh Arc, converging on each other as their pinger locators listened for the beacon from MH370's black boxes.

The military side of the search operation had been designated Joint Task Force 658, and its commander, Commodore Peter Leavy, said the two ships and their towed pinger detector equipment would be operating at a crawl of about three knots to enable them to search at depths of 3000 metres or more.

'The search using sub-surface equipment needs to be methodical and carefully executed in order to effectively detect the faint signal of the pinger,' Leavy said in a statement that day.

While the Australians and the British were proceeding

methodically and carefully in executing their sweep for the black boxes, all hell broke loose when it came to the Chinese.

Chinese media reports went wild on suggestions the Chinese vessel *Haixun 01*, operating around the southern extreme of the Seventh Arc target search area, had found MH370, or at least the pings from its black boxes. China's official Xinhua news agency reported that a beacon locator on board the Chinese search ship had picked up a signal at a frequency of 37.5 kilohertz – the black box locator beacon frequency.

It was one of several occasions where Houston had to hose down expectations.

'I have been advised that a series of sounds have been detected by a Chinese ship in the search area,' Houston said in a statement on 5 April. 'The characteristics reported are consistent with the aircraft black box. A number of white objects were also sighted on the surface about 90 kilometres from the detection area. However, there is no confirmation at this stage that the signals and the objects are related to the missing aircraft.'

Australian search authorities urgently worked to establish what the Chinese had or had not found – would it be worth sending aircraft to drop sonar buoys urgently since they could get there fast while the signal was still there? Or would it be better to send the Australian or British vessel with the beacon locator equipment which were working over the northern part of the search area?

It was one case where international political sensitivities came into play, and had to be massaged. While to the external audience and particularly the international media, the three governments principally involved in the hunt for MH370 – Malaysia, China and Australia – maintained a united front, behind the scenes one of the key jobs of Houston and his deputy at the JACC, senior public servant Judith Zielke, was to smooth things over. In remarks she probably never thought would be reported, Zielke said there were 'bumps along the way' in this process.

Zielke made her remarks at the previously mentioned Institute of Public Administration seminar in Canberra in 2017, where AMSA's Alan Lloyd had also spoken. It was not a big affair – just a relatively short session of an hour or so in which public servants were invited to hear how the JACC was set up, how it worked, and a bit about the search strategy. By that stage the Australian search had ended; that and the fact the event was relatively intimate saw the officials loosen up and make some at times revealing observations. Zielke told the IPA gathering, 'The biggest thing that I have learnt from being involved in the search is actually the huge cultural differences between all the countries involved.'

She noted China had two thirds of the passengers as its nationals.

'To be quite frank, as the outcry from the people increased when the aircraft wasn't located, the greater China's concern and engagement became,' Zielke told the small gathering. 'We were in effect dealing with China, as much as we were dealing with Malaysia, and continue to as well.' It had been necessary for the Australians to respect 'different work practices and approaches' along with 'gender issues or hierarchy issues', Zielke said.

'It's important to remember that people are, culturally, the way they are, for a reason.'

It was an important revelation for the row that was to develop in future. As it came under pressure the ATSB said its search strategy decisions had always been non-political and based on objective scientific evidence; Zielke's 'quite frank' admissions at the IPA seminar showed international political and cultural concerns did impinge, and were taken into account by the Australian search leaders.

On 6 April, Houston and his colleagues including Leavy called what journalists call a 'presser' to hold the line against headlines around the world that the Chinese had found MH370, while at the same time trying to avoid doing anything that might mean Beijing lost face.

'This is an important, encouraging lead but one which I urge you to continue to treat carefully,' Houston told journalists. 'We are working in a very big ocean and within a very large search area.'

Houston said *Echo* would go to help the Chinese vessel, but '*Ocean Shield* will be delayed while she pursues an acoustic noise in her current location'.

So, journalists instantly began to wonder, what was this? What was the 'acoustic noise in her current location' that would delay *Ocean Shield*?

'This only happened within the last 90 minutes,' Leavy told the press pack. 'We heard a report back from *Ocean Shield*, from the towed ping locator operators on board there, that they had picked up a detection. It is very, very early days.'

The next day, 7 April, Houston announced the best news in the hunt for MH370 to date.

'The towed pinger locator deployed from the Australian Defence Vessel *Ocean Shield* has detected signals consistent with those emitted by aircraft black boxes,' he told journalists. 'Two separate signal detections have occurred within the northern part of the defined search area. The first detection was held for approximately two hours and 20 minutes. The ship then lost contact before conducting a turn and attempting to re-acquire the signal. The second detection on the return leg was held for approximately 13 minutes. On this occasion, two distinct pinger returns were audible. Significantly, this would be consistent with transmissions from both the flight data recorder and the cockpit voice recorder.'

Houston described this news as 'a most promising lead' and 'probably the best information that we have had'.

But he still wanted to keep expectations within realistic bounds, telling journalists MH370 could not be confirmed as found until underwater cameras took shots of wreckage and established conclusively it was from a Boeing 777.

Houston and Leavy also advised the media pack about just how difficult the process of acoustic detection was. It was a very slow operation to tow the beacon locator device at only three knots, and with the length of cable, it took hours for the ship to turn around for a new pass. Unlike in air where sound travels in a straight line, Leavy explained, sound through the water is greatly affected by temperature, pressure and salinity.

Nonetheless, it was immensely encouraging news, and it got better. Two days later, on 9 April, Houston told journalists:

'I can now tell you that *Ocean Shield* has been able to re-acquire the signals on two more occasions – late yesterday afternoon and late last night, Perth time.

'The detection yesterday afternoon was held for approximately five minutes and 32 seconds. The detection late last night was held for approximately seven minutes. *Ocean Shield* has now detected four transmissions in the same broad area.'

And there was more good news, Houston said. The Australian Joint Acoustic Analysis Centre based at HMAS *Albatross* in Nowra, NSW, which Houston described as the Australian Defence Force's 'centre of excellence for acoustic analysis', had analysed the pings, and determined that 'a very stable, distinct, and clear signal was detected at 33.331 kilohertz and that it consistently pulsed at a 1.106 second interval'.

'They, therefore, assess that the transmission was not of natural origin and was likely sourced from specific electronic equipment. They believe the signals to be consistent with the specification and description of a flight data recorder.'

It was the best single moment in the hunt for MH370 – before or since – for hopes the aircraft would be found. While still urging caution, Houston allowed just a bit of his own excitement to ebb out.

'I'm now optimistic that we will find the aircraft, or what is left of the aircraft, in the not too distant future,' he told the media pack.

Houston said the next move would be to deploy the autonomous underwater vehicle on *Ocean Shield* to find and get images of the wreckage – but not before the possibility of narrowing down the search area through more towing of the beacon locator had been exhausted. Houston wouldn't put a fix on when that might be, but said the pings seemed to be getting weaker, which could suggest the batteries were running out.

Houston's optimism was catching; in remarks he made in Shanghai for which he was later roasted by journalists, a few days later Abbott said, 'We are confident that we know the position of the black box flight recorder to within some kilometres'.

It was a difficult period for the families of those lost on MH370. As news reports heralded the expectation that MH370 was about to be found and its secrets revealed, next-of-kin felt at least one element of closure might be at hand.

The Weeks family had been reluctant to hold a memorial service for Paul while the aircraft was still missing. One of Houston's key jobs was to brief the families – Danica got a one-on-one session with Houston every Friday, and also personal updates in between when developments called for it. Danica said the impression she got from Houston at that point was that the aircraft was about to be located.

'He did say he'd found the "ping" from the black boxes,' Danica told me. 'He said, "Go home, prepare your memorial, that's it, we're going to find the plane". So I set about preparing, doing songs, movies.'

Houston insists he always managed expectations, pointing out that at every turn he repeated the mantra that the aircraft was not found until visual confirmation of verified aircraft wreckage was in hand. But he said it was also not unreasonable for him to have been optimistic at that point based on the information provided. Houston said that, inevitably, when the series of four pings were picked up by the towed pinger locator, 'of course, we got excited'.

'We wondered if we had found it,' he said. 'There was quite a saga to this.'

The pings straddled the Seventh Arc, so all pieces of the search strategy fitted with the location of the pings. Nobody had jumped to conclusions, Houston said, and the RAN acoustic unit at Nowra was highly regarded. It had come back with a report that the signals were consistent with those from the beacon of a black box.

'That's when people started to say – it's definitely down there,' Houston said. 'I was very hopeful, but I was very guarded.' With the batteries on the beacon likely to run out at any moment, the searchers redoubled their efforts in the hunt for acoustic signals.

The cleverly adapted sonobuoys were deployed by the RAAF AP-3C Orion aircraft. As Leavy told journalists, the sonobuoys were a particularly useful tool at that point. The task force did not want to send another ship to join *Ocean Shield*, because the whole idea was to limit the sources of man-made noise. *Ocean Shield* itself had turned off all but absolutely essential equipment on board. The sonobuoys could cover a big area quickly without putting any moving parts in the water. Leavy explained the technology at a press conference.

The sonobuoys were parachuted out of the aircraft and the main component would float on the surface of the ocean and deploy a hydrophone 1000 feet below the surface of the ocean. The sonar buoy had a radio that transmitted the data back to the aircraft.

Each Orion could carry 84 sonar buoys on each mission, Leavy said.

Leavy later made an interesting revelation: the sonobuoys were single-use only; it could not have been cheap.

'When the life of the sonar buoys expires, which is generally around eight hours after they are deployed, they do scuttle and sink to the seabed,' Leavy said.

On 10 April, Houston announced another possible breakthrough: an Orion aircraft had 'detected a possible signal' via sonar buoys in the vicinity of *Ocean Shield*; just the next day, 11 April, he said it had turned out to be another red herring.

By then, it had been 34 days since MH370 went missing. The window was closing fast, but the efforts only intensified. Houston's statement that day said *Ocean Shield* was making 'more focused sweeps', while the Orions would support that effort with three more sonobuoy missions that day.

'A decision as to when to deploy the autonomous underwater vehicle will be made on advice from experts on board the *Ocean Shield* and could be some days away,' he said.

The autonomous underwater vehicle was another critical tool in the hunt for MH370. They are amazing machines. They are unmanned, free-ranging, torpedo-shaped miniature submarines which have an extraordinary array of sensors. In their bodies, usually around six metres long, most carry side-scan sonar, a multi-beam echo-sounder, a sub-bottom profiler, a high-definition camera, a conductivity/temperature/depth sensor, a self-compensating magnetometer, a turbidity sensor, and a methane and laser sensor.

The most important pieces of equipment for this search were the side-scan sonar, which can create images of things on the sea floor; the multi-beam echo-sounder, which can produce three-dimensional images; and the magnetometer, which can confirm if objects are metallic.

In some cases, the machines can message robot ships known as unmanned surface vehicles about what they are doing, using acoustic positioning telemetry. They have onboard cameras and machine-vision software that can enable them to keep an eye on what's ahead of them and dodge underwater cliffs or other obstacles. The autonomous underwater vehicles can be programmed to run a mission over many hours, returning to the surface where the information can be downloaded.

The side-scan sonar can produce some extraordinarily clear images, in a sort of sepia tone, of natural features and man-made objects on the sea floor, even though there is little or no light at extreme depths, by bouncing signals off them, much like radar.

In this case, the magnificent piece of AUV technology was called *Bluefin-21*, operated by private contractors Phoenix International.

At a press conference with Chinese journalists, Leavy spoke of the extraordinary way it would work: once deployed, *Bluefin-21* would glide around 35 to 50 metres over the seabed, looking around 300–400 metres either side of its track.

By 12 April there had been no confirmed acoustic detections over the previous 24 hours. A couple more days passed without any more pings, and, on Day 38, the searchers assessed that could mean that the batteries on the underwater locator beacons were finally dead.

The big decision was taken. As Houston put it at a press conference on 14 April:

'We haven't had a single detection in six days. So, I guess it's time to go underwater. *Ocean Shield* will cease searching with the towed pinger locator later today and deploy the autonomous underwater vehicle, *Bluefin-21*, as soon as possible.'

Houston braced journalists, the families, and the general public for a long, painstaking process.

'Each mission conducted by the *Bluefin-21* will take a minimum of 24 hours to complete,' he told the press conference. 'It will take the autonomous underwater vehicle two hours to get down to the bottom of the ocean. It will then be on-task for 16 hours. It will then take two hours to return to the surface and four hours to download and analyse the data collected. The first mission will see *Bluefin-21* cover an area of approximately five kilometres by eight kilometres, an area of 40 square kilometres.'

As always, Houston urged caution.

'And I would just say to everybody, don't be over optimistic, be realistic and let's hope, let's hope that that the very strong signal that we were receiving is actually coming from the black box because that would be a really good outcome.'

This was, effectively, the only remaining chance on Houston's watch to find MH370. He told journalists the ping picked up at the other end of the target search area by the Chinese vessel had been analysed and discounted.

'So, at the moment, this is really all we've got,' he said.

And so, as Houston put it to me, '*Bluefin-21* started doing daily trips down to the deep.'

That night, amid considerable anticipation of all those involved, *Ocean Shield* launched *Bluefin-21*. What the JACC called the 'focused underwater search area' was defined as a circle of 10 kilometres in radius around the second towed pinger detection on 8 April.

One problem with *Bluefin-21*, according to Houston, was that it had limited depth – it could only descend to about 4500 metres, and again, some of the search area was deeper than that. The JACC report of 15 April said:

'After completing around six hours of its mission, *Bluefin-21* exceeded its operating depth limit of 4500 metres and its built-in safety feature returned it to the surface.'

In the 17 April media bulletin, the JACC seemed to be placing so much faith in *Bluefin-21* that the undersea robot took on an almost independent intelligence and soul of its own, planning its own missions:

'Overnight *Bluefin-21* AUV completed a full mission in the search area and is currently planning for its next mission. *Bluefin-21* has searched approximately 90 square kilometres to date and the data from its latest mission is being analysed.'

The issue of whether *Bluefin-21* could go deep enough was solved – by taking on an 'acceptable level of risk' and going a bit deeper.

The days went by, about a dozen aircraft and a dozen ships scoured the surface of the southern Indian Ocean looking for wreckage, and *Bluefin-21* went down to the deep, producing excellent sonar images of a sea floor with nothing man-made on it.

On 21 April, the JACC media bulletin said:

'This morning, *Bluefin-21* AUV completed mission eight in the underwater search area. *Bluefin-21* has searched approximately two thirds of the focused underwater search area to date.'

More days passed, and the bulletins reported that *Bluefin-21* had searched 80 per cent, then 90 per cent, then 95 per cent of its target zone. Each bulletin had the same line: 'No contacts of interest have been found to date.'

By the end of April, despite a massive effort involving military and civilian officials from many countries, and Australian volunteers, all the many aspects of the search had, in the end, got nowhere.

Not one item viewed or picked up from the sea had been associated with MH370.

An oil slick turned out to not be aviation oil.

Bluefin-21 had looked here, looked there, but all that came back from the sonar imaging was dull, lifeless Indian Ocean seabed. It was, Houston told me, deeply disappointing.

'For everyone who was involved it was a big downer,' he said. With heavy hearts of those involved, it had to be the end of the trail for this chapter of the hunt for Malaysia Airlines Flight MH370.

It was Prime Minister Tony Abbott who took the press conference at RAAF Pearce to call it quits – while at the same time announcing the next chapter. With Houston at his side, Abbott told the media pack on 28 April:

'It is now 52 days since Malaysia Airlines Flight MH370 disappeared and I'm here to inform you that the search will be entering a new phase. I regret to say that, thus far, none of our efforts in the air, on the surface or under sea have found any wreckage.'

Abbott said the 'new phase' of the search would involve a different approach: rather than a surface search like the one just completed and a selective underwater hunt for the aircraft based on trying to find the pinger locators, the new effort would involve a massive, slow and methodical underwater survey of the seabed around the Seventh Arc.

The many aircraft from many nations whose crews had tirelessly searched the ocean's surface went back to whatever they had been doing before, as did the ships.

The JACC itself closed up shop in Perth, and moved to Canberra where most of the federal public servants returned to their regular jobs, while maintaining the coordination role for the next phase of the search.

It had, the Australian government said, been the biggest maritime search in history. It had involved 345 aerial sorties, 3500 flying hours by 26 aircraft, and 23 ships of nine nations.

Ocean Shield and *Bluefin-21* kept going with the seabed search for some weeks, looking at adjacent areas after covering the original target area based on the four 'pings'. It made sense to absolutely exclude the possibility that those contacts revealed MH370's final resting place.

Eventually, that valiant effort also had to be brought to a close. On 29 May, the JACC issued its last statement on this phase of the hunt.

'Yesterday afternoon, *Bluefin-21* completed its last mission . . . no signs of aircraft debris have been found by the autonomous underwater vehicle since it joined the search effort,' it said.

The noble vehicle, the private technicians who ran it, and the Australian crew which sailed *Ocean Shield* from which it day to day went down to the deep, had scoured over 850 square kilometres of the ocean floor looking for signs of the missing aircraft.

Ocean Shield, the JACC said, had departed the search area and headed home.

Houston soon went on to his next duty; in July, Prime Minister Abbott asked if he would take up another tough assignment – sorting out Australia's interests in the shooting down of Malaysia Airlines Flight MH17 over Ukraine by Russian-backed rebels, in which some 40 Australian citizens and residents perished. The mission statement was for Houston to 'lead Australia's efforts on the ground in Ukraine to help recover, identify and repatriate Australians killed in the MH17 crash'. Zielke took over from Houston as chief coordinator of the JACC.

There was one truly tragic aspect of the 'pings' saga yet to unfold. As Houston explained, after some time 'a different version of the interpretation of the acoustic contacts came through.'

'The ATSB basically got the scientists from the Defence Science and Technology Organisation, as it was then, to also do an analysis on all of the data. Sometime later we got the results back that the scientists determined it was not from a flight data recorder. I understand that what can happen is that the locator can sometimes pick up its own signal.'

So, the pings which had raised so much promise, and led to such a heroic undersea search effort, were never possibly from a black box; they were from the locator pinging itself. It was the ultimate heartbreak for the hunters on that stage of the grail quest – all that hope, and all that effort, involved in the underwater search had been doomed to fail from the start.

Despite everything, Houston said he was sure that during the phase of the hunt for MH370 he coordinated, all that could have been done had been done, and more.

'The surface search went on longer than would normally be the case, and that was because of sensitivities from our partners,' Houston said, without elaborating. 'When we got to the end point we thought we had done everything we could do.'

Danica Weeks said of Houston, 'He was amazing. He just did an amazing job, but he was just tasked with an impossible mission.'

SIX

NOWHERE TO HIDE

When Peter Foley went to sea in 1983 as a young cadet marine engineer with the Australian National Line, it's unlikely he thought that three decades on he would be in charge of a massive international underwater search to find a missing Malaysian jetliner.

Foley knew the ocean – before joining the ATSB in 1999, he had 16 years of seagoing experience, and he holds two engineering degrees. With the ATSB, Foley had investigated several of Australia's big maritime disasters: the grounding of Chinese coal carrier *Shen Neng 1* on the Great Barrier Reef in 2010; the *Pasha Bulker* coal carrier beaching on Newcastle's Nobbys Beach in 2007; and 2001's *Nego Kim* ballast tank explosion off Dampier, which killed eight members of the crew.

Foley had no illusions about just how hard a hunt for MH370 would be.

'On the surface, it's a hard place to be for any vessel, with swells of up to 15 metres,' he told the shipping industry journal *IHS Fairplay*. 'When a big blow is coming, you're out in middle of nowhere and there's nowhere to hide. All you can do is heave to and pick the best heading.'

It was a big ask to be assigned the job of finding MH370 where others had failed, but clearly somebody had to take on the task and Foley did have extensive maritime and investigation experience. The boss of the ATSB at the time, chief commissioner Martin Dolan, who would have appointed Foley to the task, was certainly not an expert in the skill sets required; Dolan studied French at university and became a career public servant.

The new effort to find MH370 was at that stage set as an underwater search along the Seventh Arc roughly 700 kilometres by 80 kilometres.

Tony Abbott said the project would cost some $60 million, and take about eight months.

'This is so important not just to the families but to everyone who travels by air,' Abbott said.

The new mission started to take shape in a series of meetings among the three governments which would combine their resources for the new undersea search: Australia, Malaysia and China.

On 5 May 2014 in Canberra, Australian Transport Minister Warren Truss called a press conference with his Malaysian counterpart, Hishammuddin, and China's Minister for Transport, Yang Chuantang, to announce the way ahead.

After the previous failed aerial, maritime and subsea effort, the idea was to go back to the drawing board and have another look at all the available evidence. Truss said international experts would re-analyse all the data and information likely to identify the path of MH370.

The search plan, using primarily side-scan sonar 'towfish' which are tethered to a ship on a very long cable and don't have the in-built automatic collision-avoidance capabilities of the autonomous underwater vehicles, required a switch of approach: before the actual searching for MH370 could begin, the seafloor had to be mapped. That way, the depth with which to send down the towfish, and ways to avoid crashing them into undersea terrain, could be established.

'Much of this area has never been mapped,' Truss said.

The three ministers made a show of force to drive home the unity of their governments in the task of finding MH370, and to reinforce that they had a determined plan to make it happen.

'What was discussed this morning is very structured, it is very focused, and I believe that we are on the right track,' Hishammuddin said, adding, 'there is a sense of urgency.'

Then it was Yang's turn to make a prepared statement to the media which he did in Chinese; the translation might have made it even more eloquent than the original – it was certainly promising of all things good.

'During the whole course of the search, the Chinese Government has been sticking to the principles of people orientation, positive participation, and proactive contribution, and maintaining very good collaboration and cooperation with all parties involved, which laid down a solid foundation for continuing the full ops search activities,' the translator said Yang had said.

'It is my firm belief that so long as we three countries closely collaborate with each other, materialise the joint communique seriously, could we, with our pragmatic work, respond to the great expectations of the international community, provide closure to the families of the people on board, and discharge our duties and responsibilities.'

As will be canvassed in greater detail in Chapter Eight, for the Chinese government, 'pragmatic work' would include using the guise of hunting for MH370 to spy on Australian military activity, security experts believe.

While Foley knew the difficult logistics of hunting for MH370 in the wild seas of the southern Indian Ocean, as program director of the ATSB-led subsea search he also realised the most crucial part of the job came before a single vessel dangled its towfish to catch the aircraft: working out where to look.

That wasn't easy: there was some data to work with, but, as Troadec had said in one media interview, a lot less than there had been with the infamous doomed flight, AF447. Ultimately, some assumptions had to be made about what happened to the aircraft at the end of the flight.

Foley had lots of help – an international team of experts from Boeing, Inmarsat, the US National Transportation Safety Board, European aerospace group Thales, the British Air Accident Investigation Branch, and the Malaysian Department of Civil Aviation. That panel was named the 'Search Strategy Working Group'. On top of that, Foley was able to draw on the expertise of the CSIRO; the Defence Science and Technology Organisation (later 'Group'), which is a branch of the Department of Defence with some of the best and the brightest scientists and engineers; and Geoscience Australia, which knew how to map the seabed.

In his public appearances, including before a Senate committee, Foley insists he and his colleagues approached the challenge with dispassionate logic. The starting point went back to the same elements with which the Houston-coordinated surface search had begun: the early military primary radar data showing MH370's last confirmed position in the northern part of the Straits of Malacca and heading north-west; the Inmarsat metadata of the seven satellite handshakes which provided the band upon which – but not the precise point where – the aircraft had likely ended up; and the calculations of when the plane would have run out of fuel.

The calculations and re-calculations of these variables had never stopped among the team in Kuala Lumpur and their international advisors, with refinements always being made as new information and interpretation came in.

The initial job of mapping the sea floor – known as 'the bathymetric survey' – got underway almost immediately by deploying the Chinese People's Liberation Army Navy ship *Zhu Kezhen*, though it had to spend a couple of weeks in the Western Australian port of Fremantle repairing its equipment. As will be discussed in the next chapter, Chinese government vessels spent much time in

Fremantle, where a lot of Australian naval and special forces activity happens.

In early June, the Dutch deep-water marine survey company Fugro won the private sector tender for the bathymetric work, and soon after the contract for the actual search for MH370, and its ship *Fugro Equator* was deployed.

The two vessels were anticipated to take around three months to complete the bathymetric survey of the 60,000 square kilometre search zone, the JACC, which still retained primary responsibility for media relations, said on 10 June.

The main equipment on the vessels used for the purpose were multi-beam echo-sounders, which collected the raw data used by Geoscience Australia to produce stunning three-dimensional images of the often dramatic bottom of the Indian Ocean.

Meanwhile, the ATSB, the Defence Science Technology Group, and the Search Strategy Working Group got down to the task of determining the new target zone.

On 26 June, the ATSB published a paper outlining in some detail its initial search plan and the rationale behind it, titled *MH370 – Definition of Underwater Search Areas*. It's an interesting document – it shows the detective work and logic the ATSB and its allies used to determine where to look, while at the same time admitting the very nature of it made it an imperfect science. It said three factors were important in defining the search area along the Seventh Arc: the position of the final turn to the south from the previous north-west heading along the Straits of Malacca; aircraft performance limitations; and analysis of the satellite communications data.

Going through each of these issues, the ATSB report noted the last contact from primary radar when the aircraft was heading north-west on airway N571 was at 2:22am. The satellite handshake three minutes later, at 2:25am, suggested it was still on the same track. But, the ATSB determined, the satellite handshake at 3:41am 'indicated that the aircraft was tracking in a south/south-easterly direction.'

The problem here is clear: those calculations meant there was no way of knowing, within the one hour and 16 minutes when the aircraft was out of radar range and between satellite handshakes, just when the plane turned south. So, the ATSB said in its report, it had adopted two approaches in its calculations. The first was to just use a range of possible locations for the turn. The second, the ATSB report said, was 'to analyse the satellite data independently without assuming where the turn occurred'.

So, the idea was to in parallel work out the whole range of random possibilities, and separately establish what the satellite data itself suggested was the most likely track.

On the second critical issue, aircraft performance or, essentially, the calculation of when and where MH370 would have run out of fuel, the ATSB report said altitude, airspeed and wind were the important factors.

The investigators had a couple of solid clues about these variables in the early phase of the flight. The last ACARS transmission from the aircraft, at 1:07am, provided the total weight of the fuel remaining on board. Between then and 2:22am, while the aircraft was being tracked by primary radar, its speed and consequently fuel burn could be estimated. But, the ATSB said, during the period the aircraft tracked to the south, there was no altitude or speed data available.

While there was wind information available, the ATSB said, that varied against time, altitude and location, so the only reasonable approach was to match it against a variety of possible altitudes, speeds and possible routes of the aircraft. So, again, without the data to determine just when MH370 splashed down along the Seventh Arc, the way forward was, to use a poker player's term, to work the percentages: rate the probabilities of a variety of different routes and fuel exhaustion times against known data, and identify a probability 'hot spot'.

There was, however, another critical line of thinking involved in this determination. This related to a particularly clever part of the sleuth work about what happened to MH370 at the end of the flight.

The last few handshakes were of particular interest to the investigators. The sixth handshake at 8:11am was initiated by the ground station and appeared to be the last of the normal, reciprocated, roughly hourly requests from the ground station for an update of data from the aircraft. The seventh handshake eight minutes later at 8:19am was different; it was initiated by the aircraft and took the form of a 'log-on request'.

As the ATSB commented, this was highly unusual. It meant the regular communication between the ground station and the aircraft had suffered a disruption, then been restored. There were only a few explanations for such a break, the ATSB said:

'These include a power interruption to the aircraft satellite data unit (SDU), a software failure, loss of critical systems providing input to the SDU or a loss of the link due to aircraft attitude.'

Analysis showed the scenario which worked best, the ATSB said, was a power interruption to the SDU.

The modelling of the fuel and aircraft performance data indicated MH370 would have reached fuel exhaustion at about this time, and the engines would have flamed out one after the other. But then, when that happened, as mentioned in Chapter One, after about a minute, the auxiliary power unit, the small jet engine designed to provide power for the aircraft's basic systems, would have automatically started.

The ATSB's theory was that in those eight minutes between the sixth handshake and the log-on request, the engines had flamed out, and since the engines power the electrics of the aircraft, a power interruption would have cut the satellite communication link. But after about a minute, the auxiliary power unit would have had automatically powered up, leading the SATCOM to come back on line, and initiate the log-on request at 8:19am.

And there was a further key clue in the equation.

As mentioned in Chapter One, there had been what the ATSB took to be an earlier break in the satellite transmissions, in that case, it said, most likely when somebody turned off the electrical circuit which powered them, then later turned it back on. That time, the ATSB said, there had also been a log-on request from the aircraft at 2:25am, and about 90 seconds later, 'communications from the IFE (In Flight Entertainment) system on the aircraft were recorded in the SATCOM log'.

Then the clincher: 'Similar messages would be expected after the [8:19am] log-on request, however none were received.

'This could indicate a complete loss of generated electrical power shortly after the 7th handshake. Because the location of the [8:19am] arc is also consistent with estimates of the aircraft range calculated from the remaining fuel quantity provided by the last ACARS transmission, the 7th arc is the focus of the search area.'

What the ATSB was saying, in its usual diplomatic tones, was that within about 90 seconds from the precise time of 8:19am, something must have happened on the aircraft to stop the satellite data unit from logging on the inflight entertainment system again. The ATSB did not spell it out then – it did a bit more in subsequent reports – but logic suggests two possibilities.

One is that within those 90 seconds the auxiliary power unit had itself run out of fuel, and power was again cut off to the SATCOM. The other possibility, of course, is that within those 90 seconds, the aircraft hit the water and blew to bits the satellite data unit and everything else on MH370. It meant that within 90 seconds of the precise time of 8:19am, Malaysia Airlines Flight MH370 was either in its death dive going down, or had already hit the ocean.

It was good detective work, and hugely increased the ATSB's confidence that the Seventh Arc marked a narrow band upon which the aircraft went down.

The third key question identified by the ATSB was the analysis of the satellite data. In the time since the satellite handshakes had first become known to exist, the international team responsible for decoding them had also done a lot more work. It was, to say the least, complex; what follows is an attempt to make the gist of it understandable not just to PhD level aerospace engineers and mathematicians, but to mere mortals.

The components of the satellite information system used on flight MH370 consisted of the Inmarsat Classic Aero ground station located at Perth, the Inmarsat Indian Ocean Region (IOR) I-3 satellite and the Inmarsat Classic Aero Mobile Terminal, which is the satellite data unit on the aircraft. It's a triangular system in which the ground station sends signals to the satellite, which relays them in turn to the aircraft, and vice-versa.

The ground station in turn sends the data to the clients.

From the satellite handshakes the tech heads identified and retrieved two types of metadata: burst timing offset and burst frequency offset.

The burst timing offset is a measure of how long the handshake signals take to go from the satellite to the aircraft and back. By measuring burst timing offset the scientists were able to establish the difference between a 'nominal' position of the aircraft if it were directly below the satellite and therefore at its closest possible position, and the 'actual' position at the time of each handshake. The longer it took from when the signals were sent from the satellite to reach the aircraft and vice-versa, the farther away it was.

FIGURE 6: TIME DELAYS BETWEEN NOMINAL AND ACTUAL LOCATION OF MH370

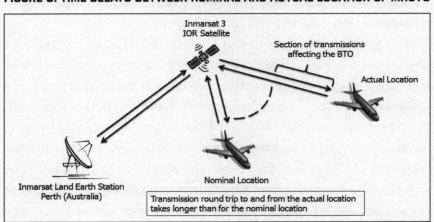

© Inmarsat / Australian Transport Safety Bureau

This produced the seven concentric rings associated with each handshake, as MH370 moved initially closer to, then farther away, from the satellite.

The first handshake at 2:25am, just after primary radar coverage was lost at 2:22am, shows MH370 was somewhere on a band which does indeed coincide with the northern end of Sumatra. The second at 3:41am puts it on a band farther west – the innermost band. The third arc, at 4:41am, is slightly to the east of the second, and all other arcs are also to the east and south. That opened up a number of conceivable routes and possible end points on the Seventh Arc, but within a restricted range based on fuel endurance.

By cross-referencing the handshakes from when the aircraft was on the ground, and the last ACARS transmission when MH370 was still over Malaysia and its position known, the investigators were able to determine that the burst timing offset–defined rings would accurately reflect where the aircraft had been along them to within plus or minus 10 kilometres.

The scientists also used a different calculation to calibrate the results: the burst frequency offset. That, hard to believe though it is, was even more complex, but it involved one element which high-school students learn about in science class: the Doppler effect of relative movement and frequency.

The general principle of the Doppler effect is that when two objects are moving towards each other the frequency increases, and when they are moving away from each other the frequency decreases. The classic example cited by science teachers is that when you stand on the edge of a highway and a big truck is coming towards you, the pitch of the noise it makes becomes higher in your ears until it reaches you, then when it passes you, the pitch falls. The scientists used the Doppler principle to make calculations against the satellite data of changes in the frequency of transmissions, which they used to cross-reference against possible flight paths. From that, they derived an indication of the aircraft's speed, which was put in a range of 375 to 425 knots.

The international team made refinements to the satellite data model to take into account other factors, such as that the satellite, while described as geostationary, actually moves in a bit of an elliptical ring itself, and that at times when it was in the shadow of the earth, it cooled down and this could affect the frequency of transmissions.

To test the accuracy of the model, the team ran various validation and verification tests. Using nine previous flights of the aircraft, 9M-MRO, and 87 other aircraft with the same SATCOM equipment in the air at the same time as MH370, the investigators tested some path prediction analysis techniques. Essentially, they compared what their model of analysis of the satellite data showed would be the track of the aircraft against the tracks actually flown. The path estimations based on the satellite data were verified as very close to the actual paths for most of the flights.

The analysis of the satellite data was an exceptional piece of ground-breaking international scientific and engineering deduction, pushing out the frontier of knowledge and done, by academic standards, very quickly. The aircraft went down in early March with the satellite data being made available a bit thereafter; by late June the work was not just done, but published in a paper.

There was, however, one final decision which had to be made before all the variables and probabilities could be put together to determine a search area: what happened at the end of the flight and, more specifically, was anyone flying the plane?

It was in many respects the most important question of all.

If no-one was flying the plane and it ran out of fuel, when the engines flamed out the autopilot would disconnect, and the aircraft would likely go into a spiral but crash pretty much straight down. If someone were flying it at the point of fuel exhaustion, the ATSB itself determined, from about 35,000 feet which was MH370's last recorded altitude, he or she could glide it another 100 nautical miles or so farther down the Seventh Arc or, for that matter, another 100 nautical miles off it.

Which way the ATSB decided to fall on this most critical determination had big political and diplomatic implications.

The ATSB, it says in its search strategy report, 'reviewed three general classes of accidents that were relevant to the cruise phase of flight.'

The first was 'an in-flight upset' which it said was generally characterised by 'normal radio communications' and 'normal en route manoeuvring of the aircraft' up until an 'upset event' which could be 'a stall due to icing, thunderstorm, system failure etc.'. In that case, there would be 'pilot control inputs' and a 'rapid loss of control'. Air France 447 was a good example of an 'in-flight upset'; everything was normal up until the pitot tubes filled with ice crystals and the autopilot shut off – there were control inputs after that, but the wrong ones, right up until the point the pilots realised 'F***, we're dead'.

The second class of accident the ATSB defined was 'an unresponsive crew/hypoxia event'. Such scenarios, the ATSB said, were generally characterised by 'failure of the aircraft to pressurise during initial climb, loss of radio communications, long period without any en route manoeuvring of the aircraft, a steadily maintained cruise altitude, fuel exhaustion and descent, no pilot intervention, loss of control.'

There are several known cases of accidents of this type, the classic being Helios Airways Flight 522. The Boeing 737 took off from Larnaca, Cyprus, on a scheduled flight to Athens, Greece, on 14 August 2005. There had been some trouble with icing on one of the doors on the previous flight, and an engineer did some tests requiring him to set the pressurisation mode on the aircraft to 'manual'. He forgot to switch it back to 'auto'.

When the plane took off, it failed to pressurise, and though within five minutes an alarm sounded warning of the problem and soon thereafter the oxygen masks dropped, the pilots mistook it for another warning which did not sound that different.

The captain reported a related air conditioning problem, had some discussion with the same engineer on the ground, but quickly became hypoxic, stopped conversing rationally, and then passed out, as did the co-pilot. The aircraft, flying on autopilot on its programmed route, reached its assigned altitude of 34,000 feet, cruised along till it got to the approach to Athens airport, and then automatically started a holding pattern.

Two Greek jet fighters scrambled to intercept the aircraft and, peering in through the 737's windows, their pilots saw a 'ghost plane' flying beside them. They saw no-one in the pilot's seat, the co-pilot slumped over the controls, lifeless passengers, some with oxygen masks on, others with their masks dangling overhead. Incredibly, shortly before the plane went down the pilots saw a flight attendant, who had apparently got his hands on portable oxygen bottles, enter the cockpit and take the pilot's seat, and wave to them. It was a brave last-minute attempt to save the plane nearly three hours into a 'ghost flight'.

But while the attendant had some flight training, and attempted two Mayday calls, he was not trained on the 737, and very soon the first engine flamed out, and the aircraft left the holding pattern and started to descend. Ten minutes later the second engine failed, and the aircraft crashed into hills about 40 kilometres from Athens killing all 121 on board.

The third class of accident the ATSB considered was a 'glide event', which it said was generally characterised by 'normal radio communications, normal en route manoeuvring of the aircraft, engine failure/fuel exhaustion event(s), pilot-controlled glide'. There are also plenty of glide events in the history of commercial aviation, the most prominent of which in recent years was the extraordinary successful ditching in January 2009 of US Airways Flight 1549 into the Hudson River in New York after a bird strike took out both engines – this fine piece of airmanship was made into the film *Sully: Miracle on the Hudson* starring Tom Hanks.

That was a short glide – the longest among airliners was Air Transat Flight 236 which took off from Toronto bound for Lisbon in August 2001, and ran out of fuel over the Atlantic due to an undetected leak. With no power the pilots managed to glide the Airbus A330 for 20 minutes covering 65 nautical miles, or 120 kilometres, to land safely in the Portuguese islands of the Azores.

As it debated which of the three 'general classes of accident' to adopt, the ATSB clearly had political sensitivities in mind. It knew that Malaysia was, under the ICAO Annex 13 protocol, in charge of the overall air crash investigation, and had the ultimate responsibility to determine what happened to MH370. The ATSB and Transport Minister Truss knew the Malaysians would not like it if they pre-empted their investigation. So, right after outlining the three 'general classes of accidents', and before revealing its conclusion on which one it would go for, in its search definition report the ATSB wrote, in bold face and italics:

'Note: Given the imprecise nature of the SATCOM data, it was necessary to make some assumptions regarding pilot control inputs in order to define a search area of a practical size. These assumptions were only made for the purposes of defining a search area and there is no suggestion that the investigation authority will make similar assumptions.'

The first of the three 'general class of accident' – an 'in-flight upset' – was pretty easy to rule out.

That scenario was characterised by normal communication and manoeuvring up until an 'upset event'. The known facts about the flight of MH370 reflected exactly the opposite – there were not normal radio communications because they were broken off, and the en route manoeuvring of the aircraft was anything but normal: doing radical turns and steering over major airports without landing.

The two remaining options, though, involved a sensitive issue. If the ATSB determined the scenario it would work on was the third one, a 'glide event', Dolan and Truss would have to front the media to say the bureau had determined that someone had most likely flown MH370 to the end. That would have represented a conclusion about what happened on MH370 and pre-empted the Malaysian investigation report.

More controversially, since the scenario of pilot hijack was already widely regarded as the most realistic, journalists would have reported Dolan had effectively confirmed the ATSB thought one of the Malaysian pilots had taken 238 passengers and crew on a Malaysian government-owned airliner to their deaths.

The 'unresponsive crew/hypoxia' scenario would have avoided this. In that case Dolan could have just told journalists the ATSB did not really know what happened on MH370, but didn't need to know because that was the Malaysians' job; the bureau's sole job was to find the plane. When asked if there was evidence of pilot involvement he could say that was not his business, but add that it looked like no-one was flying the plane at the end. That was exactly what Dolan told journalists. He was able to do so because the ATSB chose to go with the 'unresponsive crew/hypoxia' scenario, rather than a 'glide event'.

In its report, the ATSB noted that despite having 'multiple redundant communications systems' no radio communications were received in the last seven hours of the flight. It also said the SATCOM data suggested there were probably no large changes to the aircraft's track in the last five hours after the turn south.

So, the ATSB chose to conclude:

'Given these observations, the final stages of the unresponsive crew/hypoxia event type appeared to best fit the available evidence for the final period of MH370's flight when it was heading in a generally southerly direction.

'This suggested that, for MH370, it was possible that after a long period of flight under autopilot control, fuel exhaustion would occur followed by a loss of control without any control inputs,' the report said.

That line was immediately followed by another note; this time not in italics, but still in bold:

'**Note: This suggestion is made for the sole purpose of assisting to define a search area. The determination of the actual factors involved in the loss of MH370 are the responsibility of the accident investigation authority and not the SSWG.**'

The 'note' again demonstrated how driven the ATSB was about the diplomatic niceties of not saying what happened on MH370. The next line in the report was, when reflected upon, quite extraordinary in terms of the logic of the search strategy, and revealing.

'Also allowing for the fact that a maximum glide distance of 100+ NM [nautical miles] would result in an impractically large search area, the search team considered that it was reasonable to assume that there were no control inputs following the flame-out of the second engine,' the ATSB said in its report.

The statement went against all the excellent scientific logic, deduction and methodological rigour which had preceded it. The ATSB was effectively saying it was going to exclude the other main end-of-flight scenario of a controlled glide with a pilot in control because, if it went with that, the search area would be too big against the financial budget available. Better to 'assume' there was no-one flying the plane after flame-out, regardless of the evidence, so as to stay within budget.

The day the ATSB released its report on 26 June, Dolan and Truss held a media conference. The journalists immediately probed whether the pair thought MH370 had been hijacked, and were repeatedly told it was not the ATSB's job to make such a determination, but the Malaysians' job. The question and answer session began as follows:

Question: Mr Dolan, could I just ask you, since the whole
 business began, there are massive rumours and speculation

that have filled the vacuum, I suppose, but also created enormous confusion about this . . . Can you just address two issues. One is the claim that the transponders in the aircraft must have been physically turned off by the pilots. Could that have actually happened as a result of an accident – a catastrophe, like an explosion or something? And the other is the claim that the aircraft must have been under control and from the course it was taken, as indicated on radar records, and clearly tried to dodge radar.

Dolan: Those are both for the Malaysian investigation, which we are assisting. The focus of the ATSB has been on assembling the flight path of the aircraft across the Indian Ocean so we can determine the most likely place where . . . we will find it . . . questions as to why this occurred are not ones that we needed to address in determining the search area, which has been our focus.

Truss: But it would be fair to comment that it is highly, highly likely that the aircraft was on autopilot, otherwise it could not follow the ordinary path that had been identified through the satellite's findings.

By this time, various elements of the Royal Malaysian Police investigation into the loss of MH370, which had drawn on assistance from the FBI, had started to leak out. Although it was only at the rumour level then, and the rumours themselves were vague, the suggestion was that Zaharie had a fairly sophisticated flight simulator at home, and that it had shown he had 'flown' a simulated flight that ended up in the southern Indian Ocean. A journalist put a question to this effect to Truss.

'Look, again, I – we – I don't really want to comment on areas which will probably be the responsibility of Malaysia in its investigation,' Truss said. 'Although, I've heard a number of reports about the pilot simulator, some saying it hasn't been active for a year, some saying it had certain mapping and so forth on it. But I can't confirm that that's accurate or not. And it's not really relevant to us in seeking to find the evidence.'

In fact, the issue of whether a pilot was flying the plane at the end of the flight was absolutely critical to the search strategy. If the view had been taken that MH370 had not crashed, uncontrolled, pretty much straight down, as the ATSB decided to assume, but had been glided up to 100 nautical miles in any direction, there would have been two logical options.

One would be to seek a huge increase several fold in funds to search a much, much bigger area, to cover the piloted glide scenario.

The other option, if the determination was that those vastly greater funds would not be forthcoming, would be to not search at all, at least until new information more accurately pinpointing MH370's likely location emerged. Such a decision would have been rational and justifiable on the basis that the narrow search budgeted for was going to be pointless and a waste of taxpayers' money, because the odds were that a pilot had glided the aircraft outside of it.

But the ATSB decided to use the logic the other way round: to exclude the possibility that a pilot flew the aircraft to the end because it would be too expensive to mount a credible search on that basis. Instead, it decided to 'assume' the plane was unpiloted at the end.

As will be outlined later in the book, many veteran professional pilots, engineers, scientists and air crash investigators believe the evidence available to the ATSB at the time it first decided on its search strategy pointed most strongly to a pilot flying MH370 to the end and ditching it. They think the ATSB locked into the alternative 'ghost flight' and 'death dive' scenario irrationally from the start, and possibly, though perhaps subliminally, to avoid offending Malaysia.

Some suggest the ATSB effectively gave that game away in its line that because 'a maximum glide distance of 100+ NM would result in an impractically large search area, the search team considered that it was reasonable to assume that there were no control inputs'. Once committed at the start to the 'ghost flight/death dive' theory, many aviation professionals consider that the ATSB ignored – either deliberately or subconsciously – all subsequent evidence that went against that theory.

The decision to assume no-one was piloting the plane at the end enabled the ATSB to complete its search plan. All the informa- tion – the last known position in the Straits of Malacca, the estimates of speed and possible courses from there based on the satellite data, calculations of when the aircraft would run out of fuel – was put into a grand equation. While the point at which the aircraft turned south was still unknown, the analysis of the satellite data narrowed the range of possibilities considerably. All of these elements were fed into the computer, and what spat out at the other end was a band of probabilities along the Seventh Arc. With the help of the Defence Science and Technology Group scientists, the ATSB worked out a probability 'hotspot', a sort of bulls-eye where the most likely tracks were concentrated. The hotspot was considerably farther south-west along the arc than determined in the surface search.

The tricky last part of the equation was this: how wide to make the search band along the Seventh Arc. Obviously, the wider the search band, the bigger the chances of finding the aircraft, but there was only a certain budget available, allowing a maximum search area of 60,000 square kilometres at that point. Every nautical mile wider along the Seventh Arc the target area was defined, the less far up and down the arc the search could go.

The ATSB drew up an interesting spreadsheet on this calculation. At one extreme, it looked at what would happen if the width along the Seventh Arc covered the possibility of an absolute maximum 125 nautical mile pilot-controlled glide either way, or a total width of 250 nautical miles. In that case, only 70 nautical miles along the Seventh Arc could be searched – the target area would be much wider than it was long. The ATSB said, 'these search widths give impractically small search lengths along the arc.'

At the other end, the investigators referred to a study done by the ATSB and the French air crash investigation authority, the BEA, of previous cases where aircraft had plunged down uncontrolled. It found that in the case of an 'upset' followed by a loss of control, all the impact points occurred within 20 nautical miles from the point at which the emergency began and, in the majority of cases, within 10 nautical miles.

Eschewing buffers for margin of error, the calculation was made of what a target zone with a width of 30 nautical miles would look like. That produced a very long, very narrow search area going 583 nautical miles up and down the Seventh Arc.

In the end, the ATSB team decided on a formula somewhere in the middle. They used the premise that after fuel exhaustion and with no pilot at the controls, the aircraft would descend and spiral.

The team settled on a search width of 50 nautical miles – 20 to the left and 30 to the right of the Seventh Arc. That division was based on some geometric calculations about the angle at which MH370 would have crossed the Seventh Arc at the end of the flight. It enabled a search distance of about 350 nautical miles, or 650 kilometres, vertically along the arc.

The ATSB produced a map which showed the 'priority' search area in orange, along with a 'medium' search area in blue, and a 'wide' area in grey – the last one representing the sort of search one would do taking in the controlled glide scenario and if resources were many times that budgeted.

With that, Foley was all set to get the ships under his control to the target search area and their towfish in the water as soon as enough of the bathymetric study had been completed to enable them to do so safely.

The deductions looked sound, and confidence was high that Foley and his team would find MH370 – so long as the assumption that no-one was flying the plane at the end was correct.

Byron Bailey had a fair bit of practical experience in areas relevant to the disappearance of MH370.

His more than half century career in aviation involved stints as an air force flying boat navigator, fighter pilot, air traffic controller and Boeing 777 captain. He also taught aerodynamics in the RAAF. Bailey is today a commercial pilot flying various corporate twin-engine jets. So, when it comes to MH370, Bailey told me in an interview, 'All this stuff that they are talking about, I know that stuff.'

That's why he couldn't believe what he regards as the lack of professional aviation knowledge demonstrated by the ATSB, which he attributes to the bureau's officers not having his sort of experience or expertise.

Bailey was born in the early hours one night in 1944, in Worthing in West Sussex, not too far from the Royal Air Force's Tangmere air base, amid huge explosions in the distance.

'My mother told me there was a bombing raid going on – the Germans were trying to hit Tangmere,' Bailey said.

Seven years later, Bailey's family migrated to New Zealand as 'ten-pound Poms', and he went to a Kiwi school but, he said, in fact 'spent most of that time building model airplanes'.

At 17, Bailey joined the Royal New Zealand Air Force as a cadet navigator. He spent three-and-a-half years as a navigator on Sunderland flying boats. The missions varied enormously: from searching for vessels in distress, to intercepting Russian whaling fleets. Bailey navigated the last ever military Sunderland flight, from Fiji to Auckland, in April 1967. It had been great fun, but coming to the end of his six-year 'short service' commission, he could see the writing on the wall.

'There is no future in being a navigator,' Bailey said.

So, like many young men from New Zealand in those years, Bailey 'crossed the ditch', and on the first working day after the Christmas/New Year's break in 1968, headed for the RAAF recruiting office in Sydney.

'I walked in and said I would like to join the RAAF.'

Next thing he knew, Bailey was in a pilot's course where he graduated first in flying, and first academically, at Point Cook in Melbourne. By the end of 1968, Bailey was deployed to the RAAF's Pearce base in Perth to learn to fly the de Havilland Vampire, a distinctive-looking twin boom jet fighter.

Bailey spent a decade in the RAAF, moving from Vampires to Sabres and then Mirages, of which three years were at Butterworth in Malaysia. A highlight of his air force career was performing as a member of the Mirage aerobatic team in 1975. Bailey left the RAAF in 1977; there was a promotion on offer to a desk job, but he wanted to keep flying.

'I had been passed over several times for promotion because of my rambunctious attitude,' Bailey said. 'I was a good flyer, not a good officer.' To his surprise, at the age of 33, Bailey was ignored by the major Australian airlines on the basis he was too old. Needing a job, he took a five-month course as an air traffic controller, and spent 18 months working in Sydney as a tower and area controller. But it wasn't for him.

'I found the whole job way too stressful and demanding,' Bailey said.

Hanging round the airport, Bailey discovered there was work to be had moonlighting as a pilot on piecemeal jobs, starting off on a Nomad.

'Disguising my voice as a pilot when I had to talk to air traffic control, I started building multi-engine hours,' Bailey said.

He got a full-time job flying a Learjet on night cargo operations for six years, then decided to have another go at landing an airline job. Bailey went back to his native England, re-sat his exams, and flew as a first officer for three airlines, including Dan Air. Then a friend told him about a new airline in Dubai, Emirates.

'I applied, got in on the 727, and became a captain shortly thereafter,' Bailey said.

He spent 15 years with Emirates, seven of them flying the Boeing 777. By the time MH370 disappeared, Bailey had 26,000 hours in his log book. Like all professional aviators, he developed an immediate and deep fascination in the MH370 saga right from the start.

'When it disappeared over the South China Sea I was very interested,' said Bailey. 'Then came the revelation of the Seventh Arc – I thought great, they'll find it fairly quickly. But then the months started rolling by, and the ATSB were publishing absolute rubbish.'

Bailey had no doubt whatsoever that there was only one possible explanation for what happened to MH370: pilot hijack – it was the only scenario where all the pieces of the puzzle fitted together. He assumed the ATSB would come to the same conclusion.

Bailey knew someone in government who had some knowledge of the MH370 investigation. 'I rang this guy, I said, what the hell is going on? He said, "it's just a joke – the FBI have supplied us with deleted flight plan information from the captain's home flight simulator, and they think the captain did it."'

'I thought great, they are going to announce that,' Bailey said.

The ATSB made no such announcement – in fact, though the bureau had the knowledge of what the FBI had found, Truss had if anything cast doubt on it at the media conference announcing the search plan.

Bailey was amazed and rang his contact. By this time, though, the ATSB and the JACC had started holding back key information about MH370 and instilling fear in the ranks.

'I asked him again, and he said, "Please don't mention me again, one guy here has been fired because he leaked information".'

That might have been the end of Bailey's involvement in the fight to reveal the truth about MH370, but for the serendipitous fact he and the then editor of the Sydney *Daily Telegraph*, Paul Whittaker, were in the same tennis club and got to know each other.

'I kept saying, this is ridiculous, so he said, write an article, and so I did.'

In fact, Bailey wrote lots of articles on MH370, first for the *Daily Telegraph*, and then *The Australian*, after Whittaker moved to the national morning daily as editor-in-chief.

Like other major MH370 stories, Bailey's features in *The Australian* went straight onto the top ten most read online list, often going to number one, and stayed there a good length of time. In his articles, Bailey systematically took to task what he regarded as the flawed logic of the ATSB's reports.

To suggest the pilots could have been overcome by decompression and hypoxia was absurd, Bailey wrote. If the decompression was slow, alarms would have gone off and they would have reacted; if rapid, they would have immediately initiated emergency action according to protocol.

That would have involved rapidly putting on oxygen masks and selecting the transponder setting which would immediately notify air traffic controllers of an emergency.

The flight path of MH370 was also completely inconsistent with the 'unresponsive crew/hypoxia' scenario chosen by the ATSB, Bailey said. If the aircraft had decompressed and the pilots lost consciousness, Bailey said the aircraft, which would have been on autopilot, would, like Helios Airways Flight 522, have flown itself to its programmed destination, in MH370's case, Beijing. But MH370 did not do anything like that – after radio contact was lost, it flew in a deliberate fashion with several turns before the last turn and long track south. Only a pilot could have made that happen.

The ATSB's reliance on there being no control inputs – changes in course or direction – on the final long leg, Bailey said, was ignorant of the fact that this is standard operating procedure for modern airliners: they are flown almost entirely on autopilot.

Bailey said it's actually quite difficult to fly a Boeing 777 manually at high altitude, and for this reason, pilots are generally instructed to put the aircraft on autopilot after getting airborne and just a few hundred metres above the ground.

Bailey also argued that the early part of the flight showed a skilled aviator was in control. To alter course several times in such a clearly deliberate manner would require a pilot who knew exactly what he was doing and had a reason to do it.

For all those reasons, Bailey wrote in articles going right back to 2014, the ATSB's 'unresponsive crew/hypoxia' theory simply didn't stack up.

Now, over the following months and years, the ATSB, initially in off-the-record briefings to journalists, and later in oblique statements to Senate Estimates, seemed to accept that a pilot probably did hijack the aircraft. But the bureau never adequately explained why it concluded that pilot would not, and did not, fly it to the end to make sure the manifest objective of disappearing the plane was achieved. At that point in 2014 Bailey was critiquing what the ATSB had publicly stated in its own precise words: that the 'unresponsive crew/hypoxia' general class of accident was the basis for its search strategy.

Bailey was far from alone among professional aviators in identifying the 'pilot hijack' theory from pretty much the start as the most likely, and rejecting the ATSB's assumption to this day that it was a 'ghost flight' with no pilot flying it at the end. As will be outlined in later chapters, senior British captain Simon Hardy, who trains pilots on Boeing 777s, did an extensive analysis early on that asserted the only logical conclusion from the known facts was that Zaharie hijacked his own plane and ditched it. Hardy gave extensive briefings to the ATSB, starting in January 2015 and including visits to Canberra and Fremantle, on his findings. He told them exactly where he had deduced Zaharie ditched the aircraft – it was not that far off the target area defined by the ATSB, but the ATSB did not go that small extra distance to search it.

Just four weeks after MH370 went missing, former Malaysia Airlines captain Dick Evans told news media only one scenario 'ticked all the boxes'. Evans, a Western Australian, was so sure straight up that he sent emails to news outlets. One sent on 9 April 2014 said:

'Could not the lack of detectable surface debris be consistent with the aircraft making a successful planned ditching at sea when fuel was low and power available, in daylight and without significant damage, but depressurised to allow quicker water ingestion, all exits closed, then sinking intact?'

Undeterred, the ATSB instructed ships to sail to search some of the most difficult seas in the world based on the premise that the professional pilots were wrong, and conversely that the assumption that MH370 was a ghost flight at the end, with no-one flying the plane, was right.

THEORY THREE:
ONBOARD FIRE

About 40 minutes into the flight, having settled onto cruise altitude, MH370 first officer Fariq Abdul Hamid was regaling Captain Zaharie Ahmad Shah of his marriage plans.

Fariq's fiancée was the beautiful Nadira Ramli, whom he had met at Langkawi flying school about nine years earlier; she was a pilot on Malaysia Airlines' budget rival, AirAsia. Just as Fariq was mid-sentence extolling the many virtues of his beloved Nadira, the left, pilot-side windshield heater caught fire, burning out some circuits including that of the secondary radar transponder and ACARS system. Well trained for such emergencies, both pilots immediately donned their oxygen masks and Zaharie ordered Fariq to turn off the left electrical AC bus to cut power to the short-circuiting heater. In the process, though they were not to know it, the pilots turned off the satellite data unit that makes the electronic handshakes with Inmarsat.

As Fariq concentrated on controlling the aircraft, Zaharie fought the fire with an extinguisher, both pilots waiting until the immediate crisis was in hand before making a radio distress call. Pilots are trained that radio communication is the third priority in such an in-flight emergency, after flying the aircraft and setting a heading to the nearest suitable airport. The drill is 'aviate, navigate, communicate', and Fariq did just that by making sure he had control of the aircraft by making a short initial turn right, then quickly turning back towards Malaysia and setting the autopilot on course for Kota Bharu.

Then, disaster. While reaching with the extinguisher, Zaharie accidentally pulled the tube from his oxygen mask out of its socket. With nothing to stop it, the pilot's oxygen bottle started dumping the highly flammable gas at a huge rate into the cockpit, creating a violent fire impossible to control. Zaharie, since he was not in his seat, managed to make it out of the cockpit alive, but badly burnt. Fariq, still strapped in, perished in the inferno.

Then the crisis compounded. The fire weakened the bottom of the windshield and dislodged it, leading to the air rushing out of the cockpit and a sharp fall in temperature, putting out the fire. The decompression of the aircraft, still at high altitude, would cause the oxygen masks to drop, providing about 12 minutes of breathing for the passengers – not quite enough time for the aircraft to get over Kota Bharu and enable them to make a mobile phone call.

Zaharie got to one of the portable oxygen bottles and masks available to the crew before hypoxia set in. Once the fire was out, though badly injured but with the help of a flight attendant, he returned to the cockpit, but found a scene of devastation. Apart from killing his co-pilot, the fire had partly, but not completely, gutted the flight deck. Some elements, including the radio, satellite phone and ACARS system, had melted, cutting off all forms of communication.

It then became a battle of gruesome desperation and bravery, with a badly injured Zaharie returning for brief periods to the freezing, wind-blasted cockpit to try to regain control, with the aid of the flight attendant. The flight management system was sufficiently intact to set new headings, although the fire had knocked out the auto-throttle so Zaharie could not set it to descend.

On a dark night, with a smoky windscreen and some non-functioning instruments, taking over manual control would be problematic and risky. As Zaharie flew over Penang he decided to turn north-west up the Straits of Malacca, away from built-up areas, to continue the troubleshooting process, during which time he turned the left electrical AC bus back on, repowering the satellite data unit. But then, with his own and his assistant's portable oxygen tanks running out, and all the passengers and the rest of the cabin crew either comatose or dead, Zaharie accepted the game was up. He briefly removed his oxygen mask, and told the flight attendant,

'It's two of us versus the danger of killing a whole lot of people in a busy shipping channel'.

Zaharie turned the autopilot to a southerly heading, pointing the aircraft to nowhere in the southern Indian Ocean, and soon MH370 became a ghost flight, again exactly as the ATSB said.

There are a lot of attractions with this theory, which was put to me by former RAAF supply officer, retired logistics manager with Ansett, private pilot and amateur aviation sleuth, Mick Gilbert. Among other elements, it deals with the sub-mystery of why the satellite data unit was turned off for a time, then came back on.

There are plenty of precedents of onboard fires. South African Airways Flight 295, mentioned earlier, is one. Another, discussed in more detail in coming chapters, is Swissair Flight 111 which came down in 1998 off the coast of Nova Scotia as a result of a rapidly spreading fire started by an electrical short circuit, killing 229 people. Yet another example, also discussed later on, is the 1991 in-flight fire and crash in Saudi Arabia of a Nationair DC-8 in which 261 died.

The one which Gilbert focused on, though, was EgyptAir Flight 667, an accident involving a Boeing 777 in Cairo in 2011. The aircraft was, fortunately, still on the ground at the time, rather than in the air on the way to its scheduled destination of Jeddah, Saudi Arabia. As the crew were waiting for a late passenger, an oxygen fire, the result of a suspected electrical fault, broke out and spread quickly from a rupture in the tube to the first officer's oxygen mask. The blaze melted many, but not all, control features in the cockpit. The captain immediately ordered the first officer to leave the cockpit and evacuate the passengers while he fought the fire with an extinguisher, but the damage was extensive. There are photos on the web of the EgyptAir Flight 667 cockpit, showing the blackened features from the oxygen fire with some communications and navigation equipment melted, but others not.

The 'Onboard Fire' theory does rely on a lot of things happening in sequence, but air accidents very often do involve not just one improbable event, but several.

SEVEN

'GRIEF RETURNS WITH THE REVOLVING YEAR'

By early October 2014, the secret topography of the southern Indian Ocean had been revealed, the search ships were getting ready to sail, and the ATSB needed a dashing figure to front its new hunt for MH370.

Paul Kennedy was their man.

Kennedy was the lean, British-born, Perth-based project director of the Fugro survey group team whose vessels were to lead the next valiant effort to find the holy grail of aviation. The ATSB media unit produced a video, watchable on YouTube, featuring Kennedy on board *Fugro Discovery*, presumably docked at, or sailing off, Perth. He responded to some questions from an interviewer about the new underwater search for MH370. The remoteness of the search zone in the southern Indian Ocean, and the stormy seas meant the challenge was tough, Kennedy said in the video, shot by Chris Beerens from the Royal Australian Navy.

'We're more than seven days' sail from the nearest civilisation, which is Western Australia, so that's an awful long way if things go wrong,' he said. 'It's rough where we are, it's terribly rough, so you don't sleep particularly well, so fatigue is one of our biggest issues offshore.'

But Kennedy also stressed the sophistication of the search effort.

'The deep tow on board the vessel is called "Dragon". It's got three forms of sensors on board. The way I like to make an analogy: it's got ears, it can listen – that's the acoustic sensors on board; it's got eyes, that's the cameras; and it's got a nose, it's got a sniffer – it can sniff jet fuel. People say, will you find it? The answer is: if it's in the area we're searching, we will find it.'

It was derring-do, *Boys' Own* stuff, just the message the ATSB wanted to get out there to suggest Australian taxpayers' money was in the best hands for the task of finding MH370 and its precious black box flight data and cockpit voice recorders. Funnily enough, a bit later in the piece, it was Kennedy who by speaking truth to power caused the biggest single embarrassment for the ATSB – more about that later this chapter.

The underwater search directed by Peter Foley for the ATSB at the strategic level, and Kennedy at the operational level for the big Dutch-based international underwater survey group Fugro, started with great enthusiasm. No-one could doubt the degree of hard work and dedication of those who designed and supervised the new search, but as Foley told the IPA seminar, 'the heroes are the guys who are on the search vessel'.

The bathymetric work had been hard enough, involving *Fugro Equator*, the Chinese vessel *Zhu Kezhen*, the Malaysian survey ship KD *Mutiara*, and two support ships, the Malaysian naval vessel *Bunga Mas 6* and the Chinese government ship *Haixun 01*. The *Haixun 01* seemed to have to spend a fair bit of time in port; the 10 September 2014 JACC operational bulletin said it had been 'stationed at the Port of Fremantle'. The operational bulletin two weeks later said 'the Chinese support vessel *Haixun 01* continued to be stationed at the Port of Fremantle for repairs'.

Fun-loving knockabout or calculating mass murderer? Sakinab Shah, elder sister of MH370 captain Zaharie Ahmad Shah, at her Kuala Lumpur home in 2016, says he was an affectionate man who 'loved life, loved fun' and had many women friends. 'He was naughty, I admit that, but at the end of the day he always went home.'

MH370 captain Zaharie Ahmad Shah, seen here with fellow Malaysia Airlines pilots, and below, passing through security on the night of MH370's final flight. Zaharie was a well-liked, highly accomplished and respected senior flight officer and was also politically active.

Former kindergarten teacher turned political activist Fatima Pardi had a special friendship with Zaharie Ahmad Shah, 20 years her senior. The relationship ended a few months before the plane went missing, but Pardi claimed to have had an exchange of messages with Zaharie two days before the flight. She has never revealed their content.

SANJIT DAS

Zaharie's wingman, MH370 first officer Fariq Abdul Hamid was a young man engaged to be married to a fellow pilot he met at flight school. On an earlier flight he had appeared in a social media post smiling with a young blonde South African woman, Jonti Roos, who had been invited to the cockpit.

Interior of a Malaysia Airlines Boeing 777 200–ER like MH370. Zaharie Ahmad Shah would have been sitting in the captain's left–hand seat in the cockpit (above); his co–pilot Fariq Abdul Hamid at his right. Perth engineer Paul Weeks, was in the business class section, similar to that shown (below), on his way to an exciting new job in Mongolia. Brisbane's Rod and Mary Burrows and fellow adventurers Bob and Cathy Lawton were seated in economy (bottom), as were Sydney couple Gu Naijun and Li Yuan.

Brisbane couples Mary and Rodney Burrows (top) and Catherine and Robert Lawton (below) were close friends who had known each other for many years. MH370 was to be the next leg in a trip of a lifetime to Asia. Instead they vanished, leaving children and grandchildren to wonder to this day about what befell the flight and what fate their loved ones met.

Danica and Paul Weeks met at the Munich Beer Fest as young Antipodeans living in London and doing the usual European grand tour. 'I moved in with him two weeks later,' Danica recalls. The whirlwind romance and 14-year marriage ended when she farewelled Paul aboard MH370. 'Everything since then is like a blur.' Danica was left a single mother with their two young boys, Lincoln, three, and Jack, 11 months.

In the days after MH370 disappeared, friends and family of the missing gathered for candlelight vigils like this one in Kuala Lumpur. The hunt was on but with every day hopes faded.

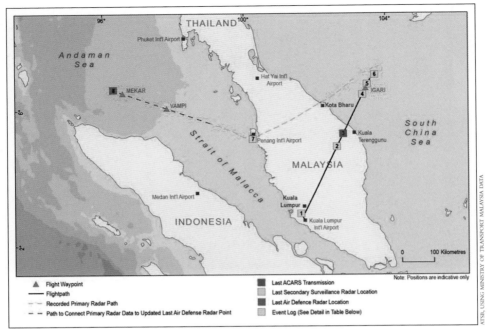

MH370 lifted into the air at 12:42am, Malaysian time, on 8 March 2014, its wheels never to touch the ground again. There were a few radio transmissions, with the eerie last one, 'Good night, Malaysian Three Seven Zero', recorded 37 minutes after take-off, at 1:19am. After that a lot of things happened in quick succession including the disappearance of the aircraft from air traffic control screens and, as military radar later revealed, a sharp U-turn back toward Malaysia. The aircraft went beyond primary radar range at 2:22am.

Nine days after MH370 vanished, on 17 March 2014, Malaysian Defence Minister and Acting Minister of Transport Hishammuddin Hussein, second from right, told media two gigantic search 'corridors' had been established after analysis of satellite data that showed the aircraft either went north-west over Asia as far as the Caspian Sea, or south-west to a desolate stretch of the southern Indian Ocean. With Hishammuddin, from left to right, were Malaysia Airlines chief executive Ahmad Jauhari Yahya, Malaysian Deputy Foreign Minister Hamzah Zainudin and Malaysian Department of Civil Aviation director general Azharuddin Abdul Rahman.

0002 P CAM 2
25-MAR-14 23:55:43
0002

The desolation of the needle-in-a-haystack hunt for MH370 can be seen in this shot taken at sunrise in late March 2014, from the stern of the Royal Australian Navy ship HMAS *Success*. The vessel's crew of 218 scoured the southern Indian Ocean during the surface search, which covered an area the size of western Europe, yet found no trace of the plane or its 239 passengers.

Kojiro Tanaka, head of the Japan Coast Guard contingent in the search for MH370, prepares notes on board a Gulfstream V aircraft en route to the southern Indian Ocean on 1 April 2014. The surface search for MH370 involved sea vessels and aircraft from many nations whose leaders recognised the urgent need to solve the mystery.

The hunt for MH370 in the early weeks after its disappearance in the southern Indian Ocean involved close cooperation between mariners, airmen, and underwater search experts. In this 9 April 2014 shot a Royal Australian Air Force AP-3C Orion flies past Australian Defence vessel *Ocean Shield* on a mission to drop sonar buoys to listen for the 'pings' from the aircraft's black boxes in a desperate bid to locate the aircraft before the dying batteries in the underwater locator beacons, only guaranteed to last 30 days, ran out.

'If this mystery is solvable, we will solve it,' Australian Prime Minister Tony Abbott told members of the 550 strong international brigade during his visit to RAAF Base Pearce near Perth Monday, 31 March 2014. Abbott had agreed to Malaysia's request to lead the next hunt for MH370 but even he admitted the search for the missing plane was an 'extraordinarily difficult exercise'.

'It's time to go under water.' On 14 April former Australian defence chief Angus Houston announced the next critical stage of the hunt for MH370. The week before, Houston had raised hopes by revealing the hunt's 'most promising lead' – two detected 'pings' possibly emanating from MH370's black box recorders. Australian vessel *Ocean Shield* launched autonomous underwater vehicle *Bluefin-21* to the deep to try to find the wreckage.

As chief commissioner of the Australian Transport Safety Bureau in 2014, the buck stopped with Martin Dolan. The ATSB's failed search strategy assumed MH370's pilots were unconscious or dead at the end of the flight and the aircraft plunged down uncontrolled after running out of fuel flying on autopilot. Four years later, Dolan admitted to *60 Minutes* that the theory might be wrong.

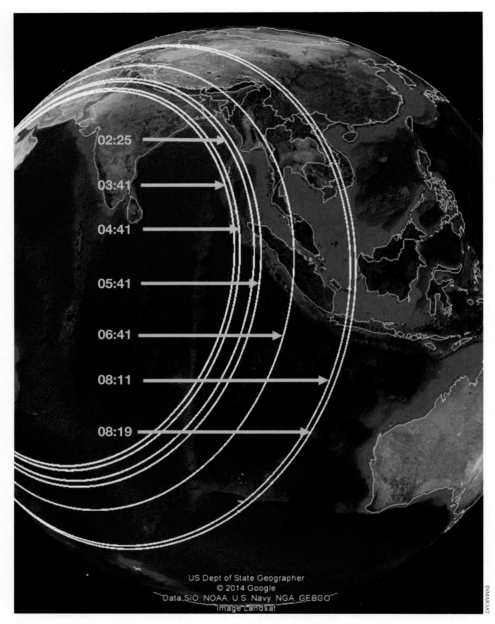

02:25
03:41
04:41
05:41
06:41
08:11
08:19

The Seventh Arc is the best clue in the grail quest to find MH370. It's the last of seven rings around the earth upon which MH370 is believed to have been at different times on 8 March 2014. The rings are derived from sophisticated mathematical calculations of how far the aircraft would have been from a satellite at each of seven mostly hourly automatic satellite transmission 'handshakes'. The first, at 2:25am, is consistent with the last primary radar tracking showing MH370 heading north-west up the Straits of Malacca, and the second at 3:41am showed the aircraft, at least initially, continued in that direction. The other five handshakes show MH370 turned left on a long track south to the southern Indian Ocean. The final transmission at 8:19am is the most critical, because analysts believe MH370 had just run out of fuel and was on its way down. The seventh 'ring' was narrowed down to an 'arc' off Western Australia by calculating how far MH370 could have flown with the fuel it had. Pilots believe the Seventh Arc does indeed show where MH370 was at the end of the flight but think, contrary to the ATSB theory of an unpiloted descent at the end, Captain Zaharie Ahmad Shah flew the aircraft beyond the search zone and ditched it, just as the sun was rising.

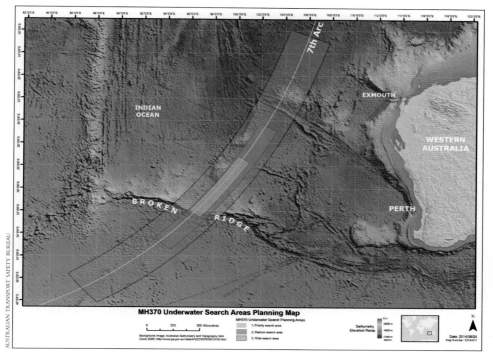

MH370 Underwater Search Areas Planning Map

How far? How much? The ATSB had to decide how far around the Seventh Arc to send the ships to look for MH370 on the sea bed. If its budget had been unlimited, the ATSB could have covered the whole of the 'wide area search' marked in grey, allowing for the possibility that a pilot flew the aircraft to the end and ditched it. But because its funds were limited, it decided to 'assume' the pilots were unconscious or dead, producing a cheaper option, divided into an orange 'priority search area' and a light blue 'medium search area'.

To the deep. On 14 April 2014, with four acoustic 'pings' detected around the Seventh Arc from what was hoped to be MH370's black box underwater locator beacons, *Bluefin-21*, a high-tech autonomous undersea robot submarine equipped with a range of sophisticated scanning devices and cameras, was deployed from the Australian Defence Vessel *Ocean Shield* to look for the aircraft on the ocean floor.

In their ever more desperate bid to find MH370, hunters ran 'towfish' over the ocean floor terrain. Data from the bathymetric surveys was analysed by Geoscience Australia and modelled to show the dramatic undersea volcanoes, valleys, and escarpment of Broken Ridge.

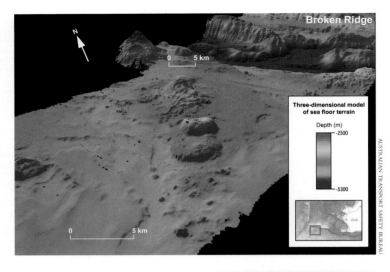

Broken Ridge

N

0   5 km

Three-dimensional model
of sea floor terrain

Depth (m)
-2500

-5300

AUS

0   5 km

While the ATSB did not find MH370, it did stumble across some fascinating shipwrecks which told their own eerie tales in the strange sepia tones of high-resolution sonar imaging. This wreck, detected by the crew of *Havila Harmony* in December 2015, was determined to be a steel/iron vessel dating from the turn of the 19th century.

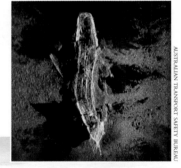

THE OCEAN INFINITY SEARCH

The ship *Seabed Constructor* led the 2018 hunt for the missing MH370 plane using mini-submarines

UNMANNED
SURFACE
VEHICLE
(USV)

malaysia

MALAYSIA

Kuala Lumpur

N
W   E
S

MADAGASCAR

INDONESIA

AUSTRALIA

Durban

The new
search area

SOUTH
AFRICA

0km   2000

Approximate search area
■ ATSB   ■ Ocean Infinity

HUGIN AUTONOMOUS
UNDERWATER VEHICLE (AUV)

Source: Ocean Infinity   Graphic: VIKI SIZGORIC

The private British-owned company Ocean Infinity launched a new search for MH370 in early 2018 using a fleet of high-tech robot mini-submarines. The Malaysian government would only pay Ocean Infinity if it found the wreckage. It finished its search in May 2018.

It floated for more than a year across the whole of the Indian Ocean, a tantalising clue to the world's greatest aviation mystery. In July 2015, French authorities recovered the MH370 right flaperon found by local council worker Johnny Begue on a remote beach on Reunion (above). Later, a flap was found on the island of Pemba, off the coast of Tanzania, shown here with the head of the ATSB's underwater hunt for MH370, Peter Foley (right).

'I saw this strange plane.' A year into a failed search effort, an unsatiated media reported locals of remote atolls in the Maldives had witnessed a mysterious aircraft with the colours of Malaysia Airlines' livery on the morning of 8 March 2014. Abdu Rasheed Ibrahim said he saw: 'the biggest plane I've ever seen from this island.'

Chinese anger boils over: Zhang Huijun, whose husband and daughter disappeared on MH370, breaks down during a protest in Beijing on 29 July 2016. She was one of many furious at the decision by Australian, Chinese and Malaysian ministers a week earlier to suspend the hunt for the aircraft once the 120,000 square kilometre target zone was covered.

Above: Australian Transport Minister Darren Chester and his Malaysian counterpart Liow Tiong Lai officially announce the end of the ATSB's subsea hunt for MH370 on 23 January 2017, at a dock in Perth with the search vessel *Fugro Equator* in the background. Directly behind the two ministers is Fugro's project director, Paul Kennedy, and, in yellow vest and sunglasses, ATSB chief commissioner Greg Hood.

Right: 'MH370 – Still hoping back soon.' These mournful words are seen here written on a mural on the 'Wall of Hope' at Kuala Lumpur International Airport.

SIMON HARDY

BYRON BAILEY

MIKE KEANE

LARRY VANCE

British Boeing 777 captain Simon Hardy, Australian former Boeing 777 captain and RAAF fighter pilot Byron Bailey, former easyJet chief pilot and RAF fighter pilot Mike Keane, and Canadian pilot and veteran air crash investigator Larry Vance have separately analysed the known facts of MH370 and concluded it was hijacked by its captain, Zaharie Ahmad Shah, flown to the end, and ditched. Hardy, Bailey and Keane have made specific predictions of where MH370 lies, in all cases just outside the south-western end of where the ATSB searched. Vance says if he had to search, he too would go where the other pilots propose.

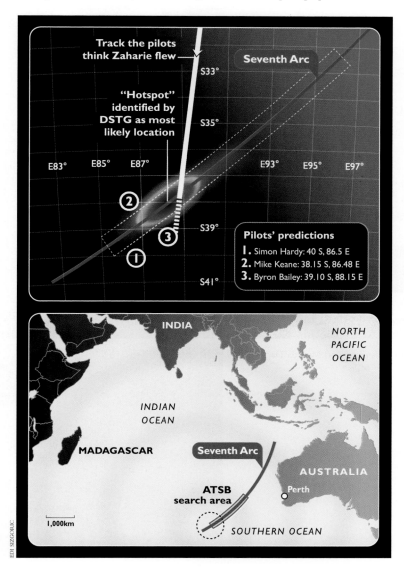

Track the pilots think Zaharie flew

Seventh Arc

S33°

"Hotspot" identified by DSTG as most likely location

S35°

E83°   E85°   E87°   E93°   E95°   E97°

②

S39°

③

①

Pilots' predictions
1. Simon Hardy: 40 S, 86.5 E
2. Mike Keane: 38.15 S, 86.48 E
3. Byron Bailey: 39.10 S, 88.15 E

S41°

INDIA

NORTH PACIFIC OCEAN

INDIAN OCEAN

MADAGASCAR

Seventh Arc

AUSTRALIA

Perth

ATSB search area

1,000km

SOUTHERN OCEAN

EDI SIZGORIC

Karla and Jayden Burrows, the children of Queensland couple Mary and Rodney Burrows who disappeared on MH370, joined families of the other Australian passengers at a memorial service held in March 2017 at St John's Anglican Cathedral in Brisbane.

Danica Weeks, who lost her husband Paul on MH370, poses for a photo with her sons Lincoln, four, and Jack, one, outside Parliament House, on 5 March 2015. Danica and extended families of the Australasians lost on MH370 had been invited to Canberra to attend a memorial event.

In Jeanette Maguire's living room in Brisbane is a memento to her sister Cathy and brother-in-law Rob Lawton, lost on MH370. The collection has a photo of the Lawtons on their wedding day, a couple of purple candles from the 2017 memorial service, and one of the china dolls Cathy used to collect.

AP PHOTO/ROB GRIFFITH

While some of the main features of the seabed in this part of the Indian Ocean were known, particularly a massive escarpment known as Broken Ridge, most of it was not. What was discovered, and later released in stunning simulated colours showing elevation, was an extraordinary world of undersea mountains, volcanoes, valleys, depressions and canyons.

It was going to be very tricky to get the towfish low enough, about 100 metres above the sea floor on its 10 kilometre armoured fibre-optic cable, to perform the sonar imaging without hitting terrain. The autonomous underwater vehicle with its capacity to independently dodge obstacles was going to be crucial for some parts of the search.

By early October 2014, about 120,000 kilometres of seabed along the Seventh Arc had been surveyed.

The weather was getting better, so the search ships and their crews readied for action, including the vessel *GO Phoenix* chartered by the Malaysian government, with equipment and experts from Phoenix International. The JACC bulletin made the low-key announcement on 8 October: the new search was on.

'On Monday, 6 October 2014, *GO Phoenix* arrived in the vicinity of the search area and, following system checks and vehicle deployment, underwater search operations commenced on the Seventh Arc.'

Foley had told the IPA seminar his greatest fear was that in the massive seas, someone would be killed. It was a long, grinding job for both the crews out on the water, and the planners in Canberra and Perth. Foley got up early enough to review the sonar reports at 5:30am every day. The JACC team met to discuss the progress of the search each day, with a Malaysian representative present.

Out on the ocean, the multinational crew of *Fugro Discovery* worked 12-hour shifts seven days a week, for periods of six weeks. And week by week, the JACC issued its operational bulletins, which reported the coming and going of ships, the difficulties of the weather, the steady rise in the number of square kilometres searched, and the lack of any sign of MH370.

By the start of March 2015, with the first anniversary of the disappearance of MH370 looming, 24,000 square kilometres, or more than 40 per cent of the 60,000 square kilometre target zone, had been searched. The Australian, Malaysian and Chinese governments had always said that while finding MH370 was essential in order to determine what went wrong, as with all air crash investigations, they also said the search effort's key objective was to provide closure for the families of those lost. The first anniversary was, therefore, a big deal.

'We all got taken down to Canberra, 25 of us, all the rest of the extended family,' said Danica Weeks.

The government set up a briefing session, with Transport Minister Truss, Foreign Affairs Minister Julie Bishop and ATSB boss Dolan. Prime Minister Abbott showed up for morning tea.

'I'm firing questions at Martin Dolan,' Danica said of the briefing session, saying she also engaged in sparring matches with Zielke. 'Judith has been wonderful, but we do fire each other up. I was asking, what are they doing? There was really no directive of where to search. Did they leave on a wild goose chase?'

Danica has a favourable impression of how the ATSB dealt with her, and particularly Foley.

'Peter Foley is an incredible man,' she said.

After the briefing, the families were then brought into the House of Representatives to hear the speeches. Abbott's speech, according to Danica's assessment, was 'weak and nul and void'.

'My pledge is that we are taking every reasonable step to bring your uncertainty to an end,' Abbott, in remarks addressed to the families, told Parliament.

But in a remark he probably didn't really have to add on that occasion, Abbott said, 'I can't promise that the search will go on at this intensity forever. But I do reassure the families of our hope and our expectation that the ongoing search will succeed.'

By contrast, Danica said, opposition leader Bill Shorten's speech was 'wonderful'. It was certainly more ambitious. He started out quoting the English poet Shelley.

Winter is come and gone.

But grief returns with the revolving year.

'Shelley wrote those words nearly 200 years ago when mourning the loss of his friend John Keats,' Shorten said. 'Today, as we pay our respects to the 239 souls lost aboard MH370, we offer our heartfelt condolences to those for whom a year has come and gone yet their grief abides.

'Our hearts go out to you, the people they loved. None of us will know your sorrow.'

The session finished with a minute's silence. Then, the families went home, the politicians went back to politics, and Foley went back to reviewing the sonar reports every morning at 5:30am.

It was pretty monotonous for the search crews, as they made one long pass towing the towfish, then another long pass. It was, Kennedy had said, what the crews called 'mowing the lawn'. There was, however, the rare moment where something actually happened, like finding a shipwreck. The first such discovery, in May 2015, must have caused huge initial excitement for those on the ship in question, *Fugro Equator*.

Foley said in a media statement at the time that the sonar imaging returns, at 3900 metres, had 'aspects that generated interest, multiple small bright reflections in a relatively small area of otherwise feature-less seabed'.

The autonomous underwater vehicle was deployed for a low-level pass with a camera, and came back with intriguing images of an anchor and a scatter of small, cricket ball-sized black objects taken to be pieces of coal.

It was a fascinating find, but not what they were looking for.

'On the optimistic side,' Foley said, 'it's shown that if there's a debris field in the search area, we'll find it.'

A second shipwreck was discovered later on, and the clear image of its outline in the strange brass-tinged tones of the sonar imaging was released, showing surprising detail with the ship's bowsprit, or pole on the bow, clearly visible.

By April 2015, 60 per cent of the target 60,000 square kilometres had been searched, and the hunt was due to come to a finish by the end of May if MH370 were not found.

It was a hard one for the governments; no-one wanted to stop the search, but the issue was where to draw the line.

It was time for the three governments to decide the next move. Truss; the new Malaysian transport minister, Liow Tiong Lai; and Chinese Transport Minister Yang met in Kuala Lumpur.

The decision was taken to double the search area to 120,000 square kilometres if the existing 60,000 were found to not contain the aircraft.

'Ministers recognise the additional search area may take up to a year to complete given the adverse weather conditions in the coming winter months,' they said in a statement.

There was an implied suggestion, though, that this would be the end of the trail.

'Upon completion of the additional 60,000 sq km, all high-probability search areas would have been covered,' they said.

The Australian and Malaysian governments agreed they would share the cost of the search – China, even though it had by far the most nationals on the aircraft, would not cough up any cash, but Yang continued the fine words of moral support.

'The Chinese side is ready to stand by, as always, by our fellow friends Australia, as well as our Malaysia friends,' he said.

The Chinese also insisted, however, that they were contributing to the search in kind, by supplying vessels. But a bit later on, while

reading the weekly JACC search report bulletins, I noticed something a bit odd: the Chinese government ship *Dong Hai Jiu 101*
almost always seemed to be docked in, or lying just off, Fremantle,
not searching. *Dong Hai Jiu 101* just kept having extraordinarily
bad luck, forcing it to return to port. At one stage it lost its towfish,
due, the JACC said, to the 'failure of a tow cable connector'. Then a
crewman was injured, forcing another trip back to port. Eventually,
it seemed the boat just gave up and returned to hang around
Fremantle.

'Projected weather conditions for the next several weeks preclude
the effective deployment of search equipment from this vessel,'
the JACC reported. '*Dong Hai Jiu 101* will remain at anchor off
Fremantle until weather conditions improve.'

When I put questions to the new head of the JACC, Judith
Zielke, who as mentioned took over from Houston after he moved
to deal with MH17 in Ukraine, she would not reveal how many days
the Chinese vessel had spent conducting actual underwater search
operations. (For the record, the battles I had with the JACC, which
was clearly suppressing information to the media, only occurred well
after Houston left the JACC.)

Faced with a brick wall from the JACC, I instead did an analysis of
weekly operational bulletins, and had it crossed checked by another
journalist. *The Australian* broke the story that, in the more than six
months since it joined the search for the missing airliner, *Dong Hai
Jiu 101* had its equipment in the water looking for MH370 for somewhere between a minimum of 17 days, to a maximum of 30 days.

Throughout the coverage of the MH370 saga, I went through
a three-stage process in trying to establish the truth. The first was
to ask the ATSB and the JACC what the truth was. When they
would not answer that question, the next stage was to submit an
FOI request for that information. If the agencies refused to release
the information sought under FOI, the next stage was to report that
it had been suppressed, and name the officer who had suppressed it.

(Sometimes there was a fourth stage: getting a senator to ask the same officers the same questions in Senate Estimates.)

The FOI request was made for documents revealing how many days the *Dong Hai Jiu 101* had spent looking for MH370. Not long after, *The Australian* reported the first of many failures by the ATSB and the JACC to be transparent about the search – a document existed, the JACC said, but would be suppressed. *The Australian* reported that the JACC knocked back the Freedom of Information request, stating that to release the document 'would cause harm to the Australian government's relationship with other governments'. The JACC had decided to use the exemption under the FOI Act relating to 'documents affecting national security, defence or international relations'.

So, just what was *Dong Hai Jiu 101* doing while its sailors were sitting around, twiddling their thumbs, in or just off Fremantle? According to some of Australia's leading security experts, the answer is pretty simple: the Chinese ship was spying. Western Australia is home to the Australian submarine base near Perth at HMAS *Stirling*; the elite Australian army Special Air Service Regiment, also in a suburb of Perth; the Australian Defence Satellite Communications electronic spying station at Kojarena near Geraldton; and the North West Cape naval communications station near Exmouth. *The Australian* broke the story.

'From my past intelligence experience I would be surprised if a vessel like the *Dong Hai Jiu 101* did not have an intelligence collection role,' said Clive Williams, a former Australian army officer and former Director of Security Intelligence told *The Australian*. 'WA is of course a target-rich environment in terms of various Australian defence activities. The People's Liberation Army Navy has a strong interest in the Indian Ocean where "research" activity is conducted by Chinese ships including its hospital ship, the *Peace Ark*.'

Australian Strategic Policy Institute executive director Peter Jennings also said the *Dong Hai Jiu 101* 'would as a matter of routine be noting any activity into and out of Fremantle and HMAS *Stirling*, which all adds to a database of ship movements and observed capabilities.' But Jennings said the real value of the *Dong Hai Jiu 101*'s activities was 'learning first-world techniques, tactics and procedures' from Western experts.

Greg Barton from Deakin University said the ship would probably be spying 'as a matter of course'.

'Apart from actual intel, it would also represent an opportunity to gauge their signals intelligence capacity in terms of working out what they can pick up at that sort of distance, such as working out how well their hydrophone instrumentation can track submarine movements,' he said.

The story was widely read and drew nearly 100 comments. A commenter named 'Christopher' wrote:

'I think it's time to thank the Chinese very much for their efforts in locating MH370 and escort their vessel with all appropriate pomp and ceremony that should be shown to such a good neighbour and trading partner back to the South China Sea.'

A particularly amusing element to all this was that the Australian government had hailed the deployment of *Dong Hai Jiu 101* as a sign that the Chinese were prepared to put skin in the game, with a press statement thanking the Chinese government 'for its contribution and the captain and crew for their efforts in the search for MH370'.

It took them a few days, but the Chinese embassy eventually issued a statement which did not actually deny *Dong Hai Jiu 101* was spying, but described the suggestion as 'wild speculation'.

A few months later, after doing just a little bit of actual searching for MH370 after *The Australian* broke the story it had likely been spying rather than hunting, *Dong Hai Jiu 101* dropped off its underwater robot in Fremantle and headed home to Shanghai.

As the hunt for the Boeing 777 registered as 9M–MRO kept drifting along with no result, the international club of MH370 watchers started looking back at earlier theories, including the more mysterious.

Early on, there had been reports that locals on some tiny islands in the Maldives, an independent archipelago nation in the Indian Ocean south-west of Sri Lanka, had seen a big aircraft flying low soon after 6:00am on the morning of 8 March 2014. Somehow, a year later, journalists decided to revisit the reports, some flying to the extremely remote coral atolls. *The Weekend Australian*'s national chief correspondent, Hedley Thomas, got to the 60-hectare island of Kuda Huvadhoo, and talked to locals including Abdu Rasheed Ibrahim, 47, a court official and keen fisherman.

'I watched this very large plane bank slightly and I saw its colours – the red and blue lines – below the windows,' he told the newspaper in a story published in April 2015.

Even though Thomas was cautious and balanced in his reporting, canvassing countervailing opinions suggesting the aircraft could not have been MH370, the story created a huge stir, being picked up by several British and US newspapers.

But it got shot down pretty quickly – most effectively by French daily *Le Monde*'s Asia-Pacific correspondent Florence de Changy, who published a story two months later headlined 'The Plane which Wasn't MH370'.

De Changy observed locals had the mystery aircraft flying in what would have been a different direction from a line from the Straits of Malacca – rather than coming in from the east, they said, it arrived from the north-west.

De Changy determined there was another island 50 kilometres south-east of Kuda Huvadhoo called Thimarafushi, which had a new airport opened six months before MH370 disappeared.

On the morning of 8 March 2014, civil aviation records showed a flight touched down on Thimarafushi at 6:33am, a twin-engined

De Haviland Dash 8 carrying 50 people. It was operated by Maldivian, an airline whose livery is red, white, and blue, like Malaysia Airlines.

So, de Changy put paid to the Maldivian option.

But just a month after her story came out, MH370, or at least a chunk of it, did show up on another island in the Indian Ocean.

Reunion, about 6000 kilometres north-west of Perth, is one of those tropical Indian Ocean islands east of Madagascar which, like Mauritius and the Seychelles, the British and French kept fighting over during the Napoleonic wars.

In 1810 the British Royal Navy seized it off the French for a few years, but France got it back under the Congress of Vienna in 1815, and it's a French overseas department to this day. Reunion is known for its big, active volcano Piton de la Fournaise, its sugar cane and rum, and a rich ethnic mix of descendants from mainland Africa, India, China, Madagascar and France who make up its 900,000 inhabitants.

It was on a beach on the island's north-east at Saint-Andre in late July, 2015, that local council worker Johnny Begue and his team of eight had started their regular job at 7:00am of keeping the local coastline clean. Begue had taken his morning break a bit before 9:00am and went for a stroll to look for a suitable stone to grind up some spices. He saw a piece of debris washed up on the pebbles, and realised it had some sort of significance. About two metres long, it had a distinctive curve and length, and there were screws on it that had not gone rusty.

'I knew immediately it was part of an aircraft,' Begue told the Associated Press. It just didn't occur to him it might be from the greatest aviation mystery of modern times and help solve it.

Begue got his workmates to help him bring the thing farther up the beach so it wouldn't wash away again. The question then was, what to do with this interesting piece of plane? Begue's initial thought was that he and the blokes he worked with could do something local. Maybe make it into a memorial to whomever it involved – he and the boys could set it on the lawn and plant some flowers around it. Begue resolved to call his favourite local radio station and tell them about how he'd found this thing that looked a lot like a part of a big plane.

It was pretty soon afterwards that the French gendarmes arrived in force at the beach. They cordoned off the area, securing the piece of debris. The French did not waste any time: keeping it under tight security at all points and the media away, they bundled the piece up and put it on a plane to Toulouse to be examined by a military aviation laboratory. The French and aviation experts around the world had no doubt, once the first few photographs hit the media, what the interesting piece of junk Begue had stumbled on actually was: a flaperon from MH370.

The possible implications were immediate, obvious and huge.

If it were a piece of MH370, it meant, conclusively, that the aircraft had come down in the ocean and everyone had to be dead. Those next-of-kin, particularly in China – egged on by conspiracy theorists – who had sadly but understandably held out hope that the plane had somehow flown the other way to land in a remote location in central Asia, would now have tragic solid evidence to the contrary.

Jayden Burrows, the son of Rodney and Mary Burrows, told News Corp he had struggled with mixed emotions since the plane's disappearance.

'After 16 months of no information it will be a bit of a relief if it does turn out to be the plane . . . it's been extremely challenging.'

In a touching move by the Reunionnais locals in Saint-Andre, that weekend residents held a special mass to pray for all those aboard MH370. Father Guy Hoareau led parishioners at Cambuston Catholic Church in an evening mass.

Eighteen-year-old student Sophie Ingra said the mass, attended by about 200 people, was a positive move after all the grief for the families.

'It's important for us to share the bad feelings and look forward with hope,' she said.

It took only a week for the French to confirm the piece of debris had been a part of MH370 – it was a flaperon from a Boeing 777 and one of the serial numbers matched 9M-MRO. No doubt the French moved fast, since the discovery was, for all but the most devoted conspiracy theorists, the final proof that the aircraft and the people on board could be no more. Malaysian Prime Minister Najib Razak again took it upon himself to break the news.

'Today, 515 days since the plane disappeared, it is with a heavy heart that I must tell you that an international team of experts have conclusively confirmed that the aircraft debris found on Reunion Island is indeed from MH370,' he told the media.

The second implication of the discovery was that the working assumption that MH370 had come down in the southern Indian Ocean now appeared sound – the arrival of the flaperon at Reunion was consistent with the pattern of current and drift in that vast body of water.

The ATSB, which had all the drift-modelling from the surface search, quickly ran through it and issued a statement on its website – it was no doubt happy to do so since it supported its working hypothesis. The discovery of the flaperon at Reunion, it said, was 'consistent with the currently defined search area.'

The third implication was that the discovery of the flaperon enabled drift-modelling gurus around the world to get to work. These scientists try to work out where things will drift to if you know where they start from, dubbed drift-modelling. Then there is 'reverse drift-modelling': working out where objects started from if you know where they drifted to and ended up.

The ATSB got the experts at the CSIRO to start the reverse drift-modelling exercise, but independently, a European group of oceanographers began such an exercise, as did a team at the University of Western Australia.

Those were the initial implications, but there were two more which were to play out importantly over time: the French getting their own bit of MH370 and hence a valuable piece of currency in the overall bid to find out what happened to the aircraft; and a new concrete challenge for the ATSB and its 'ghost flight/death dive' theory.

From the start the French had a stake in MH370: four of their nationals were on the flight. Laurence Wattrelos, 52, was returning from a beach holiday in Malaysia with two of her three children, Hadrien, 17, and Ambre, 14. Hadrien's girlfriend, Zhao Yan, 18, was also on the flight. The teenagers had reportedly been attending the French school in Beijing. The *Wall Street Journal* reported that Laurence's husband, affluent engineer and business executive Ghyslain Wattrelos, flew into Beijing from Paris the same day flight MH370 went missing, and was expecting to be reunited with his family. He was instead met by two French diplomats, who broke the news of the missing flight.

The French had a different and, to many observers, better approach to MH370 than the Australians. Whereas Australian government agencies timidly asked where MH370 might have come down, avoiding embarrassing the Malaysians by making any inquiries about what actually happened on board, the French set themselves the task of determining who or what had killed its four citizens.

From the start, French authorities treated the disappearance of

MH370 as a matter for judicial inquiry into the deaths of Wattrelos' family group. The flaperon, found on French sovereign territory, was going to be securely held by French judicial authorities to that end, and not turned over to either the ATSB or the Malaysians.

When it came to the debate of whether MH370 came down in an unpiloted crash, as the ATSB maintained, or was flown to the end and ditched as many in the professional aviation community believe, the flaperon was and remains central.

Flaperons on airliners sit on each wing, and serve two functions. For take-off and landing, they operate as flaps: the pilots deploy them to configure the aircraft for greater lift and slower speeds. When lowered, they sit in line with the flaps. In cruise, the flaperons serve a different function: they are moved up and down in conjunction with the ailerons to enable the pilots or autopilot to bank the aircraft in turns. A passenger with a view over the back of the wing can see the flaperon move – not much, up and down in cruise flight, keeping the wings level, and at a slightly higher deflection in a turn.

Even just the photographs printed in the media of what the flaperon had looked like when it was sitting on the beach and then being manhandled by French officials made a number of things abundantly clear. Firstly, it was no longer attached to the aircraft. While that might seem pretty obvious, it meant some force had torn it from its mountings – either in the air or when the aircraft hit the water.

Secondly, it was mostly in one piece. That became a critical element in the ensuing debate: if the aircraft had come down in a pilotless crash, why wasn't it smashed to bits on impact?

Thirdly, the flaperon had clear damage to the trailing edge, that is, the part in line with the back of the wings. Sufficient force must have been applied to do that damage.

It wasn't long before one of the world's leading air crash investigators, Canadian Larry Vance, expressed a view on exactly what all that meant: MH370 must have been flown to the end and ditched. It was, in his view, the only explanation for the pattern of damage to the flaperon, and the fact it existed intact rather than in dozens of tiny bits.

Vance, about whom a great deal will be said in the later chapters of this book, concluded the only possible explanation for the damage to the trailing edge of the flaperon was that it had been lowered for a controlled ditching, and only a pilot alive at the end of the flight could have made that happen.

'I do some general media here in Canada to do with accident investigation, and when I was asked about the flaperon that was recovered from MH370 I expressed my opinion that it proved that the flaps were extended, with all the ramifications of that regarding the intentional act,' Vance said.

Vance maintained that if the aircraft had come down in a high-speed dive, all its hollow component parts including the flaperon would have been exploded into dozens of pieces by the hydro-dynamic force, and not left pretty much intact. Conversely, the trailing-edge damage was only consistent with it having been lowered with the flaps by a pilot, and dragged through the water on ditching, before being torn off altogether, he said.

The search kept going, the ships 'mowed the lawn', and each week the JACC put out its operational bulletins on the progress. By December 2015, 75,000 square kilometres of the expanded 120,000 square kilometre target zone had been covered. That month, the ATSB issued a report which explained some of the continuing work which had been done, but also, between the lines, tried to defend the assumptions that had been made in using the 'unresponsive crew/hypoxia' scenario as the basis for the search strategy.

In a section titled 'Ditching Considerations', it said: 'A controlled ditching scenario requires engine thrust to be available to properly control the direction and vertical speed at touchdown and to provide hydraulic power for the flight controls including the flaps.'

As per its previous report, the December report said the analysis of the satellite data unit transmissions suggested the aircraft had run out of fuel.

'This evidence is therefore inconsistent with a controlled ditching scenario,' the ATSB said.

But this was one of several aspects of the ATSB report the former fighter pilot and Boeing 777 captain Byron Bailey took to task as being wrong and, he claimed, the sort of conclusion a government agency might come to if it did not have professional pilots familiar with the aircraft advising it. Bailey pointed out that with the automatic deployment of the auxiliary power unit, after both engines flamed out, the flaps could still be lowered.

Famously, one of the first things Chesley 'Sully' Sullenberger did when he lost both engines in flight and had to ditch his aircraft in the Hudson was tell the first officer, Jeff Skiles, to start up the auxiliary power unit which, among other things, enabled him to lower flaps.

After the famous interchange where Sullenberger told air traffic controllers 'we're gonna be in the Hudson', the transcript specifically refers to the flaps being down.

'Got flaps two, you want more?' Skiles asked Sullenberger in the minute before landing on the river, referring to the second of several options for how far to deploy the flaps.

'No, let's stay at two,' Sullenberger said.

Sullenberger did exactly what the ATSB report said could not be done after dual engine flame-out on MH370: he lowered the flaps and conducted a controlled ditching, in his case getting all 155 people on the aircraft off it in one piece.

In January 2016, now writing in *The Australian*, Bailey again dissected the ATSB's search strategy, and repeated his claim that he had been told by a government source that the FBI had found evidence that Zaharie had 'flown' a similar flight to the southern Indian Ocean on his home computer simulator.

When I put that to the ATSB, its MH370 spokesman Daniel O'Malley said:

'The ATSB cannot comment on the accuracy of an alleged conversation . . . the ATSB is not responsible for the investigation of the accident; that . . . belongs to the Malaysian government.'

The ATSB, and Transport Minister Truss, did their best to marginalise Bailey, the former writing an extensive piece on the 'Correcting the Record' section of its website, and the latter writing letters to the editor of *The Australian*.

The ATSB set up its 'Correcting the Record' site in June 2015 to attack critics in the media of its hunt for MH370, and of 11 posts over the next two years, all but two of them related to MH370.

The ATSB maintained its line that 'for search purposes, the relevant facts and analysis most closely match a scenario in which there was no pilot intervening in the latter stages of the flight'.

It was not just *The Australian* that started asking questions as to whether the ATSB was looking in the right place. On ABC radio, ATSB chief Martin Dolan was asked by reporter Sarah Dingle: 'So is it worthwhile, then, changing the search parameters to consider whether the pilot deliberately took MH370 down?'

Dolan said: 'We have certainly considered that as a possibility; all the evidence we have at the moment says that that is very unlikely.'

The problem for the ATSB was that if its 'ghost flight/death dive' theory was right, surely it should be able to find MH370?

The months passed, and it didn't. There was a bit of excitement here and there, such as when one of the search ships lost its towfish when it crashed into an underwater mud volcano. It was recovered in early February using a marine robot that plucked it from a depth of 2550 metres. Mostly, though, the gruelling, monotonous business of hunting for MH370 continued without spectacle – but the debate about whether the hunters were looking in the right spot heated up.

After seven years as ATSB chief commissioner, Dolan retired in the first half of 2016. He was replaced on 1 July that year by Greg Hood, who had started out a career in aviation as an air traffic controller in the RAAF. Hood, who held glider and private pilot licences, had been head of air traffic control at Airservices Australia before moving to head up the ATSB.

By the start of July 2016, Foley's team had searched 110,000 of the 120,000 square kilometre target zone.

Then, all at once, the public relations war shifted against the ATSB.

The ATSB's efforts to steer around Bailey's claim that the FBI had found the critical flight simulator data on Zaharie's computer, and that Australian investigators had known about it, were blown out of the water. *New York* magazine revealed it had obtained a secret Malaysian police report on the findings of the FBI analysis of the hard disk drives on Zaharie's flight simulation computer, which showed waypoints for a simulated flight eerily similar to the zigzag route MH370 actually took. The simulated flight, conducted only a month or so before MH370's disappearance, also flew up the Straits of Malacca to the Andaman Sea, then took a sharp turn south before ending in the southern Indian Ocean.

New York magazine quoted one excerpt from the report that showed investigators regarded the find as significant: 'Based on the Forensics Analysis conducted on the 5 HDDs obtained from the Flight Simulator from MH370 Pilot's house, we found a flight path, that lead [sic] to the Southern Indian Ocean, among the numerous other flight paths charted on the Flight Simulator.'

Then, around the same time in July, there was another blow to the ATSB's effort to defend its 'unresponsive crew/hypoxia' theory.

The news agency Reuters reported the ATSB's pin-up boy, Fugro's Paul Kennedy, now thought the whole premise of the $200 million search had been wrong from the start. The way Reuters reported it, Kennedy had decided the ATSB had erred in determining the search area based on its 'ghost flight' and 'death dive' scenario.

Reuters reported Fugro now thought it had been 'scouring the wrong patch of ocean for two years.' Kennedy said he now believed the 'rogue pilot' theory, in which a fully conscious pilot glided the aircraft down to the sea, was probably right after all.

'If it's not there, it means it's somewhere else,' Kennedy told Reuters. 'If it was manned, it could glide for a long way. You could glide it for further than our search area is, so I believe the logical conclusion will be, well, maybe that is the other scenario.'

Kennedy went into specifics of the 'other scenario'; he said a skilled pilot could glide the plane approximately 193 kilometres from its cruising altitude after running out of fuel.

The Reuters story went viral – like other big new breaks on MH370, everyone ran it. It can still be found through a Google search on the *ABC News* website, dated 21 July 2016, headlined, 'MH370 may have been gliding in its final moments, leaving wreckage outside search zone, experts say'.

As a case of biting the hand that feeds, it doesn't get better than this. For about 18 months the ATSB had been fighting a running battle against senior airline pilots including Bailey, Hardy and Evans who had promoted the theory that Zaharie hijacked his own aircraft and flew it right to the end and ditched it in a deliberate effort to disappear it. Meanwhile, the ATSB and Transport Minister Truss had consistently described the controlled glide scenario as 'very unlikely' and stuck to the bureau's preferred 'unresponsive crew/hypoxia' end-of-flight model.

So now, the ATSB's $200 million action man, Kennedy, seemed to be siding with the enemy – Bailey and the other pilots – in supporting the 'rogue pilot to the end' theory. To make matters worse, the story came out just a few days before ministers from Australia, Malaysia and China were to meet again to discuss the next move.

Fugro went into full PR damage control mode to try to mitigate the distinct impression implied by Kennedy that the pilots were right all along.

'Fugro wishes to make it very clear that we believe the search area to have been well defined based on all of the available scientific data. In short, we have been thoroughly looking in the most probable place – and that is the right place to search,' Fugro said in a statement.

The statement did not, however, claim Reuters misquoted Kennedy.

Between Kennedy's suggestion that the 'pilot hijack' theory was right, and the confirmation of the FBI discovery of the simulated flight, Bailey claimed he had been vindicated and that the ATSB and Truss had been hiding the truth for two years while sledging him.

'How is it that a taxpayer-funded government department can be so devious?' Bailey asked in *The Australian*.

By late July 2016, with only about 10 per cent of the designated search area of 120,000 square kilometres yet to be covered, the three governments backing the search had to decide what their next move would be if that were completed and the aircraft not found. It was a tough call, and as the country officially in charge of the investigation into the disappearance of Malaysia Airlines Flight MH370, and the one putting up the most money to find it, the Malaysian government held the whip hand in making it. While Malaysia is no longer a poor country, the government faced a dilemma in whether it could write a blank cheque in the hunt for the aircraft when that money could otherwise go to, for example, schools, health or economic development.

The government's new Transport Minister, Liow Tiong Lai, brought his counterparts together in the Malaysian administrative capital of Putrajaya on 22 July. At the end of the meeting, Liow announced the verdict at a press conference: 'In the absence of new credible evidence, Malaysia, Australia and China have collectively agreed to suspend the search upon completion of the 120,000 kilometres.'

'I must emphasise that this does not mean that we have given up on locating MH370. If there are any new credible news, or credible new evidence, we will continue to work together,' he said. 'The families and loved ones of the passengers and crew of MH370 remain a priority.'

The new Australian Transport Minister, Darren Chester, said every effort had been made to find the aircraft with the best minds and the best technology.

'This decision has not been taken lightly nor without some sadness and we want to emphasise our work is continuing.'

The final stage of the ATSB-led hunt was caught in a pincer movement of governments saying they had to find MH370 within the remaining search area or call it quits, and more and more independent observers saying they were not finding it because they had the wrong theory of what happened.

Then commercial television, and its huge popular impact, weighed in against them. It was one of the Nine Network's star reporters, Ross Coulthart, on its flagship program *60 Minutes* Australia, who started putting all the pieces together that the ATSB might have got it wrong with its 'ghost flight/death dive' theory. Coulthart had watched an episode of the Canadian Broadcasting Corporation's nightly news show *The National*, and on it was Vance talking about the flaperon and what it meant. Coulthart immediately appreciated the international implications.

Here was one of the world's most experienced and applauded air crash investigators who, if correct, had pointed out the elephant in the room missed, or ignored, by the ATSB. Coulthart decided to do a story for *60 Minutes* on Vance's findings and other aspects of the MH370 debate.

By this time, there had been a few other major developments. The discovery of the flaperon by chance by Johnny Begue on Reunion prompted huge interest among the official investigators, but also the international club of MH370 devotees, as to whether other parts of the aircraft might have washed up. Some members of the MH370 families, but others who were not next-of-kin including the high-profile American lawyer Blaine Gibson about whom more will be said later, started campaigns to recover them by visiting countries on and off the south-east coast of Africa. In May 2016, the rear edge of the left outboard flap was found and recovered on an islet off Mauritius.

The following month, an even bigger and more significant part of the aircraft, the right flap, was discovered on Tanzania's Pemba Island, mostly intact, and was sent to the ATSB for analysis in Canberra. Again, dates and letters and numbers enabled a conclusive determination it was from MH370. The flap showed trailing edge damage very similar to that of the flaperon.

Coulthart's story aired, prime time, on Nine on Sunday, 31 July. It quoted Vance saying, in stark terms, the ATSB's 'ghost flight/ death dive' assumption was wrong.

'Absolutely. Somebody was flying the airplane at the end of its flight. Somebody was flying the airplane into the water,' Vance said.

Coulthart went through the FBI findings that Zaharie had practised a similar flight on his home simulator. He brought out the details of the evidence of the flap and flaperon. He also interviewed Danica Weeks, who said, 'If you look back over the last two-and-a-half years and the actions of the Malaysians, it just tells me that they are hiding something. Something is not right here. I have been patient. I have given them the benefit of the doubt. For me the gloves are off now.'

Coulthart, a fellow aggressive journalist I've known since we were both young reporters covering NSW state politics in the 1980s, had not lost his touch. He grilled Foley, asking him if, in fact, he had known all along about the FBI finding that Zaharie had practised a death flight to the southern Indian Ocean on his home flight simulator.

Coulthart: You don't deny the existence of that report, do you?
Foley: Absolutely, it exists.
Coulthart: We have it here.

Foley: Yeah, yeah.

Coulthart: We found a flight plan that leads to the southern
Indian Ocean.

Foley: Mmm. Correct.

Coulthart: As a taxpayer, who has seen an enormous amount
of money spent on an investigation – not least the victims –
I would want to know about this report, showing that the
captain tracked a flight path into the southern Indian Ocean.
Don't you think the public has the right to know this?

Foley: I think, as we would strongly argue, it should form a part
of the final report.

Coulthart: What about the interim factual analysis, why wasn't it
put into the interim factual analysis?

Foley: That's a question for the Malaysians, Ross.

Incredibly, Foley admitted to Coulthart – while he was still
directing the search on the basis that no-one was flying the plane
at the end – that the French analysis of the flaperon suggested the
contrary.

'We have also seen some analysis from the French that suggests
that it's a possibility that it was in a deployed state,' Foley admitted.

Then Coulthart asked, 'Doesn't the visual evidence on the flaperon suggest that the flaperon was extended?'

Foley responded, 'Yes.'

It was extraordinary. Coulthart had got Foley to admit, effectively,
that a key part of the evidence suggested the 'ghost flight/death
dive' theory was wrong. But the ATSB stuck with the search plan,
regardless.

The reaction of the ATSB and the JACC to the adverse media
was to suppress what families of those lost thought should have been
public information, in what was a clear attempt to sideline journalists
who sought to unveil the truth about their likely errors in the hunt
for MH370.

EIGHT
AN INCONVENIENT TRUTH

Daniel O'Malley sounds just like what Americans call 'a regular guy'.

He has a solid American accent, and is well spoken and courteous, even to the point of calling journalists, or this one anyway, 'Mr Higgins'. He ends conversations with, 'Thanks for your call, Sir, good to hear from you,' even when you've been corresponding with him for years. In fact, O'Malley is a dinkum Aussie who went to Canberra Grammar School. But he spent time in the US, graduating with a master's degree in medieval history from Ohio State University.

When I was researching a story on US-born then NSW Premier Kristina Keneally's failed bid to lose her Toledo, Ohio accent in favour of an Aussie drawl through speech lessons, speech experts explained that some accents are dominant, and the American accent is one of them. Australians who go to the US pick up the American twang and can't easily lose it when they return; but Americans coming to Australia keep their American accent and can't learn to speak 'Aussie'.

So, O'Malley, like Keneally, is stuck with talking Yank.

O'Malley's an accomplished science-fiction writer – his first novel, *The Rook*, was released in 2012 and won the Aurealis Award that year for Best Science Fiction Novel. But O'Malley's day job was as media officer for the ATSB, and for a period he had the specific title of spokesman for the MH370 search.

O'Malley had started off with a helpful, bright and open approach to journalists when it came to MH370. To my eye, in the US he had acquired not just an American accent but an American view of democracy: that government agencies and those who work for them have a duty to serve the public and release information about what the government, paid for by American citizens, is doing. O'Malley was initially very cooperative and tried to release as much information to me as he reasonably could.

But by the time his second novel, *Stiletto*, came out in 2016, things were starting to get a bit hairy. The ATSB was coming under serious pressure about whether its 'ghost flight/death dive' theory was right. There were suggestions, denied by the bureau, that some within its own ranks were having second thoughts – the alternative theory of a controlled ditching put forward by more and more professional pilots and some air crash investigators was gaining sway in the media.

It's not hard to see from where O'Malley got some of his inspiration for his novels. One reviewer wrote of O'Malley's 'mixture of characters with superpowers and bureaucratic paranoia'.

As the pressure grew on the ATSB, O'Malley and his colleagues in the media unit found themselves having to dodge questions about MH370 – not of their own choosing, of course, but because the bureau would either not pass information on to them, or order them not to pass it on to journalists.

The flight simulation revelation from Zaharie's home computer was a classic. When *New York* magazine broke the story of Zaharie's simulated flight, opposition transport spokesman Anthony Albanese told *The Australian* the government had a duty to the families of the victims to explain what information it had. Instead, the ATSB failed to reveal the existence of the flight simulation, then downplayed its significance, saying it showed 'only the possibility of planning'.

The degree to which the ATSB, and then Transport Minister Truss, had obfuscated in June 2014 when the flight simulation death flight story first came out was starkly revealed much later, by the bureau itself.

It had received the information right at the time the FBI did the analysis in early 2014, took it seriously, and used it in considering where a ditched aircraft might be found. The admissions came out in the ATSB final report on the search, released in October 2017. It admitted that 'data from the Pilot-in-Command's (PIC) home flight simulator was recovered and analysed in March/April 2014. This information was provided to the ATSB on 19 April 2014.

'Six weeks before the accident flight the PIC had used his simulator to fly a route, initially similar to part of the route flown by MH370 up the Straits of Malacca, with a left-hand turn and track into the southern Indian Ocean. There were enough similarities to the flight path of MH370 for the ATSB to carefully consider the possible implications for the underwater search area.'

O'Malley could have said that on 8 January 2016, when I asked about it, but he either wasn't told or was instructed not to discuss it. Clearly the full facts did not fit the ATSB policy of: trying to discredit Bailey and other critics of their search strategy; sticking in lockstep with the Malaysians in not releasing information; and downplaying the possibility of pilot hijack.

The new key to defending the ATSB's working proposition that MH370 ended up in a 'ghost flight' and 'death dive' was the interpretation that the satellite data suggested a rapid and accelerating descent. It was all based on eight seconds of data.

The work on the Inmarsat automatic electronic 'handshakes' with MH370 had kept going, even as Foley's undersea search continued. The Defence Science and Technology Group had been looking at the last log-on request from MH370's satellite data unit at 08:19:29am. It was followed eight seconds later, at 08:19:37am by a log-on request acceptance – the return of the handshake from the ground station to the satellite and back to the aircraft. The team led by an eminent mathematician at DSTG, Neil Gordon, used the burst frequency offset analysis to see what those two signals said about whether the aircraft was in level flight, or ascending or descending. Gordon's team came to the conclusion the aircraft was descending at a rate of between 2900 feet per minute and 15,200 feet per minute when the Seventh Arc was crossed. Eight seconds later the rate of descent had increased to between 13,800 feet per minute and 25,300 feet per minute.

The ATSB concluded in early 2016 that such rates of descent ruled out a controlled unpowered glide with the intent to extend range. But Bailey and other professional aviators said this rate of descent could easily be explained by a pilot wanting to point the nose down on fuel exhaustion to avoid a stall, rapidly descend to a warm and breathable level, and get out of the early sun at altitude. Additionally, other aviation experts said that, while they believed the satellite data was solid in establishing the Seventh Arc, they held doubts about its reliability in measuring ascent or descent.

The ATSB decided it had to do something publicly to suggest this element was right, and that others thought so. So, it turned once again to those it had hailed – rightly – as the best and the brightest, the experts of the Search Strategy Working Group. The JACC bulletin of 27 July 2016, sought to discredit the increasingly popular 'controlled ditching' theory, saying that 'for the purposes of defining the underwater search area, the relevant facts and analysis most closely match a scenario in which there was no pilot intervening in the latter stages of the flight'.

'The last satellite communication with the aircraft showed it was most likely in a high rate of descent in the area of what is known as the 7th arc,' the bulletin said.

'This is indeed the consensus of the Search Strategy Working Group.'

The 'consensus' line was reported internationally, including by China's Xinhua news agency, and Malaysia's Bernama news service.

Then, without announcement or explanation, the following day, 28 July, the JACC bulletin was amended to remove the 'consensus' line. The sentence, 'This is indeed the consensus of the Search Strategy Working Group,' just disappeared into the ether, with no word as to why.

Richard Godfrey, who is a member of the Independent Group of scientists, engineers and other experts following the MH370 saga, first picked up the change in the bulletin, and told me about it. Godfrey, a British aerospace engineer, said the most likely explanation for the 'consensus' line removal was that one of the experts on the strategy group panel said they did not support such a conclusion. It might be the case, Godfrey suggested, 'that it was assumed there was a consensus, but then some party complained and the published report had to be changed.'

While the bulletin was issued in the name of the JACC, it was prepared by the ATSB. When I asked for an explanation of why the 'consensus' on their rapid descent theory had disappeared, a bizarre thing happened. All of a sudden, people who had previously been very helpful went totally quiet when asked to explain why the best and the brightest were all in agreement on the death dive one day, but not the next.

A JACC official who had previously been helpful would not return calls, texts or emails. Nor would ATSB spokesman O'Malley. When I finally got him on the telephone line, O'Malley said in his polite American voice, 'I'm going to have to ring you back'. He then hung up. He never did ring back.

It was problematic to report the loss of consensus without the JACC or the ATSB explaining it, but given the absolute wall of silence, eventually it had to be done in the public interest. On 12 August 2016, *The Weekend Australian* published the story.

'An Australian government agency has secretly retracted its claim that international scientists and air crash investigators had reached consensus that Malaysia Airlines Flight MH370 went down quickly in a "death dive" rather than being flown to the end by a "rogue pilot",' the newspaper reported.

'The backdown indicates that the Australian Transport Safety Bureau no longer commands unanimous support among its global advisory group for a public relations narrative it is running in conjunction with the Malaysian government and Malaysian Airline System Berhad.'

The ATSB, extraordinarily, denied the story, even though the evidence was there in black and white. The same day the story came out, the bureau put a post on its website under 'Correcting the Record'.

'An article published . . . by Mr Ean Higgins on 12 August 2016 falsely accuses the ATSB of "secretly retracting" information from a Joint Agency Coordination Centre operations update on 27 July,' it read.

The ATSB reiterated its claim that its analysis of the final two satellite communications from the aircraft to the ground earth station showed the aircraft was in a high, and increasing, rate of descent.

'All the members of the Search Strategy Working Group have reviewed DST Group's analysis and no objections to the analysis have been provided,' it said.

In denying it had secretly retracted information the ATSB was, of course, telling a falsehood. It did retract the 'consensus' line, it did so without any public announcement, and its media officers would not talk about why it was done or even acknowledge the fact it had been done. *The Australian* set about to expose the truth.

In the armory of journalists, one of the better weapons is the federal Freedom of Information (FOI) legislation. It doesn't always work; if a government department or agency really doesn't want you to get your hands on the truth, they have a variety of ways of claiming they don't have to provide it. But when it does work, it can be hugely effective.

There's a bit of an art to the FOI request. One trick is to always make it in formal terms, starting out by saying you want to make 'a Freedom of Information request under the relevant statutes', thus reminding those who receive it that you know your rights under

FOI law. Another is to be as precise as possible about what you seek, keep it to one thing at a time, and keep the request tight but at the same time inclusive of all possible material.

In this case, the identical requests to the ATSB and the JACC were:

'In this FOI request, I seek material, including, but not necessarily restricted to, emails, notes, letters, minutes of meetings or telephone conversations, instructions, or other documents, which go to the reason the "Consensus" line cited above was deleted, including why, by whom, in what circumstances, on whose instructions, and if it was at the request of a member of the Search Strategy Working Group, a foreign government, or any other party be it an individual, agency or other entity.'

On the JACC side, the FOI request was handled by chief coordinator Judith Zielke. She agreed to release the material, though excluding names of officers citing privacy provisions. The released material proved the ATSB had told a falsehood in saying the 'consensus' line had not been secretly deleted. The documents show that just a few minutes after the 27 July bulletin was issued, an ATSB senior investigator warned colleagues by email this was an 'error' and that the sentence should be taken down.

'It is certainly not yet the consensus position of the SSWG . . . 2 parties are yet to make a formal response on the subject,' the investigator said.

The email chain shows another ATSB senior investigator agreed and gave instructions for the sentence with the 'consensus' line to be removed from the ATSB's and the JACC's websites. But the ATSB did not retract the sentence until the next day, by which time it had been reported internationally, including in Malaysian and Chinese publications. When *The Australian* exposed the ATSB's falsehood, the JACC finally issued a public admission:

'The information was retracted when it was learned not all working group members had, at that stage, provided formal responses. Subsequently a consensus view was reached.'

The ATSB and the JACC – represented by decent young individuals like O'Malley – could have just said so first up when *The Australian* first queried why the 'consensus' line had been removed.

But it turned out O'Malley and the others had been instructed by their superiors not to divulge any more information to me.

The Australian's fight for the truth about whether the international experts did really agree with the ATSB's 'death dive' interpretation had led to the first attempt by the bureau and the JACC to restrict the newspaper's enquiries. In a letter to the editor-in-chief of *The Australian*, Paul Whittaker and cc'ed to me, dated 12 August 2016, Zielke wrote that the government agencies had imposed an information ban.

'If Mr Higgins attempts to make contact, he will not receive any assistance from either the Department or the ATSB,' Zielke wrote. 'The Department and the ATSB will continue to respond to media inquiries from other journalists [at *The Australian*].'

The idea that a government agency would dictate which reporters would be allowed to ask questions goes against all the principles of press freedom and independence, and was roundly rejected by the editors of *The Australian*. In the letter to Whittaker, Zielke tried to justify banning me on the basis that I had engaged in 'harassment' of staff. This, she claimed, included 'sustained and persistent questioning on issues to which answers have been provided' and 'threatening to name staff if they do not acquiesce to requests'.

The editors wrote to Zielke stating that while my pursuit of the MH370 story had been determined, apart from one communication whose timing and tone could have been more considerate, my reporting was in keeping with the principles of good, robust journalism. After a few days of negotiation, Zielke lifted the ban.

The exercise shows how even senior public servants can fail to grasp the practical fundamentals of journalism in a democracy. 'Sustained and persistent questioning' is exactly what journalists should engage in when government agencies respond with non-answers to questions in the public interest. And while government media officers hate being named when they don't provide real answers to legitimate questions, it is good practice to name them when it looks like the agency, department or minister's office is withholding the truth.

In a career spanning nearly four decades, I have observed a marked decline in government transparency, engagement and willingness to provide information. In the 1980s when I first entered journalism, federal government ministers, departments and agencies felt a duty to answer legitimate questions, and more often than not did so. That is the way it should be, but since then that sense of duty has steadily evaporated, and media officers often seem to think that a bland response made of bureaucratic blancmange, which does not answer the question but makes nice irrelevant statements, is good enough. It's not good enough, and it should be called out, naming both the ministers and senior public servants who whip up the blancmange and the media officers who dish it out.

The Search Strategy Working Group 'consensus' story is a good example. When as outlined, in July the ATSB and JACC media flacks mysteriously went silent, I went to the office of the then transport minister, Darren Chester. It was a compendium of questions which over the weeks the ATSB and the JACC had refused to answer. The questions emailed to Chester's office on 30 July 2016, included:

1/ Why was the line 'this is indeed the consensus of the Search Strategy Working Group' removed?

2/ Was it because a member of the SSWG saw the bulletin, and asked that that line be removed because he or she does not share that consensus view?

3/ If so, who objected?

4/ Is it the case that there is no longer a consensus among the SSWG on this question?

Question series B:

1/ Is it correct that the ATSB, and/or the DSTG, has received a request from members of the IG group (another prominent

member is Duncan Steel), and this information has not been
provided to those seeking it?

2/ If so, why?

Question series C:

1/ As a journalist himself, is Mr Chester concerned that a
government agency under his portfolio, the ATSB, is consistently
failing to answer questions from the media about MH370?

2/ What action will the Minister take to ensure the ATSB, a
taxpayer funded body with a media unit whose officers
have their salaries paid for by the taxpayer and whose role
is presumably to inform the public via the media, answers
questions from the media about MH370?

Chester's media officer, Brie Colley, responded with the following
email on 1 August:

Please find below:

Quotes attributable to Darren Chester, Minister for Infrastructure
and Transport.

'There is an enormous amount of data which has been collected
in the search for MH370 and the Australian government has
already given an undertaking that it will be provided as open
source information when possible.

'I am confident in the ATSB's expert analysis and remain hopeful
the aircraft will be located in the 120,000 km sq highest priority
search area.'

As exemplified here, ministers are increasingly hiding from issues
by having their media officers come up with meaningless mother-
hood statements rather than answers.

The practice of warning media officers they will be named if they
don't answer questions might sound aggressive, but it goes to the
principle of making them, and in turn their bosses, take responsibility

for their responses or non-responses. It can also be very effective in getting answers – once trained with the Pavlov effect of being named, media officers become far more attentive.

On one occasion, in June 2017, O'Malley did not respond to a question on when exactly the ATSB would be releasing its final report on its failed search for MH370, prompting outrage from Danica Weeks. *The Australian* quoted Danica as saying, 'If the ATSB had crossed their "t's" and dotted their "i's" on the search, why would it take nine months to produce a report? It's inconceivable.'

The next sentence in the story was: 'Despite the plea from Ms Weeks, Mr O'Malley would not provide a clearer timeline for the release of the report, or explain why it had been delayed.'

Three months later, when O'Malley again failed to answer a similar question after three days, I wrote him an email:

Hi Dan -

Are you going to answer this question, or do I write:

'ATSB spokesman Daniel O'Malley refused to say whether the bureau would meet its latest deadline in releasing its long-awaited report on its failed search for MH370.'

Cheers,
Ean

That worked a treat: this time, O'Malley came back with an answer the same day, at 4:47pm, 13 minutes before the deadline set by me.

Dear Mr Higgins,

Thank you for your email. Owing to the extensive review and consultation process, and the size of the report, we now anticipate that the ATSB's final MH370 report will be released in the first week of October.

Regards,
Dan

The warning that he would be named if he did not answer the question by deadline had the desired effect: O'Malley no doubt applied pressure on one of the ATSB officers to come up with the goods. Most reporters would describe such practices as holding media officers and their bosses to account in a bid to get answers; some senior public servants regard it as bullying and grounds to ban whole government agencies from answering questions of high public interest.

I was curious about the inside machinations that led Zielke to send the letter of complaint and banning to Whittaker, and put in an FOI request to the ATSB and the JACC to this effect. The FOI request sought: 'All material, including but not limited to documents, emails, reports, minutes and transcripts of meetings, relating to communications among JACC staff, ATSB staff, and ministerial staff that went towards the decision to issue that letter from Ms Judith Zielke . . . to *The Australian.*'

To their credit, the ATSB and the JACC provided not all, but at least some, of what I applied for. What emerged was very revealing. The material provided showed a flurry of activity among a number of officials, some expressing concern they might be named for not answering questions, and discussing what sort of action could be taken against me in the form of contacting the editors, banning me from information, and even complaining to a federal media industry body.

It was another example of how the public service often seems to have little grasp of real-world media practice, but does display a keen desire to try to suppress journalists when they are persistent and poke around where bureaucrats prefer they didn't.

THEORY FOUR:
TERRORIST HIJACKING GONE WRONG

The plan of the jihadists was brilliant, or so they thought: take control of a big jetliner, fly it to a Taliban-held airstrip in Afghanistan, and hold the passengers and crew, and the aircraft itself, to ransom. And they knew Captain Zaharie Ahmad Shah and co-pilot Fariq Abdul Hamid had just the weakness for a particular temptation to make it work. Zaharie was known to like young attractive women generally; Fariq had been known to flirt with them on invitations to the cockpit. Days after MH370 disappeared, the Australian television program *A Current Affair* made headlines internationally showing Fariq getting friendly with South African blondes Jonti Roos and Jaan Maree and an unidentified Malaysia Airlines captain.

So when it came to the MH370 flight on 8 March 2014, about half an hour after take-off, three passengers – two men and a pretty young woman travelling together – asked a male flight attendant if they could visit the flight deck for a brief photo opportunity. The flight attendant asked permission over the intercom to enter the cockpit, was let in, and said, 'Captain, two gentlemen and a young lady have asked to visit the flight deck'.

Zaharie inquired, 'Is she a good sort?'

'Yes, sir, a real good-looker, la!'

'Fine, 10 minutes from now should be perfect, after we pass IGARI.'

Just after Zaharie signed off with 'Good night, Malaysian Three Seven Zero', the flight attendant brought the trio of passengers to the cockpit door, and they were let in. Seconds later, the two men and the woman pulled out guns they had reassembled on board made out of plastic with 3D printers and which can escape detection by metal detectors.

'No distress call, captain, do exactly as I say, and no-one gets hurt,' the hijack leader said.

'Turn off the transponder and the ACARS, then turn this aircraft towards Penang.'

Meanwhile, back in the passenger cabin, a fourth hijacker had similarly pulled out a plastic gun, and seized the mobile phones of all the passengers and cabin crew. The lead hijacker was well briefed in aviation and the plan – he ordered the slow right turn onto Airway N571 after Penang, heading in the general direction of Afghanistan.

To throw off any military aircraft which might give chase based on primary radar picking up the aircraft and observing it heading north-west on N571, at 2:45am, when they had calculated MH370 would be out of radar range, the terrorists ordered Zaharie to turn sharp left on a heading of 188 degrees, near due south. The intention was to 'jink', or throw any pursuers off the trail by unexpectedly changing course over the area not covered by radar for some minutes, then set a new heading with a right turn towards Afghanistan.

It was all going fine, the hijackers thought. But they had not counted on the pluck and initiative of some of the passengers and crew. One of the passengers, a former army sergeant in an aisle seat, whispered to a well-built individual who knew martial arts on the other side of the aisle. When the hijacker passed by on his patrol up and down the cabin, the sergeant asked the hijacker, 'Where are you taking us?'

As the hijacker turned his gun on the sergeant and told him to shut up, the martial-arts instructor jumped to his feet, and grabbed the hijacker in a headlock as the sergeant tried to seize the gun. The gun went off, and the bullet blew a hole in the window, causing rapid decompression. In the struggle the hijacker fell over the seated and strapped-in passengers beside the shattered window and got sucked out of the aircraft, as the oxygen masks dropped.

The cabin turned foggy from the rapid decompression, and as the hijackers in the cockpit turned their attention back towards the cabin upon hearing the shot, Zaharie and Fariq sprang to their feet and grappled with them. Fariq tore the gun from the hand of the woman jihadist, and shot both her and one of the male hijackers dead. But the other male terrorist shot Fariq, grievously wounding him, and killed Zaharie. Fariq got off one last shot before he collapsed, killing the remaining hijacker.

It was all over in seconds. The cockpit of MH370 was awash with blood, with two dead pilots, three dead hijackers, and the cockpit door closed and locked as ordered by the terrorists to prevent any counter-hijack attempt. MH370, with the autopilot set on the track south, well away from any mobile phone coverage, flew on. After 12 minutes, the chemically generated oxygen ran out for those passengers who had got their oxygen masks on. A couple of flight attendants had reached the portable oxygen bottles, but after a time they too ran out. MH370 was a ghost flight, exactly as per the ATSB's theory, crashing down after running out of fuel, but just outside the area searched by only about a nautical mile.

Among those who like this theory – a lot – is Geoffrey Dell. Dell had an extensive career as a transport accident investigator, before moving to Central Queensland University as an associate professor. To him, this is the only scenario that 'doesn't require a string of implausible simultaneous unrelated failures and errors'. Given the pilots' known penchant for attractive women, Dell said, 'the would-be hijackers wouldn't have to threaten a flight attendant . . . just simply include a young woman in the hijack team and just ask for a photo opportunity with the captain on the flight deck.

'If the crew did then find an opportunity to try to regain control of the flight and a fight ensued, it's plausible that it could easily have resulted in the death or incapacitation of everyone who can fly the aircraft,' Dell said. 'Then the [autopilot] would have continued to fly the aircraft.'

Again, there's an excellent precedent for this theory: famously, of course, the 'flight that fought back' on 9/11, United Airlines Flight 93. The Boeing 757-222 was on its way from Newark, New Jersey, to San Francisco on 11 September 2001 with 44 people on board when four Al-Qaeda terrorists claimed to have a bomb. Having smuggled box cutters on board, they took over the aircraft, killing the pilots. Flight 93 was the last of the four airliners hijacked that day as part of the monstrous plot hatched by Osama bin Laden.

After the hijackers, one of whom had learnt to fly, took over the aircraft, some passengers contacted loved ones on their mobile phones. They learnt that New York's World Trade Center twin towers had already been taken out in airliner murder-suicide attacks, along with a section of the Pentagon, and could see the writing on the wall. A group of them met in the galley, decided the bomb was probably a fake, and resolved to launch a counter-attack against the terrorists to retake the aircraft.

Armed with cutlery, fire extinguishers and other improvised weapons, and using a drinks cart as a battering ram, they overpowered at least one terrorist, and tried to smash their way through to the cockpit. The cockpit voice recorder was recovered and the transcript revealed the shocking last few minutes.

'Roll it!' passenger Tom Burnett is heard shouting.

'In the cockpit!' screams another passenger. 'If we don't, we'll die!'

At 10:01am, a hijacker shouts, 'Allah is the greatest!' and asks another jihadist in the cockpit, 'Is that it? I mean, shall we put it down?'

As the passengers continued their ram raid, Flight 93 nose-dived into a field near Shanksville, Pennsylvania, about 20 minutes' flying time from Washington, DC, where the target was the US Capitol building where Congress was in session that day.

So, it's yet another case of fact being at least as strange and dramatic as what might have happened on MH370.

NINE

'X' MARKS THE SPOT

The failed efforts by the ATSB and the JACC to restrict *The Australian*'s quest to get to the truth of MH370 only made the editors more keen that I should dig deeper.

The next logical phase for me was to try to get to the bottom of whether the experts on the Search Strategy Working Group had, or had not, supported the ATSB's 'death dive' theory based on the satellite data – was there really a consensus? The revised line from the ATSB was that 'all the members of the Search Strategy Working Group have reviewed DST Group's analysis and no objections to the analysis have been provided'. But it is one thing to say there were 'no objections', and another to say there was a positive 'consensus' that the analysis was right. Which was it?

The views of the international experts were of critical importance: the ATSB had based its whole search strategy on the premise MH370 ended in a rapid, accelerating, uncontrolled descent, and that assumption was in turn predicated on the interpretation of the satellite data. Once again, FOI was the way to go; either you get the truth, or you can report the truth is being suppressed, and who suppressed it. I asked for 'the formal responses on this topic from each of the following members of the Search Strategy Working Group: Air Accidents Investigation Branch (UK); Boeing (USA); Department of Civil Aviation (Malaysia); Inmarsat (UK); National Transportation Safety Board (USA); Thales (UK).'

The ATSB found these documents, no problem. They sent me a letter listing each of them as email exchanges – a dozen in all – with the dates they were sent in July and August, 2016. But while the ATSB found them and catalogued them, they were not going to release them to *The Australian* because, the ATSB seemed to suggest, to do so might annoy the government of another country.

'I have decided to exempt the documents . . .' the ATSB's then general manager of strategic capability, Colin McNamara, wrote, 'because disclosure of those documents would, or could reasonably be expected to, cause damage to the international relations of the Commonwealth, or would divulge information communicated in confidence by or on behalf of a foreign government or an authority of a foreign government.'

McNamara also said ICAO Annex 13 investigation standards required that governments not release information 'unless the competent authority designated by that State determines, in accordance with national laws, that their disclosure or use outweighs the likely adverse domestic and international impact such action may have on that or any future investigations'.

The wording of McNamara's letter of refusal said a lot about the mindset of the ATSB. The letter itself said a 'competent authority' could in fact release such documents if 'their disclosure or use outweighs the likely adverse domestic and international impact'. Many would have thought public transparency would have outweighed any niggle about displeasing a foreign government – the documents sought were fundamental to whether $200 million of Australian, Malaysian, and Chinese taxpayers' money had been wasted on a search based on false assumptions. Many would have also thought that if for no other reason, the documents should have been released to show the ATSB had nothing to hide, and that is exactly what the families of the MH370 victims thought, and said. On the third anniversary of the loss of MH370 *The Australian* published a story about McNamara's refusal of the FOI request, naming him as the decision-maker.

'Three years after Malaysia Airlines Flight MH370 disappeared, Australian officials refuse to release related documents because this could damage international ties, apparently with countries including Malaysia,' the story ran.

When the families of the Chinese nationals on MH370 read the story, they were outraged, and the association representing them issued a media statement.

'China families of the missing of flight MH370 react with displeasure at the refusal of access under Freedom of Information by *The Australian* to documents relating to the search for MH370,' the association's statement said. 'Is avoiding offending the Malaysian authorities more important than discovering the truth?'

For the Chinese families, it was another case where, in their view, the truth was being suppressed and, they claimed, data manufactured to support what they saw as a false conclusion of what happened to MH370.

'The world has been misled into a delay of almost three years,' the families' statement said.

If an FOI request is refused, the applicant has the right to seek an internal review. I did so, quoting the statement from the Chinese families, and asking: 'Does the ATSB actually know that the members of the Search Strategy Working Group would object to the release of the communications I seek, or does it just assume it?'

Internal reviews of FOI requests are usually carried out by senior officers, and in this case, the new ATSB chief commissioner, Greg Hood, took it on himself. Hood upheld the rejection of the FOI request by McNamara, but focused more on draconian laws which can put public servants and consultants in jail for two years if they release information about an air crash investigation. Hood's letter rejecting the FOI request said documents connected with Australia's assistance to Malaysia in looking for MH370 were 'classified as restricted information' covered by subsection 60(2) of the Transport Safety Investigation Act 2003, stating 'that a person commits an offence if: (a) the person is, or has been, a Commissioner, staff member or consultant; and (b) the person discloses information to any person or to a court; and (c) the information is restricted information'.

On the face of it, this is pretty extraordinary legislation in a democracy – even in a murder trial, under the TSI Act if a public servant or consultant were called to give evidence under oath and disclosed restricted information about an air crash investigation, he or she could be jailed for two years for doing so. (On the other hand, if for that reason the person called to give evidence refused to do so, they could presumably be jailed for contempt of court.)

The ATSB website has an explanation of the statutes under which it operates, and says there are some exceptions to the information ban.

'The ATSB has the power to disclose restricted information if he or she considers that it is necessary or desirable for transport safety,' the website says. The nagging suspicion among the MH370 families is that the net result of the various laws is that the ATSB releases information when it serves its own interests, and does not release it when it works against its own interests.

The Australian reported on the ATSB's refusal of the FOI request in April 2017.

Victor Iannello, an engineer and one of the leading members of the Independent Group of MH370 watchers, also criticised the ATSB's suppression of the expert opinions on the satellite data.

'Why would the information about MH370 requested by *The Australian* cause damage to international relations?' Iannello asked on his blog. 'With the failure of the underwater search to locate [MH370], it is essential that we reassess what assumptions went into the analysis.'

At this point, Hood wrote a long letter to the editor posted on the ATSB's 'Correcting the Record' section, in late April 2017.

'It is particularly regrettable that Mr Higgins' articles have now led to some of the MH370 next-of-kin expressing doubts about the ATSB's conduct of the search, and by implication, our commitment to finding the aircraft,' Hood wrote.

Regrettable for whom, the ATSB? As has been shown and will be shown again, the families and the aviation community have, as interested individuals, used their right of free speech to express doubts about the ATSB's conduct of the search because it may have been based on wrong assumptions.

Hood did not stop there: he then went on to issue yet another comment, this time public in the same post on 'Correcting the Record'.

'You can perhaps now understand why I find Mr Higgins' approach to attacking the credibility of the search unwarranted. The ATSB reserves its rights not to interact with Mr Higgins,' Hood wrote.

There has been some speculation that the 'consensus' of the Search Strategy Working Group was a pretty soft one, that the views varied as to whether the satellite data was good enough to really conclude MH370 was in a rapid and accelerating 'death dive' at the end. In August 2016 *The Australian* asked one of the most experienced and respected air crash investigators in the US, former airline captain John Cox who served on many big National Transportation Safety Board investigations, what he thought.

'I do not believe there is sufficient data in the Inmarsat data to draw any conclusion on the rate of descent,' Cox said.

Later, Cox expanded on his views.

'The satellite data is very helpful, but the axis of greatest ambiguity is the vertical axis. Therefore, it is difficult to get an accurate descent rate. This is particularly true when looking at short time intervals. At this time I think the satellite data is valuable but not conclusive.

It is possible that the airplane descended at rates other than what the satellite data indicates in the last minutes of flight.'

An Inmarsat spokesman declined to comment, but a source close to the company said it was aware of the debate.

'The data logs from the satellite "pings" do not, in themselves, provide a measure of absolute altitude,' the source said. 'The logs are just one of a number of variables (including direction of flight and speed) that the international investigation team has used to determine the most likely flight path.'

At the Institute of Public Administration seminar in 2017, the man who had led the research into this part of the satellite handshakes, mathematician Neil Gordon, himself spoke of the limitations of the data, saying it only provided 'vague hints'. Gordon, who heads the DSTG's data and information fusion group told the audience:

'The key thing to remember: there is lots of uncertainty feeding into this . . . you're never going to end up with an "X" marks the spot.'

Referring to the Doppler effect analysis, as mentioned back in Chapter Six, Gordon said there was 'a piece of metadata attached to this which you can use to give some vague hints about the speed and direction that the aircraft was doing'.

The ATSB has never answered the key question implied in Iannello's comments: why is it able under the law to release information from the MH370 investigation which it claims supports its theory of what happened, but not release information which might go against it? The double standard became quite apparent when, in September 2016, as more heat was coming on the ATSB, Foley gave an interview to the Australian Associated Press. He told the news agency Australian analysis suggested the MH370 flap recovered had not been deployed when it hit the water but was retracted inside the wing.

'The rate of descent combined with the position of the flap – if it's found that it is not deployed – will almost certainly rule out either a controlled ditch or glide,' he said. 'If it's not in a deployed state, it validates, if you like, where we've been looking,' Foley told AAP.

Now, at that stage, the Malaysian investigation was still underway, the flap was being tested by Boeing, and the official findings about the flap had not been released. The ATSB had clearly decided it wanted to reveal the preliminary information regardless.

As 2016 entered its last weeks, the ATSB was in a fix. There were only a few thousand square kilometres of the 120,000 square kilometre search zone yet to cover and, as mentioned, in July the transport ministers had said if MH370 were not found in that remaining patch, the search would be suspended unless and until 'credible new evidence leading to the identification of a specific location of the aircraft' emerged.

So, in early November, the ATSB again gathered the best and the brightest. The Search Strategy Working Group experts were called to a three-day meeting in Canberra. The bureau called it a 'First Principles Review', going back to basics on the fundamentals of the hunt thus far. Transport Minister Chester opened the closed-door summit, and issued a statement saying the international panel of experts would 'inform the remainder of the search effort, and develop guidance for any future search operations'.

At the opening of the conference on 2 November, the ATSB also released a new report, titled *MH370 – Search and debris examination update*.

That report included a few new details from further drift-modelling, debris examination, and satellite data analysis, but in essence purported to reinforce the ATSB's 'death dive' theory and where it was looking. Additional analysis of the burst frequency offsets, the ATSB said in the report, 'is consistent with the aircraft being in a high and increasing rate of descent at that time'. The wing flap debris analysis 'reduced the likelihood of end-of-flight scenarios involving flap deployment'. Preliminary results of the CSIRO's drift analysis indicated it was 'unlikely that debris originated from south of the current search area', which tended to go against pilots Hardy's and Bailey's proposed target zone.

Now, the timing, form and build-up to the First Principles Review – not to discount the quality and impartiality of the members of the Search Strategy Working Group – smacked of being a last-ditch attempt by the ATSB to come up with a plan supported by an international panel of experts to continue the search in a new area. It had the aura of providing the scientific-sounding 'credible new evidence' the ministers demanded of where MH370 might be found.

At the time of the meeting, the ABC ran a report in which the journalist said he had talked to sources who told him that was precisely the objective of the First Principles Review – to develop a case for the ATSB to go to the three governments to seek further funding to expand the search area beyond 120,000 square kilometres.

'Australia is understood to be using the meeting to put together the best scientific thinking, along with a sound and reasonable business plan that will make it impossible for Malaysia and China to back away from,' the ABC claimed.

It was another case where the ATSB denied the story, and again used the 'Correcting the Record' section of its website to say the ABC had published 'misleading media reporting on the First Principles Review into the search for MH370'.

The suggestion that the purpose of the meeting was to mount a new bid for funds and to continue the hunt and make it impossible for China and Malaysia to resist was 'not correct', the ATSB said in 'Correcting the Record'. 'This is not the purpose of the meeting and the agenda is not to expand the search area,' the ATSB said.

Well, guess what. The First Principles Review came up with a plan to expand the search area by 25,000 square kilometres farther north along the Seventh Arc, which would have required a further injection of funds and the support of Malaysia and China. The report of the review sounded pretty much like a spruik for a renewed search, saying it had 'identified a remaining area of high probability between latitudes 32.5°S and 36°S along the 7th arc'.

That report was published on 20 December 2016. At that stage, the search of 120,000 square kilometres was nearing its end by a matter of weeks. But sources have suggested that by this time – as the ABC report implied – the ATSB was fairly confident, based on the optimism expressed in the First Principles Review that the aircraft lay to the north, that the three governments would approve continuing the hunt. The feeling at the ATSB was said to be that the ministers would regard the findings of the report to be just that 'new evidence' they said they needed to extend the search.

The ATSB confidently mapped out the new 25,000 square kilometre search zone in its December report.

To the ATSB's surprise, and the disappointment of the families and the international aviation community, the governments didn't budge. In mid-January 2017, the last ship on the ATSB-led hunt for MH370, the *Fugro Equator*, pulled in its towfish for the last time, and headed back to Perth, ending the search. A few days later, Liow and Chester visited the vessel in port, and held a media conference. They stuck to the script of the July meeting: the search would not resume without a new breakthrough. Liow said his government needed 'more empirical evidence before we move to the next search area'.

Hood was present and it was pretty clear from his body language that he was, quite understandably, a bit upset to have had to announce the ATSB had failed, and that the governments had decided to not proceed to the new target zone identified by the Search Strategy Working Group. Asked why the ATSB wouldn't expand the search area further north, he said, 'That's a question for the governments'.

'It's highly likely the area now defined by the experts contains the aircraft but that's not absolutely for certain,' he said.

Hood later said ATSB would have liked to continue searching to bring closure to the families.

'Everybody wants to do the right thing – everybody's got hopes,' Hood said. 'Having met a number of family members personally, they continue to have protracted and prolonged grief. I'm profoundly sorry for these people.'

I arranged to have the following question asked of Hood at the press conference by Victoria Laurie, one of *The Australian*'s reporters in Perth: Was it time to revisit theories that one of MH370's pilots had hijacked the plane, piloting it to the end? Hood repeated the usual line: analysis of the wing flap suggested it was retracted, and the satellite data had shown a rapid rate of descent 'which is suggestive of the aircraft not being in control at the end of the flight'.

The ATSB had spent $198 million of taxpayers' funds: $115 from the pockets of Malaysians; $63 million from Australians; and, notionally, $20 million from Chinese – Beijing's main contribution was the supposed cost of the deployment, mainly in Fremantle, of the suspected spy ship *Dong Hai Jiu 101*.

An interesting question is whether Hood and Foley regret they did not search all of the relatively small area that the highly experienced Boeing 777 captains Simon Hardy and Byron Bailey identified as being where MH370 would be had Zaharie flown it to the end and ditched it. Hood did not respond to that question when I put it to him in late 2018.

Hardy had given the ATSB every opportunity to explore his theory of where to look. He told me he spoke 'at length' to the ATSB in January 2015, and visited Foley and his colleagues in Canberra and Fremantle in May 2015 and again in May 2016. He said he 'continued exchanges until end of search in January 2017 and beyond'.

Had Foley directed that the search vessels cover about 7000 more square kilometres based on the alternative theory that Zaharie had glided the aircraft (or taken it down with engines just turning over) about 100 nautical miles farther across the Seventh Arc, he and Hood would have won either way. Had they searched those 7000 square kilometres and found MH370, they would have been heroes. If it were not found, they could have put paid to Hardy and Bailey by saying they had looked where they suggested and it wasn't there.

But to do that, the ATSB would have had to at least implicitly, and perhaps publicly, say it believed a serious possibility was that a Malaysian pilot hijacked a government-owned airliner and flew 238 people of diverse nationalities to their death. That was perhaps politically a bridge too far at least at that time, so that alternative 7000 square kilometres where the senior pilots believe MH370 lies remains unsearched to this day.

Next, it was up to the private sector to have a go at finding MH370.

TEN

NO CURE, NO FEE

At first glance, upper-crust Englishman Anthony Clake would seem an unlikely candidate to want to set up a Texas-based underwater survey company and risk about $100 million to try to find MH370.

The fact he did reflects the powers of addiction to the mystery and the urge to solve it.

Clake studied philosophy, politics and economics at Queen's College, Oxford. He then went to what Britons call 'the City', or the financial markets hub in London, where he was instantly acknowledged as a wunderkind. He joined hedge fund Marshall Wace in 2001 and was co-developer of the Trade Optimised Portfolio System (TOPS) which somehow sorts through investment ideas to pick winners. He was made partner in 2004 and was among those to benefit in 2015 when US private equity firm KKR bought a 25 percent stake in Marshall Wace.

By 2017, and at the tender age of 37, Clake was filthy rich, and could spend a fortune on things and causes that interested him. Clake made news in 2017 when he reportedly gave £50,000 to a 23-year-old fashion student to spend on supporting the Brexit campaign (he was perfectly entitled to do so).

Clake and some other British investors somehow developed a fascination with marine undersea survey technology and, as you do if that's the case and you are swimming in pounds sterling, they decided to not just learn about it and follow it as a hobby, but put hundreds of millions of dollars into setting up a company to do it. That company is Ocean Infinity, based in Houston.

Ocean Infinity's website describes the company as 'ocean explorers mapping the unknown'.

'We go to unmapped locations to survey the seabed using the most advanced fleet of autonomous vehicles in the world,' it says.

Clake and his well-heeled mates decided they needed someone to run the show, and chose another unlikely Brit with a posh accent, Oliver Plunkett, to be chief executive of Ocean Infinity. Plunkett told me in an interview he is, by profession, a barrister, but somehow worked out that what he really likes to do is negotiate big deals.

Ocean Infinity's owners decided it would be fun to try to find MH370, and sent Plunkett to talk to the Malaysian government with the aim of doing a deal to make it happen. He did, and as a result, in January 2018 a futuristic scene was played out in a remote swath of the southern Indian Ocean in a new quest to find the Boeing 777 registered 9M-MRO.

An impressive but somewhat bizarre-looking ship with a massive helipad perched over its bridge and a gigantic crane on the rear deck stopped dead in it tracks. One after another, the crew launched eight orange torpedo-like unmanned mini-submarines. And with that, a new, audacious capitalist bid to find MH370, after the previous search run by Australian bureaucrats failed, was on.

The people who work for Ocean Infinity are a crack international team of engineers, information technology gurus, hydrographic surveyors, underwater robot submarine experts and others. The company's shareholders took a big gamble on their own ability.

A few months earlier Plunkett had put a juicy offer to the Malaysian government. Ocean Infinity proposed to launch a new hunt for the aircraft on a 'no find, no fee' basis – the Malaysian government would agree to pay a sizeable sum if the company found it. But if no wreckage was found, the owners of Ocean Infinity would have gone to all that effort for not a penny's compensation, and have blown their dough.

Malaysia's talkative Deputy Transport Minister Abdul Aziz Kaprawi had given some indication of the size of the deal. The government's cabinet, he said in October 2017, had agreed 'to prepare a special allocation to the Ministry of Transport amounting to between $US20m and $US70m if MH370 aircraft wreckage is successfully found within 90 days'. The sliding scale of reward was based on where the aircraft was found – $US20 million if it were discovered in the first section of the search plan agreed with the Malaysian government; $US70 million if it were tracked down in the last section.

So keen were the people who run Ocean Infinity to get started they ordered the captain of the vessel they had leased, the *Seabed Constructor* owned by the Swire group, to set sail from Durban in South Africa for the new search zone, even though a final contract with the Malaysian government had yet to be signed.

David Griffin, a CSIRO drift-modelling scientist, met the Ocean Infinity people in London, where a lot of the company's brains are located, to brief them on where he thought they should look.

'It's a very impressive organisation,' Griffin said. 'They have got terrific equipment.' Ocean Infinity planned to deploy eight top-of-the-range autonomous underwater vehicles at a time on independent search missions, enabling it to scan the seabed for MH370 much faster than in the ATSB search. Just as the new search was about to begin, Plunkett granted me an exclusive interview. On the way from its last port of call in Durban, Plunkett said, the crew and scientists had conducted some trial dives.

'We have had some pretty good results, as far as I can tell, a dive down to 5800 metres, which is pretty cool,' he said.

Ocean Infinity is a pretty serious mob. Putting them side-by-side against the search led by the ATSB, what Ocean Infinity was doing made the previous hunt look like kids' stuff. Where the ATSB-led search had used at best three ships at a time, each with a single towfish or autonomous underwater vehicle, Ocean Infinity used eight AUVs simultaneously. Ocean Infinity also had the option to guide the AUVs using eight robot surface boats, but in the end decided they were not required. The issue, however, was this: no matter how sophisticated the technology, one is unlikely to find what one is looking for unless one has the right strategy of where to look. Plunkett more or less said as much:

'I think assuming all of the aviation analysis is right, then I think we have a realistic prospect of finding it.'

The search strategy for Ocean Infinity was, in essence, pretty simple: look progressively farther north up the Seventh Arc from where the ATSB search had finished its failed hunt. The plan had been developed in conjunction with the client, the Malaysian government, the ATSB and the CSIRO drift-modelling experts. The first area to be searched would, in fact, be the 25,000 square kilometres to the immediate north of the ATSB's original 120,000 square kilometres where it looked for, and didn't find, MH370.

Since the first search, a lot of new work had been done by the drift-modelling gurus. Helping them do so was the fact that more and more bits of MH370 had been found washed up on the other side of the Indian Ocean, some by the aforementioned Blaine Gibson, who had become a sort of self-styled Indiana Jones figure.

Gibson, an American lawyer, spent three years combing beaches of Africa and islands off it looking for pieces of MH370, often sporting a hat very much like the fedora worn by actor Harrison Ford when he played professor of archaeology Henry Walton 'Indiana' Jones in the swashbuckling films. Gibson, who worked with locals in various countries to find debris from the plane, loved the sense of drama and mystery he said surrounded his quest. In an interview with *The West Australian* in 2018, Gibson said he encountered intimidation, stalking, death threats, defamation and assassination as he walked the beaches.

'For whatever reasons, some people are very upset that I and other private citizens are finding pieces of the plane,' he told the newspaper.

There was at least one really murky event that certainly did happen. In 2017, Houssenaly Zahid Raza, the Honorary Malaysian Consul in Madagascar, was gunned down in the capital Antananarivo in an apparent assassination. Raza had been due to deliver what were claimed to be more pieces of MH370 to investigators in Kuala Lumpur. The assassination fed suggestions from Independent Group blogger Victor Iannello among others of a dark conspiracy to stop MH370 wreckage being recovered. However, others speculated that Zahid, of French Malagasy ethnicity, was murdered as a revenge for yet another bizarre plot: his alleged involvement in the 2009 abduction of several residents of Indo-Pakistani descent. At the time of writing, an investigation into Zahid's death was still underway.

By 2017, 18 pieces of MH370 had been identified as being 'very likely' or 'almost certain' to originate from MH370, with another two assessed as being 'probably' from the aircraft. These are shown overleaf.

The ATSB relied on the fact that some items were from within the fuselage, and that the debris indicated 'there was a significant amount of energy at the time the aircraft impacted the water' to conclude the pattern was 'not consistent with a successful controlled ditching'.

However, those who support the controlled ditching theory insist there is no suggestion on their part that it would leave an aircraft wholly intact – rather, it would break into a few main chunks which would sink, leaving some debris but far less than in an uncontrolled high-speed crash. This is what happened to Ethiopian Airlines Flight 961, a Boeing 767 which was hijacked on 23 November 1996, en route from Addis Ababa to Nairobi. The three Ethiopian hijackers ordered the captain, Leul Abate, to fly to

Australia where they intended to seek asylum. Abate told them it was impossible, the aircraft did not have anywhere near enough range, but the hijackers ignored him.

The aircraft ran out of fuel and Abate ditched it just off a resort in the Comoros Islands off the eastern coast of Africa. There is spectacular vision on the web of the cartwheeling aircraft breaking up. While 125 of the 175 passengers and crew on board along with the hijackers died – many because they inflated their life jackets prematurely and it made it more difficult for them to get out – Abate was still praised for saving as many lives as he did.

The value of the wreckage to the drift-modellers was in where all the bits of it were found. It was, in fact, over quite a wide geographical area, from the southern tip of South Africa up to an island off northern Tanzania, and also including Mozambique on the African mainland, plus the islands of Madagascar, Reunion and Mauritius.

Also of significance was where debris was not found: not one piece was discovered in Australia even though there were many efforts to track some down. According to the drift-modelling expert David Griffin, this actually restricted how far south MH370 could be, because at a certain point south debris would have been expected to have washed up on Australian beaches.

Relatively early on in the piece, drift-modellers working independently from the CSIRO came to the view the ATSB was looking too far south. The Euro-Mediterranean Centre on Climate Change in Italy, and scientists at the University of Western Australia, working separately from each other, both said it should have been clear to the ATSB early on that they should have moved their ships much farther north.

The University of Western Australia scientist who led that institution's independent drift-modelling study, Charitha Pattiaratchi, said as soon as the flaperon was discovered in July 2015, it was pretty obvious the ATSB was looking in the wrong place.

FIGURE 7: ITEMS RECOVERED THAT WERE IDENTIFIED AS VERY LIKELY, ALMOST CERTAIN OR PROBABLY FROM MH370

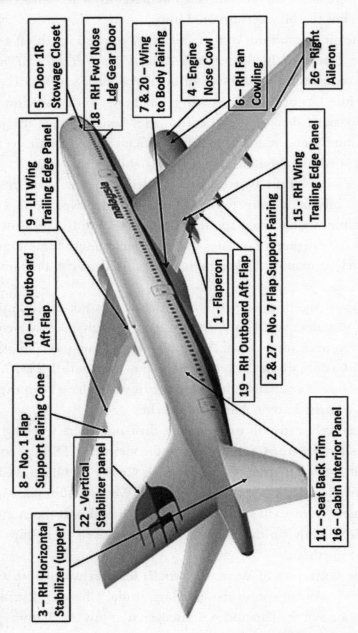

5 – Door 1R Stowage Closet

18 – RH Fwd Nose Ldg Gear Door

7 & 20 – Wing to Body Fairing

4 - Engine Nose Cowl

6 – RH Fan Cowling

26 – Right Aileron

9 – LH Wing Trailing Edge Panel

15 - RH Wing Trailing Edge Panel

10 – LH Outboard Aft Flap

1 - Flaperon

19 – RH Outboard Aft Flap

2 & 27 – No. 7 Flap Support Fairing

8 – No. 1 Flap Support Fairing Cone

11 – Seat Back Trim
16 – Cabin Interior Panel

3 – RH Horizontal Stabilizer (upper)

22 - Vertical Stabilizer panel

FIGURE 8: THE ITEMS FROM MH370 WERE RECOVERED FROM MOZAMBIQUE, TANZANIA, SOUTH AFRICA, MAURITIUS, MADAGASCAR AND REUNION ISLAND

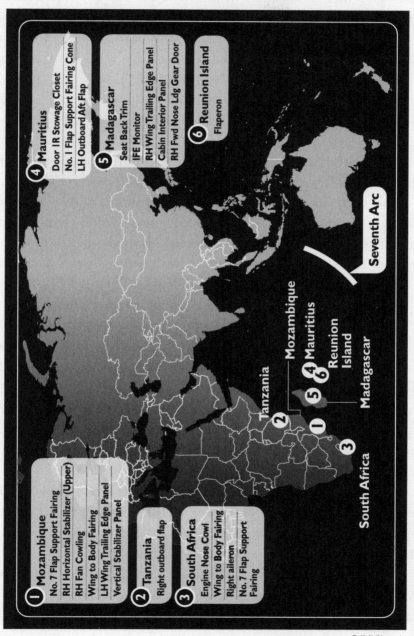

© Edi Sizgoric

'We got time on the supercomputer in Perth, which is the fastest computer in the southern hemisphere,' Pattiaratchi explained. It showed clearly that the aircraft must have been farther north, because it would have taken another three months for the flaperon to get to Reunion had it started as far south as where the ATSB was searching.

'We said that in September 2015,' Pattiaratchi said.

It took the ATSB another 15 months to come to the same conclusion, during which time it had stuck to its original search strategy focusing on the southern band of the Seventh Arc. That was the call of the ATSB; it does not discount the fact CSIRO drift-modellers had been doing a lot of very sophisticated work over that time.

The trick with drift-modelling, it turns out, is that items of different shape, size and weight drift differently with the same winds and ocean currents. The drift models have been developed from US tracking buoys over 30 years, which may not move the same way or speed as parts of an aircraft wing like a flaperon or a flap. So, the CSIRO built some Boeing 777 flaperon replicas and cut them down to resemble the damage found on the one discovered on Reunion. The researchers also got their hands on a real Boeing 777 flaperon, and set them all adrift with radio transmitters off Tasmania, beside free-floating buoys. The goal was to see how differently a damaged flaperon drifts, and refine the model to get a more accurate picture of where the starting point lies. The ATSB released the new drift-modelling in April 2017, and said, 'We are now even more confident that the aircraft is within the new search area identified'.

Griffin said the new data could in fact narrow down the 'highly likely' zone where the wreckage would be to 8000 square kilometres, or even 4000 square kilometres, essentially on the southern end of the new proposed search area of 25,000 square kilometres.

Not long after that, the ATSB and its CSIRO allies came up with yet another, intriguing new set of clues as to where MH370 might be. From the start of the surface search on 18 March 2014, Australian authorities had gone to other national governments and agencies seeking satellite imagery of possible debris. They had all been checked out and found to be junk of one form or other. But the new evaluation of the drift-modelling showed a likely location of MH370 farther north. With this and the benefit of knowing what MH370 debris looked like from what had been washed up and recovered, the ATSB decided to have another review of the satellite imagery.

Early in 2017 the French Ministry of Defence gave the ATSB four military intelligence satellite images from their Pleiades 1A spy satellite, which had been taken on 23 March 2014 to the north-west of the Seventh Arc, in an area not covered by aircraft during the surface search. The ATSB immediately saw them as significant. The drift-modelling of the debris showed the best new promise to be on the Seventh Arc at around latitude 35 degrees south. The French spy satellite images were captured just where MH370 debris was likely to have drifted to the north-west in the two weeks after MH370 went down – if it had started at 35 degrees south on the Seventh Arc.

The original French analysis in March 2014 had identified four possible objects which may be debris in the satellite images. In 2017, the ATSB asked Geoscience Australia to reanalyse the images and determine whether the objects, or others, were potentially man-made. It was intense, painstaking work, with experts poring over the satellite images at the greatest possible resolution.

In August 2017 Geoscience Australia came up with a report concluding that of at least 70 identifiable objects in the four satellite photos, 12 had been assessed as 'probably' man-made and a further 28 'possibly' man-made. The resolution was not good enough to determine conclusively that the objects were aircraft debris – they were, essentially, white blobs. But even to the naked, untrained eye, some of the blobs appeared vaguely rectangular and the sort of thing a busted-up bit of plane might look like as a blob.

The ATSB passed the results of Geoscience Australia's analysis to CSIRO to perform a drift study to determine with greater precision where the objects identified in the imagery were likely to have been on 8 March 2014, two weeks before the images were taken. Griffin and his colleagues got back to work, and determined that based on the new French military satellite images, the aircraft could be located quite precisely. The report said: 'We think it is possible to identify a most likely location of the aircraft, with unprecedented precision and certainty. This location is 35.6 [degrees south], 92.8 [degrees east].'

At the time it all looked a bit like an orchestrated campaign by the organisations involved to persuade the three governments that they had discovered the new evidence, pinpointing a final resting place for MH370 which the ministers said they needed to renew the search. Griffin, who said he for one 'obviously' wanted the hunt to recommence, explained: 'I think everyone who has been involved in the search in the ATSB is absolutely determined to bring it to a successful outcome.'

In any event, it worked: the owners of Ocean Infinity were convinced it was worth a shot and they were prepared to take the financial risk of only getting paid if they found MH370 in 90 days, and the Malaysian government accepted the deal.

The agreement was signed amid a bit of fanfare and an invited media pack on 10 January 2018 in the Malaysian administrative capital Putrajaya, with Plunkett and Liow officiating.

Liow, who had described the deal in a rather poetic fashion as 'no cure, no fee', spelt it out in more detail. The Malaysian government would pay Ocean Infinity $US20 million if the plane were found within the first 5000 square kilometres of the agreed search zone, $US30 million if it were discovered within 10,000 square kilometres, and $US50 million if it were located within an area of 25,000 square kilometres. Beyond that area, Ocean Infinity would receive $US70 million, Liow said. He also said the clock was ticking: the hunters had 90 operational days to find the aircraft, or they would not get a dime.

'They cannot take forever or drag it on for another six months or a year,' he said.

And so, a few days later *Seabed Constructor*, with half of Ocean Infinity's total workforce of about 45 employees aboard, along with the ship's crew from Swire, and two Malaysian naval officers, started the next hunt for MH370.

The strategy had divided the band of the Seventh Arc to be searched into four 'sites', each one north of the other, and the 'sites' were divided up into 'areas'. Each week, the Malaysian government issued a bulletin reporting just how much had been searched, along with a multicoloured map.

The hunters made good progress: weather was good, the equipment worked well, and the eight autonomous underwater vehicles did their job. After the first fortnight, the *Seabed Constructor* had covered 7500 square kilometres – pretty much all of Area 1, Site 1 on the map – and headed to Fremantle for resupply and crew change. The Malaysian government duly reported the state of play in its second bulletin, saying no bits of plane had been found, but displaying some interesting geological formations of what looked like underwater sand dunes.

As the search got underway, a sensational international fight broke out between Australian officials and the families of those lost on MH370. It was a classic case of 'it seemed like a good idea at the time': then Prime Minister Tony Abbott first mooted it in 2014 – a permanent national memorial to MH370. It got the go-ahead from the Western Australian government in late December 2017, which set the site at Elizabeth Quay in Perth and put out a tender for the project valued at $126,000 – plus GST. The cost of the memorial was to be shared between the federal and state governments.

The tragic mistake was typical of governments: nobody seemed to have asked the people to whom it was aimed if they wanted it. The proposal caused a storm of anguish among the families, particularly in China where the overwhelming majority of the passengers on MH370 were from. They basically regarded the move as an effort by Australian politicians to kill off their loved ones once and for all with a plaque of their names. The association representing the families of the Chinese nationals on the flight issued a media release saying 'China family members are incensed at being notified of the intent to proceed with an MH370 memorial by the Australian government, contrary to their and Australian family members' expressed wishes'.

'We hereby reiterate that we now firmly oppose the establishment of a memorial to MH370 at Elizabeth Pier in Australia.'

The view was that their loved ones were missing, not confirmed dead, and would remain so until – if and when – the aircraft were found. In what also seems to be another common error of government, both the minister and public servants rubbed salt into the wound by saying, effectively, the families would damn well get the memorial whether they liked it or not. A spokeswoman for the new federal transport minister, Barnaby Joyce, said at the time the plan for the memorial would proceed 'to honour the passengers and crew of the missing aircraft'.

'The monument will acknowledge those who were on board the aircraft and also recognise Australia's unique involvement in the search effort,' the spokeswoman said. 'Australian-based families have been consulted and will continue to be engaged during the design process.'

It went from bad to worse. The news site *Free Malaysia Today* reported that Judith Zielke, the senior public servant who, as head of the Joint Agency Coordination Centre, still held the principal all-of-government role of maintaining contact with the families, wrote to the Chinese families saying the memorial 'has received widespread support from the Australian families of those on board MH370'.

In fact, I could not find a single Australian family member who did support the idea, and Zielke did not take up the offer to name any. Danica Weeks launched herself into the fray, all guns blazing. In an email exchange with the Chinese families, she told them not to worry, as 'she [Ms Zielke] knows my opposition to the memorial, the same as you'.

'I called her on who she has consulted in Australia as she NEVER asked me about it and she said the other Australian families,' Danica wrote to the Chinese families. 'So I contacted them and they too said they had not been consulted! So trust me I don't know who she spoke to here and who gave the go ahead, definitely no-one in the Australian families I know!'

Teresa Liddle, whose sister Mary Burrows disappeared on MH370, said Zielke 'never approached me' about whether she would support a memorial, and said to me, 'I am totally opposed to it'.

'I just disagree that they declared them dead,' Teresa said, saying this was the effect of announcing a plan for a memorial.

Amanda Lawton, whose Brisbane parents Bob and Cathy disappeared on MH370, said, 'I've still not received any info regarding the memorial.'

It was an early battle in a war over the memorial which was to last many months.

MH370 is a mystery, and at the time, elements of the Ocean Infinity search looked mysterious in the public eye. The company did not say much to the media, although I got more access than most. Early on something really cloak-and-dagger happened: the *Seabed Constructor* 'went dark' and disappeared just like the aircraft it was trying to find.

Ships carry an Automatic Identification System transponder, something like aircraft transponders, that lets maritime authorities know where they are. Various website apps can track the ships, and members of the international MH370 club did so with gusto. But, like the transponder on MH370, the ship's transponder can be turned off, and that's just what happened with the *Seabed Constructor* early in the search. The Twitterati watching this went ape, particularly since those tracking *Seabed Constructor* had observed the ship making a big wide circle before it went dark. The MH370 rumour mill worked overtime – had Ocean Infinity found the aircraft? Then there was an even more sensational rumour: *Seabed Constructor* was secretly retrieving sunken treasure.

The wooden shipwreck discovered in 2015 during the previous ATSB-led search for MH370 had all but dissolved over the esti-mated two centuries it had been there (marine archaeologists had determined the type of anchor was not made after about 1820). But Paul Kennedy, the head of Fugro in Australia, had told a conference in Perth in 2016 that a large chest was the only big thing left intact, at about 4000 metres.

'It's a big chest, it's about three metres long, maybe one-and-a-half metres wide. And it's still closed,' he said at the time.

Eventually, an Ocean Infinity spokesman said the *Seabed Constructor* 'went dark' just to take a look at what turned out to be the under-water sand dunes.

'As highlighted in the weekly report, there were a couple of points of interest identified last week. These turned out to be of no signifi-cance,' the spokesman said. 'Ocean Infinity did not want to give the impression they had found the wreckage.'

Mystery kept dogging Ocean Infinity and the new hunt. The ABC ran an extraordinary story that the Malaysian investigation had, in effect, been the subject of an internal military coup of sorts.

'A power struggle has emerged in the Malaysian-led investigation into the disappearance of missing Malaysia Airlines Flight MH370 over the Indian Ocean four years ago,' the ABC story went.

'Four civilian air crash investigators, including the lead authority on analysing black box flight data, have been sidelined over reported budget constraints.'

The ABC quoted the lead aviator, Colonel Lau Ing Hiong, who

confirmed his secondment to the search team but said he was just there in case the black boxes were found.

There were other rumours: that the ATSB was somehow mixed up in all this, and that its operatives had been secretly dropped off on the *Seabed Constructor* when a vessel from Fremantle, the *Maersk Mariner*, had made a rendezvous with it.

The secrecy with which the ATSB and the JACC continued to carry out their residual roles when it came to MH370 did not help. For weeks, they refused to answer questions from *The Australian* as to whether or not the ATSB still had an officer on the investigation team. It was one case where the truth could only be wrenched out by senators.

The Australian Senate has a number of committees, and one of the things public servants hate is that they have to periodically appear before public hearings known as Senate Estimates to be grilled by senators on things they won't tell journalists. In this case, I made some suggestions to cross-bench Senator Rex Patrick from South Australia as to what to ask ATSB boss Greg Hood and JACC head Judith Zielke when they appeared before a senate committee in February. Hood at first tried to distance the bureau from the MH370 affair, saying 'the ATSB's formal involvement in the search concluded last year'. But under cross-examination by Patrick, Hood admitted the ATSB did have continued involvement in the investigation into 'what happened on that flight'.

'Australia has an accredited representative on that investigation team,' Hood revealed.

The ATSB had been particularly sensitive on the matter, with its spokesman Paul Sadler referring questions to the JACC, while Zielke did not respond and her spokesman referred inquiries to Malaysian government authorities. It may be that the ATSB, knowing that what was likely to be a controversial final report of the Malaysian investigation into MH370 was coming out within months, was trying to minimise public exposure of ATSB involvement. Zielke, in answers to questions from Patrick, did scotch the wild rumour that Australian officials had been on *Seabed Constructor*.

A few months later, as Malaysia enjoyed a major resurgence in democratic expression, the JACC and the ATSB went the other way. Zielke had another attempt at shutting me down when I was starting to think about writing this book, or at least an extended feature about the ATSB and the JACC's restrictive Freedom of Information and media policies. Saying I was considering writing a 'long form' piece on this topic, I emailed ATSB spokesman O'Malley to re-check the details he had told me about why he talked American, and spokesman Sadler about some aviation journalism awards for which he had been a runner-up. That prompted Zielke to mount another failed attempt to have me taken off the MH370 story. In a letter to Editor-in-Chief Paul Whittaker, dated 18 April 2018, Zielke wrote 'we will no longer be responding to inquiries from Mr Higgins'.

'Should you assign another writer to the story, we will accommodate their request for information.'

The editors ignored this intervention as a further attempt by an unelected public servant to curb freedom of the press and dictate which journalists should cover a story. They instructed me and other reporters on the paper to write more, harder stories about MH370 and the role of the JACC and the ATSB.

The weeks passed, and the weekly Malaysian government updates showed the area searched by the *Seabed Constructor* moving steadily north, with no hint of MH370. Those who knew the background to the search strategy knew this was not good news: the plan had been based on the CSIRO/ATSB assumptions and the drift-modelling, and that had put the aircraft most likely in the area first searched. When the two arms of the 'Phase 1' section had been covered, it eliminated the three most likely spots which Griffin and his team had identified.

Critics of the search strategy started re-emerging in the media, saying the whole Ocean Infinity approach was wrong from the start because it was still based on the ATSB's insistence that the MH370 was a ghost flight at the end, and crashed down rapidly after running out of fuel while flying on autopilot. Pilots Simon Hardy, Byron Bailey, and a new entrant to the debate, New Zealander Mike Keane – a former RAF fighter pilot and chief pilot of Britain's largest airline easyJet – started making noises again. They maintained the place to look was just outside the southern section of the ATSB-led search, allowing for Zaharie having glided (possibly with the engines barely turning over) the aircraft up to 100 nautical miles after fuel exhaustion and ditching it.

In the exclusive interview with Plunkett, I asked the Ocean Infinity chief executive if it were possible *Seabed Constructor* could be sent to the pilots' preferred zone if the new search of the ATSB defined area came up blank. Plunkett chose his words carefully.

'I wouldn't rule it out,' Plunkett said. 'We are ultimately providing a service to the government of Malaysia.'

What happened, in fact, is the government with whom Plunkett had struck the original deal got turfed out in the most extraordinary political upheaval in Malaysia since independence from Britain in 1957.

The Prime Minister who had served in that role since 2009, Najib Razak, was a member of Malaysia's political elite, educated at an English-language private school before earning a degree in economics from the University of Nottingham. His father and uncle had been Prime Minister before him, and when his father died in 1976, Najib was elected to his seat in Parliament.

In the six decades since independence, Malaysia had, overall, been a success story among developing countries, with solid economic growth, steadily rising levels of prosperity and wealth distribution, political stability and, notwithstanding race riots in the 1960s, a fairly harmonious mix of Malays and ethnic Chinese and Indians.

This stability had been based on a sort of tacit agreement among the racial groups. The Malays would be first among equals, hold primary political power, and enjoy some degree of affirmative action. But there would be opportunity for all and power sharing. For six decades, that power sharing was orchestrated through the Barisan Nasional coalition, made up of the dominant United Malays National Organisation and other ethnically defined political groupings, including the Malaysian Chinese Association and the Malaysian Indian Congress.

By 2013, the winds of change were blowing. At elections in May that year, the Barisan Nasional and Najib were returned with the most seats in the first-past-the-post electoral system, but lost the popular vote. Five years after that, Najib and his government found themselves even more out of favour. The government had introduced a deeply unpopular six per cent goods and services tax, and Najib had become mired in a scandal involving billions of dollars in an allegedly embezzled Malaysian state-owned investment fund. Najib strenuously denied any wrongdoing, but the whiff of alleged corruption was in the air.

Although it would be impossible to measure, some Malaysian political observers also said the loss of MH370, and just four months later, Malaysia Airlines Flight MH17, might have had some impact on the national mood.

The two tragedies were, of course, in essence quite different and there is absolutely no common causal link between the two. But they both had the elements of malevolence, bizarre ill fate and lack of closure.

Malaysia Airlines Flight MH17 took off from Amsterdam on 17 July 2014, bound for Kuala Lumpur, with 298 aboard. Three hours later the Boeing 777-200ER – a sister airliner to MH370 – was flying over what was known to be dangerous territory: rebel-held eastern Ukraine, where Russian-backed separatists had been fighting a messy war of independence. ICAO had warned airlines of the risks of flying over that disputed patch – just a month earlier, a Ukrainian Air Force Ilyushin Il-76 aircraft was shot down, showing the pro-Russian rebels had anti-aircraft weaponry. Some carriers had heeded ICAO's warning and decided to avoid the conflict zone, but not Malaysia Airlines.

At 4:20pm local time, a Buk surface-to-air missile blew MH17 apart, and what was left of the aircraft and the passengers and crew fell to the ground in flames. One passenger was found wearing an oxygen mask, suggesting the horrifying scenario some were conscious for a period after the missile hit.

International investigators got on the case, and the Netherlands and Australia announced in May 2018 they believed the missile was transported to Ukraine from a military unit in the Russian city of Kursk.

Russian President Vladimir Putin has repeatedly denied his country's involvement in the shooting down of MH17; the Russians have come up with various imaginative theories such as that a Ukrainian jet fighter took it out. While international investigators are working on a case for prosecution, Putin's stone-walling against any suggestion his citizens, or the Ukrainian separatists effectively under his protection, were involved will make bringing the guilty to justice difficult.

Although the cause of the disappearance of Malaysia Airlines Flight MH370 has yet to be conclusively determined, deliberate human intervention to take the aircraft down trumps any sort of accident such as fire or mechanical failure as the most likely cause.

Angus Houston, having been involved deeply in both tragedies, observed in my interview with him that five years on, the common element is unfinished business for the families of those lost on MH17 and MH370.

'They have not reached closure yet,' Houston told me. 'Both suffered greatly, it's a very unfortunate sets of circumstances. I hope at some stage MH370 is found, and as for MH17, I hope whoever ordered the firing of that missile is held to account in the International Court of Justice.'

Neither MH17 nor MH370 could seriously be said to be the Malaysian government's fault in any direct sense. But some commentators suggested that so close together and in combination, they somehow produced a feeling that while the gods had smiled on an independent Malaysia for more than half a century, something must have displeased them enough to smile no more. When Flight MH17 was shot down, Najib declared the date 'a tragic day in an already tragic year'.

At the end of 2014, the *Malay Mail* wrote in a comment piece that the two Malaysia airline tragedies 'managed to galvanise a nation torn by the divisive 13th general election the year before, as people came up with independent campaigns to express their solidarity with the stricken carrier and with each other'.

In 2018 the Malaysian political opposition to Najib got its act together, and in a many ways peculiar, but highly successful move, went back to the future in selecting a leader. That was Mahathir Mohamad, the charismatic but controversial Prime Minister from 1981 to 2003. During those two decades, Mahathir had overseen a period of prolonged and strong economic growth and modernisation, but also a crackdown on civil rights and the media and a campaign of annoying western countries including Australia. When in 1993 Mahathir boycotted an APEC summit in Seattle, Australian Prime Minister Paul Keating called him a 'recalcitrant', and Mahathir in turn talked about running a 'buy Australian last' campaign.

At the age of 92, Mahathir came back as the leader of the opposition coalition Pakatan Harapan, heading into the national elections. Even more extraordinarily, Mahathir said that if elected, he would seek a royal pardon for his former deputy with whom he had fallen out and had persecuted, Anwar Ibrahim, and ultimately hand over power to him. You may recall from Chapter One, Anwar was the distant relative by marriage of MH370 pilot Zaharie Ahmad Shah, and was convicted of sodomy hours before Zaharie captained the Boeing 777 into the sky. If, as some suspect, Zaharie had hijacked MH370 as a political protest over the conviction of Anwar, it would be a bewildering closing of the circle.

There was a big personality element to the election campaign. Mahathir had groomed a young Najib for office, but now called that mentorship 'the biggest mistake of my life'. While Mahathir and Pakatan Harapan were popular in the polls, election analysts were not convinced they could win because the government had engaged in a redrawing of electoral boundaries which favoured Najib's coalition.

The Australian's South-east Asia correspondent, Amanda Hodge, got an interview with Mahathir during the election campaign, and as an aside, asked if he had any thoughts about MH370. Did he ever. He said he did not think the Najib government had engaged in a cover-up, but he did think the aircraft might have been taken over remotely using technology said to be installed to thwart a hijack.

'It was reported in 2006 that Boeing was given a licence to operate the takeover of a hijacked plane while it is flying so I wonder whether that's what happened or not,' Mahathir told Hodge.

So it was against this volatile backdrop of a sensational election campaign in the first part of 2018 that *Seabed Constructor* calmly plied the waves of the southern Indian Ocean looking for MH370 with the eight orange autonomous underwater vehicles. By the end of April 2018, the Ocean Infinity search had covered more than 70,000 square kilometres, or two thirds of the total target zone and, again, had not found any bit of an aircraft. The company had kept a low profile, getting on with the job.

The election on 9 May, was electrifying. Mahathir's coalition romped in with 121 seats, enough to form a simple majority and take control of parliament. Barisan Nasional's vote collapsed, leaving it with 79 seats compared to 133 at the 2013 election. It was the first change of government since independence. Mahathir was sworn in as prime minister the next day, making him a role model and pin-up boy for those in their 90s around the world – the oldest national world leader by a long shot.

Mahathir's ministers were sworn in over the days after that, and right from day one, the new government started issuing some conflicting remarks about the hunt for MH370. The new transport minister, Anthony Loke, in his first remarks in the role, told journalists his first priority was to find MH370.

'Of course a major issue for the ministry . . . is to continue searching for MH370,' Loke said.

But Mahathir seemed to have a different view – he was worried the Ocean Infinity deal might be another big-spending project of Najib's that the new government needed to quash, or at least examine.

'We want to know the details of this, the necessity of this, and if we find it is not necessary, we will not renew,' Mahathir said after chairing his first cabinet meeting.

'We are reviewing the contract and we need to terminate it if not useful,' he said.

Loke changed his tune accordingly and, referring to the contract with Ocean Infinity, told journalists hours later: 'This morning I raised this in cabinet and agreed to extend to 29 May.'

Asked if that meant no more extensions, he said: 'Yes.'

The reality was, though, that it was all a bit academic. By that stage Ocean Infinity had covered its target search area, and its hunt had not found MH370. It was time for the *Seabed Constructor* to move on to its next assignment. Clake and his British investor mates had made a brave effort at public interest entrepreneurship to solve an aviation mystery, given it their best shot, and blown their dough.

It had been a noble, private sector venture using brilliant technology which had worked superbly, and shown how such a search could be done expeditiously. In four months, Ocean Infinity had covered about the same amount of territory as the ATSB had covered in more than two years. The company was gracious in announcing the end of its unsuccessful grail quest. In a statement, chief executive Plunkett said:

'While clearly the outcome so far is extremely disappointing, as a company we are truly proud of what we have achieved in terms of both the quality of data we've produced and the speed with which we covered such a vast area, the likes of which has not been seen before.

'There has not been a subsea search of this scale and we hope that in the future we will be able to again offer our services in the search for MH370.'

It had, indeed, been a massive subsea hunt – but again, it had been based on the extension of the theory that the aircraft was unpiloted at the end, and crashed down rapidly after running out of fuel while flying on autopilot. Like the ATSB, Ocean Infinity had not looked in the relatively small search area farther south proposed by Boeing 777 airline captains Simon Hardy and Byron Bailey based on their alternative scenario of a pilot flying the aircraft to the end, and ditching it.

Just as the Ocean Infinity search ended, an authoritative new independent assessment claimed to have determined once and for all that the ATSB's 'ghost flight' theory was wrong, and the pilots' claim MH370 ended in a controlled ditching was right.

ELEVEN
KING AIR, A WING, A PRAYER

It was a night training flight out of Ottawa to quiet airspace beyond North Bay on a Beechcraft King Air a couple of decades ago, and Larry Vance was in command with an equally experienced fellow Canadian air crash investigator flying the plane as co-pilot.

'We were about 20 minutes flying time north-west of North Bay, at an altitude of 10,000 or 12,000 feet, when suddenly the airplane started to shake violently, and the right wing dropped,' Vance told me.

'My co-pilot kept control with left rudder and aileron. The aileron control started oscillating back and forth. We had no idea what had gone wrong, and the shaking was very bad.'

Vance had a long history flying the King Air, a twin turboprop, including as a trainer for a number of years. One thing he knew about it he found rather disturbing at that moment.

'A sister airplane to the one we were flying had shed a wing a few years previously, and the pilots were killed,' Vance said.

As a result, all the King Airs in the Canadian government fleet had had their wings reinforced with a support strap on the wing spars, and Vance's brain immediately went to a suspicion that the strap on the aircraft's right wing had given way.

'I remember that when the wing had fallen off the other King Air we had concluded that the initial violent gyrations of the airplane would have broken the necks of the pilots. We comforted ourselves with the thought that at least they would not have had to ride the airplane down to impact alive. While our airplane was still shaking violently, I remember consciously forcing myself to untighten my neck muscles.'

As the terrifying moments ticked by, the wing was still there, and Vance and his co-pilot decided they needed a plan to keep it that way.

'We decided that we would do everything we could to keep the same flight profile that we were at – the same airspeed and power setting – the same flaps up, gear up configuration – so as not to disrupt anything aerodynamically.'

After what was probably less than a minute, the shaking, which Vance immediately as a veteran air crash investigator identified as what in aviation is known as 'flutter', subsided to something less than what he thought would break the airplane apart.

The pilots got a clearance and radar vectors to North Bay, and started their descent, keeping their airspeed steady.

'My co-pilot was flying, and I was helping her by pushing on the left rudder, to keep the airplane from yawing to the right,' Vance said. 'It took anywhere from three quarters to full rudder, and I remember my leg getting tired so I put both feet on the left rudder to hold it.'

Vance could have used the rudder trim – a compensation system that would have reduced the pressure he had to use on the rudder – but gut feel told him it was best to leave all the controls as they were.

During the descent, the severe flutter came back. Vance and his co-pilot were again sure the plane would come apart, but within about a minute, it again subsided somewhat.

'I remember thinking that if that violent flutter were to happen one more time, that would be it.

'We lined up on final and selected the gear down, but we left the flaps up, again with the idea of not changing anything. We briefed about what might happen on the landing, given that we had almost full left rudder applied. The left rudder would mean that the nose wheel would be turned to the left on touchdown.

'In the end, that was a non-issue – as soon as the main wheels touched the runway the shaking stopped.'

Vance and his co-pilot taxied in and shut down, and went into the terminal building to call back to home base. His bosses sent another King Air over to North Bay to pick them up.

'One thing that I recall is that when I tried to fill in the logbook, to leave it with the damaged airplane, at first I could not get my hand to work to write the information. I remember how weird that felt.

'On the way home in the recovery airplane my co-pilot and I talked it over some. We shared how nice it felt knowing that we were both going home to our families instead of having our TSB comrades trying to figure out what had happened to cause us to crash.'

Vance's fellow Canadian air crash investigators did determine the cause of the near-fatal flutter: a bolt holding the rudder trim had broken, allowing the rudder trim to vibrate out of control.

'As it turned out, our decision to not use rudder trim was a good one, because what was causing the severe flutter to stop was that a piece of the broken bolt had aligned itself at an exact position where our constant foot pressure on the rudder was holding it steady,' Vance said.

'If we had moved the trim, and the bolt had fallen out completely, it might have been game over for us.'

Vance knows a lot about planes – a lot about flying them and a lot about finding out why they crash.

So when he saw the ATSB stick with its 'unpiloted aircraft/high-speed dive' theory about MH370 when the aircraft's flaperon and flap were examined, photographed and analysed, he just couldn't believe it. He felt compelled to write a book, *MH370: Mystery Solved*, which transformed the international debate about what happened to the aircraft.

Vance started flying in 1967 at the age of 18 by winning a coveted flying scholarship through the Canadian Air Cadet Program. After getting his commercial licence, instrument rating and instructor rating, he worked as a flying instructor for nine years at what was then the Moncton Flying Club in New Brunswick, spending most of that time as chief instructor.

In 1978 Vance joined Transport Canada, the federal regulator equivalent to the US Federal Aviation Administration and Australia's Civil Aviation Safety Authority, as a civil aviation inspector.

'TC had its own fleet of aircraft, which included various types of light twin engine aircraft, including light turboprops, and I flew all of those,' Vance said. 'They also had DC-3s, and I was a captain on the DC-3 – that ages me, I guess, there are not many of us left.'

In 1984 Vance, by then an accomplished pilot who had flown for 17 years, joined what was then the Canadian Aviation Safety Board, now the Transportation Safety Board of Canada.

He was an air crash investigator, but he still flew himself; to get from A to B as part of doing his job and also to maintain proficiency as a flyer.

'With CASB and TSB it was mostly transporting people – including me – to various accidents,' Vance said. 'We all did that type of flying, because it was part of keeping our flying currency, which was a job requirement.'

One of the advantages of this rule was that when TSB air crash investigators, who were pilots like Vance, flew themselves and their colleagues to an accident site, it provided immediate street cred when they stepped out of the captain's seat to meet airline or other representatives.

'They see you at the controls, and you get out and introduce yourself, and they think, well, this guy is for real,' Vance said.

Vance believes in accuracy – he makes clear he was never an airline pilot, though he did learn to fly an airliner.

'The closest I got to flying a transport category was training to pilot proficiency status on the Boeing 737 – I completed a full training course on that aircraft with an airline,' he said.

When it comes to air crash investigation in Canada, Vance literally wrote the book – several in fact. He was the principal author of several of the TSB's original investigation manuals – everything from its 'Site Safety and Biohazard Manual', and its 'Accredited Representative Manual' for foreign investigations, to its 'Major Investigation Manual/Checklist'.

Vance now runs a private aviation consultancy in Ottawa, HVS Aviation, where among other things he teaches air crash investigation techniques, and accepts commissions from legal firms to investigate accidents. He's been involved in more than 200 air crash investigations over his career as field investigator in charge. In the 1985 crash of an Arrow Air DC8 with 256 fatalities in Gander, Newfoundland, he conducted studies to determine how airframe icing may have been involved. In 1991, he went to Saudi Arabia to lead the investigation of the operational and human factors involved in the crash of a Nationair DC-8 where 261 died – in that case, a tyre known to be underinflated but not dealt with caused an onboard fire. The plane came down with flaming bodies falling out along the way as the cabin floor collapsed.

The most famous air crash investigation Vance worked on was Swissair 111. It's one of the best known in the air crash business – that the investigation team found the originating cause was extraordinary; they were working in some of the most difficult circumstances imaginable. Vance was the deputy lead investigator on Swissair 111 and wrote the TSB's final report on the 1998 crash off the coast of Nova Scotia. He was also the one to give briefings to the families.

'People accuse me of being insensitive to families,' Vance told *The Ottawa Citizen*.

'I don't mind taking the question . . . How many grieving families have you talked to after an airplane accident? I've done it by the hundreds. Don't tell me that I don't have any sympathy. I've had people faint in my arms.'

Swissair 111 took off from New York's John F. Kennedy Airport in the evening of 2 September 1998, bound for Geneva with 229 passengers and crew on board. The flight was known as 'The United Nations Shuttle' for regularly transporting UN staff from UN headquarters in New York to Geneva which has many UN agencies. About an hour into the flight, the pilots noticed an odour in the cockpit; it got worse, and it was not long before they knew they had a fire on board. Canadian air traffic control offered the pilots a vector to Halifax, Nova Scotia, and they headed for it. But they were too high and had too much fuel to land safely, so the Swissair pilots requested a dump; Halifax controllers turned them around back over open water at St Margaret's Bay. As Vance described the procedure: 'Every airport, or at least every "sophisticated" airport, has areas designated for potential fuel dumping. It is not that dumping fuel is particularly dangerous – it typically dissipates before reaching the ground – but it is more logical to dump fuel over unpopulated areas or over water than to do it over built-up areas.'

Minutes later, the fire started to engulf the electrical systems, and one by one they collapsed. Lights progressively went black on the cockpit dashboard as the autopilot stopped working and instruments went dead. The captain went back to fight the blaze, as the co-pilot tried desperately to fly the plane manually. Eventually, all the control systems were knocked out, and the aircraft plunged into a steep dive into St Margaret's Bay.

The investigation determined the Swissair pilots never had a chance.

'It turned out that the decision to dump fuel made no difference in the outcome of the accident,' Vance said. 'No matter what, once the fire started they had no chance of making the airport because of the speed the fire spread. Given the location including the high altitude of the aircraft that they were starting from, they could not have landed in time.'

The air crash investigation by Vance and his colleagues was long and tedious. When the McDonnell Douglas MD-11 hit the water, it did so at 560 kilometres an hour, at 350 times the force of gravity, and was pulverised into two million pieces. An exhaustive dredging operation, bringing up more and more small pieces, enabled Vance and the other investigators to painstakingly chart the course of the fire. It took five years in all, but the Canadians eventually worked it out.

The fire ignited from an arcing event – a short circuit – in a wire feeding the inflight entertainment system. It was a tiny wire running through the ceiling above the rear of the cockpit, and it chaffed against a metal bracket until its insulating material wore through to the copper conductor.

It was a small short circuit, but big enough to set fire to the nearby metallised mylar insulation blankets, which were very flammable.

The fire spread at a ferocious rate and progressively disabled the plane.

'We recovered 98 per cent of the wreckage, including over 200 miles of wiring,' Vance said. 'From that mass of wiring we found the specific arc that started the fire, an arc that was too small to see with the naked eye. Quite an achievement.'

Vance's final report made a variety of recommendations, particularly about the lack of wisdom in having insulating material which, rather than retarding fires, accelerated them. The proposals were taken up by the international aviation community – one of the key principles of air crash investigation is that, although it may be long, labour-intensive and costly, finding out the cause of an accident can ultimately make flying safer.

In 2001, Vance and his team received a Government of Canada Certification of Recognition 'for overwhelming compassion, humanity and dedication to duty in the aftermath of the Swissair tragedy'.

The Swissair 111 investigation was a triumph of meticulous recovery and analysis of aircraft wreckage. While the technical data from the flight data recorder, and the exchanges on the cockpit voice recorder were useful, it was the wreckage which proved the key to unlocking what happened on Swissair 111.

And that's why, when wreckage from MH370, including a right flap and right flaperon, washed up on the other side of the Indian Ocean, Vance was astounded that the ATSB kept going with its theory that the pilots were incapacitated at the end of the flight and it crashed down rapidly from a high altitude into the sea, just like Swissair 111. Vance saw instantly, comparing photos of the MH370 flap and flaperon with what happened to Swissair 111, that MH370 did not go down in a high-speed crash. The two pieces of the plane were both mostly intact – they would have been smashed into tiny bits had MH370 gone down the way Swissair 111 did.

'There wasn't anything remotely big enough or intact enough in Swissair 111 to be even recognisable as a flap,' Vance said.

But both the flap and flaperon of MH370 had trailing edge damage, consistent with being dragged against the waves when lowered in a controlled ditching. Vance thought the ATSB should have right then and there abandoned its search strategy because, he believed, the premise on which it was based was clearly wrong. But it didn't: the ATSB continued with it for another 18 months when, according to Vance, it should have known it had almost no chance of finding MH370. As he wrote in his book *MH370: Mystery Solved*:

'To me, it is inconceivable that any investigator, or anyone who claims to have investigation expertise, would not automatically think their way through this, and do the calculations. They should realize that the high-speed diving crash theory supported by the official investigation simply does not make sense, based on this evidence alone.'

Vance's book published in May 2018 had a massive impact on the MH370 debate. But what enabled Vance to get his hands on the high-resolution photographs of the wreckage to make a detailed determination involved another case of a determined journalist pushing the ATSB to reveal the evidence it initially said wasn't there. Vance explained:

'The original thoughts about writing the book came when I was preparing material for my investigation courses, where we were coming up with findings that were different from what was coming from the official investigation.'

Ross Coulthart, the Nine Network reporter mentioned earlier who presented the Australian edition of *60 Minutes* story in 2016 looking at whether the ATSB's 'ghost flight' theory was wrong, a year later decided to have another crack at it. He wondered if more high-quality images of the MH370 wreckage parts could be found. Those could be shown to Vance, who could use his professional eye to examine them in more detail. While the ATSB had released some photographs of the wreckage, Coulthart suspected there might be more, and contacted the bureau.

'Initially they tried to tell me that all the photographs I needed were already publicly released, but I said I wanted a copy of ALL the high-res images taken of any of the recovered wreckage confirmed as MH370, assuming, correctly, that they had such images,' Coulthart explained. 'I did have to FOI the photographs that Larry used to do his analysis.'

'It lasted a few months and the ATSB were initially toey on the phone about my request but – to be fair – they did eventually honour the law and they released them – onto their website!'

Coulthart had Vance delve into the photos of the wreckage, looking for what in the air crash investigator trade are known as 'witness marks'.

'After the ATSB put those high-resolution photos of the flap section and other wreckage pieces on their website, we were off to the races, investigation-wise,' Vance said.

What he found further astounded him.

'I honestly thought that the official investigation would be able to figure it out from that flaperon, and then the section of flap that became available,' Vance said. 'When they failed to see the evidence, my team and I put together some pretty extensive technical notes – to be used for the training courses. It was when I was working extensively with those technical notes that I decided that the only way to put the whole mass of evidence together in an understand-able way was to put it in a book form – in language that could be understood by most people.'

Vance worked on the book with two of his colleagues who like him had enjoyed long careers with the TSB as air crash investigators and now work as independent consultants: scientist and engineer Terry Heaslip, and aircraft maintenance engineer Elaine Summers.

Ted Parisee, who did the graphics work for Vance's book, special-ises in the study of crash dynamics.

'Collectively, we have well over one hundred years of continuous service in professional aviation accident investigation,' Vance wrote.

While Vance corresponded with me over the time he was writing, he kept the totality of his findings intact to be released at a time, and in a fashion, of his choosing, in one hit. That was, Vance said, to be when the search by Ocean Infinity ended, because he did not want to have the book publicly cast doubt on the rationale of hunt while it was still going.

In early May 2018, as it looked like the search for MH370 by Ocean Infinity was approaching its end, Vance executed his media strategy for the release of his findings.

Vance gave me first go at his book, providing a worldwide scoop. On 14 May, *The Australian* published a news story about *MH370: Mystery Solved*.

'One of the world's leading air-crash investigators has produced compelling evidence that a pilot on Malaysia Airlines Flight MH370 hijacked his own aircraft and flew it to the end to perform a controlled ditching, contrary to the assumptions of the Australian investigators who led the first failed underwater search for the aircraft.'

The Australian ran two edited extracts from Vance's book. The main one got to number two on the newspaper's most read online list, and stayed in the top 10 for more than a day, indicating an extraordinary readership and interest. The main extract, of about 2000 words, meticulously mounted a case that the ATSB had made the wrong assumptions about what happened on MH370 during the latter part of the flight.

Vance wrote straight out that his and his colleagues' analysis showed the 'ghost flight' and 'death dive' theories were wrong.

'The evidence shows that the aeroplane was under the complete control of a pilot throughout the flight, and at the end of its flight, MH370 was intentionally ditched (landed in a controlled way) on the ocean surface,' Vance wrote.

It was a pretty big call: if Vance was right, it meant the ATSB had blown huge amounts of Australian, Malaysian and Chinese taxpayers' money. The implication, Vance wrote, was that they should have stopped burning public cash once the flaperon washed up on Reunion.

'The physical evidence available from examining the flaperon should have proved to the ATSB that the aircraft's flaps were extended (down) when it entered the water, and that the aeroplane was at a speed consistent with a pilot-controlled ditching.'

Vance knew from the start that he was going to have to prove his case beyond reasonable doubt before a sort of undeclared international tribunal of aviation experts who, as part of the MH370 club, would critically assess it and comment on it via mainstream and social media. The main extract in *The Australian* outlined the gist of his argument. Vance drew on his direct experience with hundreds of air crash investigations, including Swissair 111.

'If MH370 had experienced a high-speed diving crash, it would have produced tens of thousands of pieces of floating debris,' Vance wrote. 'Only about 20 pieces of wreckage confirmed to be from MH370 have been recovered to date.'

Had MH370 come down the way the ATSB says it did, hundreds of additional wreckage pieces with honeycomb-type construction would have been created and washed up, along with seat cushions, luggage pieces, life jackets, neck pillows and other floating items, and this would have arrived on the coast of Africa in significant amounts.

'The reason that more floating debris has not appeared is that it was never created in the first place. There was no high-speed diving crash.'

This part of Vance's analysis tallied with the argument put forward by international airline pilots Bailey, Keane and Hardy: it holds that Zaharie flew the aircraft to the end to ditch it, in order to sink it in as few pieces as possible and limit the debris field.

Vance rejected suggestions by some observers that the flap and flaperon might have fallen off in a high-speed dive as a result of flutter and, drifting down on their own at a lower speed, escaped the more catastrophic damage that would have resulted had they been attached at the time of impact. There would have been signs of repeated pounding on the flap and flaperon in a high-speed diving crash, and there were no such marks found on those parts.

Vance then turned to the parts of the flap and flaperon which did exhibit damage. There was some damage to the flaperon, and the flap, on the trailing edges, that is once again, the rear of those parts when assuming the orientation of the aircraft flying forward. Noting that the flaperon is made primarily of composite material, Vance wrote, 'we see at the trailing edge that it has been shredded away progressively, from the back towards the front . . . it looks like it has been eaten away, or eroded'.

This did not fit with the theory of a high-speed diving crash, but was fully consistent with a pilot flying the aircraft to the end, flaps extended, to ditch it.

Vance said MH370 would be in a slightly nose up attitude, flying at about 140 knots (259 kilometres per hour), and slowing down.

The force of the water contact would rip the engines off very quickly, and the flaps and flaperons would be next, their trailing edges touching the tops of the swells and waves which would erode them, until the entire flap system would be dragged through the water, and ripped off.

The trailing edge damage on the flaperon and the flap, which would have been lowered in parallel, was very similar, Vance observed.

In the book itself, Vance turned to other witness marks of a more complex nature, looking at the high-resolution photographs of the flap, rather than the flaperon. As he pored over the photographs, Vance noticed what were, to a seasoned air crash investigator, interesting potential clues: some cracks, and some smudges. Vance noted that the two parts recovered on the other side of the Indian Ocean, the right flap and the right flaperon, would have been adjacent to each other on the aircraft, the flaperon more inboard, but separated by a small gap to allow free individual movement. The two aircraft parts are hollow, with a cavity known as a 'seal pan' contained by end plates on either side.

Vance looked at a very clear photo of the left end plate of the flap, which would have been adjacent to the right end plate of the flaperon.

Even a casual observer can detect a V-shaped smudge on the end plate near the trailing edge, a small crack near it, and a large crack in the widest part of the flap near the middle. The cracks were not evidence of puncture, Vance noted, but compression fracture.

To Vance, those witness marks were clear indicators of the direction of the forces involved in the final moments: the flap and flaperon had been pushed into each other sideways, or 'spanwise', when the aircraft made progressive contact with the water. While the pilot would have landed wings level, as he lost airspeed one wing – it turned out to be the right – would have dipped and touched the ocean, forcing it back and inwards and causing those cracks as the flaperon impacted the flap spanwise. It provided further evidence, Vance argued, that MH370 had been ditched; the witness marks were consistent only with that scenario, and not a high-speed unpiloted dive.

The smudge marks backed up this assessment, Vance wrote. Fixed to the edges of the flaperon are synthetic rubber 'rub strips' which fill some of the gap between it and the flap to improve aerodynamic flow. Vance says it is plain that the V-shape marks on the flap match the shape of the rub strips, and further show a pivoting sideways force pushed the flap into the flaperon when the right wing hit the water.

Vance also came up with an alternative explanation for the damage around the entry hole for the flap support track, which the ATSB claimed indicated the flap was retracted. He believes the damage came about when the support track and the carriage assembly were violently pulled out of the hole in the flap when the extended flap hit the water, and they were left attached to the aircraft.

This could only happen if the wing was going forward, while at the same time the flap was being held back, Vance wrote, and that again was consistent with a controlled ditching with flaps down and not a high-speed uncontrolled crash.

Vance then concluded:

'All of the evidence I used to explain what happened to MH370 was available to the official investigation, and yet they failed to uncover it.'

In psychology there is a well-established concept known as 'motivated cognition'. It's a case where, subconsciously, new facts or developments are perceived and interpreted by a person in such a way as to support the most convenient conclusion. As the Iresearch.net psychology website describes it, people's motives influence how they process new information.

'They are relatively more likely to trust small samples of infor- mation consistent with desired expectations (even when they know that small samples can be unreliable) and are more critical of messages threatening desired beliefs . . . Judgments of frequency and probability are also influenced by motives.'

Vance suggested this sort of phenomenon may have befallen the ATSB. He claimed it had, rather than objectively assessing each clue when it came in, ignored some and focused on others, leading it – perhaps subconsciously – to stick to a conclusion that was convenient. In particular, he said, the bureau had placed too much store in complex and debatable satellite tracking data never used before for this purpose, rather than relying on comparatively old-fashioned but proven, solid and methodical wreckage analysis.

'By the time the flaperon was found, the safety investigation had already declared that MH370 was an unpiloted airplane that ran out of fuel. It appears they examined the flaperon, and the section of the flap, with that evidence . . . in mind,' Vance wrote.

It was, Vance said, a convenient fit with their rationale for continuing to search in the area where their original calculations told them the wreckage would be, and provided justification for all the money spent, and for the further commitment of resources.

'It served the purposes of those who were dismissing the possibility of pilot involvement,' Vance wrote.

Vance's conclusion on where MH370 might be differed from those of Keane, Bailey and Hardy. The airline pilots thought Zaharie had flown an essentially straight line after fuel exhaustion and ditched the aircraft at maximum distance. Vance took the view that it was, essentially, pointless to search anywhere: if a pilot deliberately flew the aircraft to the end, he could have flown it in any direction in the final minutes, creating a massive search area.

In the conclusion to *MH370: Mystery Solved*, Vance said 9M-MRO 'probably will be found someday, but most likely it will be a long time from now. It will rest where it is until eventually someone finds it by using a technology that has not yet been invented.'

As always, I gave the ATSB every opportunity to respond to Vance before putting the extracts and news story to print, and as always, by that stage of the game, the ATSB passed up the chance.

On 10 May, three days before *The Australian* went to press with the Vance extracts and the news story, I wrote to ATSB spokesman Paul Sadler outlining how Vance had claimed the ATSB got its assumptions wrong in coming up with, and sticking to, the 'ghost flight/death dive' theory. I asked for the response of the ATSB's search leader, Peter Foley.

Neither Sadler nor Foley responded.

But the timing was such that Australian democracy was again going to force the ATSB to front up before a national audience to address these questions. Another round of Senate Estimates was coming up, and once again, I liaised with cross-bench Senator Rex Patrick to develop a series of questions to put to the ATSB. Patrick was keen.

'In any circumstance where $200 million of taxpayer money has been spent and credible sources raise questions as to the approach or efficacy, some form of inquiry is worthy,' Patrick told *The Australian* in a lead-up story about how he and other senators were going to approach Foley and Hood.

Considerable anticipation developed about the imminent Senate Estimates hearing, fuelled also by a fresh treatment of the MH370 mystery by *60 Minutes*. The Nine Network's story, which filled a whole program and ran the night before *The Australian* published the extracts from *MH370: Mystery Solved*, took the form of a panel discussion among key members of the international MH370 club, including the former ATSB boss, Martin Dolan. The program mostly re-covered material and theories and counter-theories already known, but the panel discussion style made for some engaging television.

60 Minutes reporter Tara Brown (Coulthart had by then left Nine) posed the question:

'Was MH370 a catastrophic accident or mass murder?'

The answer the panel eventually arrived at, pretty much unanimously, was the latter. There was one particularly interesting new element to the *60 Minutes* program: some deft positioning and repositioning by Dolan. The former ATSB boss in charge during most of the first subsea search for MH370 performed an exquisite segue during the course of the program from expressing full confidence that the ATSB's 'ghost flight/death dive' theory was right, to acknowledging that maybe it wasn't.

Dolan started off with the standard ATSB line that MH370 was not controlled by a pilot at the end.

'I still think the weight of the evidence – which is why the search has been concentrated where it is – is that, for whatever reason, it's unlikely there were control inputs at the end of the flight, and therefore the aircraft spiralled into the water and crashed,' Dolan said.

But as the program went on Dolan became increasingly open to the other possibility; that a pilot had in fact flown the aircraft to the end, and outside the ATSB's search area.

'If we don't end up finding the aircraft in the search area, then the conclusion is that we focused on the wrong set of priorities, yes,' Dolan said. 'There are two viable theories – that someone was at the controls of that aircraft and applying control impulse at the end of flight or they were not, and there's evidence that supports both of those theories.'

They were important concessions, and helped set the scene for a similar acknowledgement by Foley barely a week later. Even though it did not say a lot that was new, the power of television is such that the *60 Minutes* program generated worldwide publicity along the lines that an international group of experts had cracked the MH370 mystery – concluding 'the pilot done it'.

'MH370 experts think they've finally solved the mystery of the doomed Malaysia Airlines flight,' headlined *The Washington Post*.

Although on the program only Hardy and Vance had specifically claimed Zaharie had flown the aircraft to the end and ditched it, Dolan's admission that the search strategy could have been wrong because it excluded that possibility upped the pressure on the serving ATSB officers who were about to be confronted at Senate Estimates. All eyes were upon the ATSB when Hood, Foley and chief legal officer Patrick Hornby took their seats in the interrogation chamber that constituted the Senate Rural and Regional Affairs and Transport Legislation Committee at Parliament House on 22 May 2018.

One of the excellent modern democratic qualities of the Senate Estimates process is that it is streamed live. This hearing when the ATSB was in the hot seat was watched contemporaneously by many in the international MH370 club around the world. Hood read out an initial prepared statement saying 'at the ATSB, we exercise great care not to engage in conjecture or speculation', and handed over to Foley. After some initial questioning about the Ocean Infinity search, Labor Senator David Chisholm said:

'In recent media reports the investigators have been heavily criticised for sticking to the "ghost flight" theory. Do you have any response to that?' Foley could be seen to bristle. 'Firstly, I'd like to re-characterise it as not a ghost flight and not a death dive,' he replied evenly. 'This is a construction – and quite an ugly one – by . . . a journalist.'

Foley had seemed to pause after the word 'by', as if he were going to name the journalist.

It is worth noting here that the terms 'ghost flight' and 'death dive' were taken up by media organisations around the world as graphic, but accurate and descriptive layman words for the ATSB's 'unresponsive crew/hypoxia' and 'high and increasing rate of descent' theories.

Just as Dolan had on *60 Minutes*, Foley started off with the line that the ATSB remained confident its scenario of what happened to MH370 at the end was the correct one based on the evidence. He went over the satellite data, the fuel calculations, the satellite 'reboot' thought to indicate fuel exhaustion followed by the automatic deployment of the auxiliary power unit. Then he came to the discovery of the flaperon, and the flap, which he again maintained analysis showed had not been deployed, so that in all, as always, 'the most likely scenario at that point was that the aircraft was probably descending in an uncontrolled manner'.

But then, again like Dolan, under further questioning from Chisholm, Foley started to open up the possibility a pilot was in fact in control at the end.

'We haven't ever ruled out someone intervening at the end,' Foley said, while adding, 'it's unlikely.'

Then Patrick took over the cross-examination, asking a difficult and significant question of Foley. Patrick established that while Foley claimed the satellite data showed the aircraft in rapid descent at one point late in the flight, he could not know what the aircraft did after that.

Patrick: You've based the modelling on what happens when
no-one is in charge of the aircraft. You've gone to Boeing.
They've described the rudder movements and the perturbation
and you've modelled that.
Foley: Correct.
Patrick: But you actually have no data points to say, 'From that
point, that is correct.' If, for example, there was someone
still in control of the aircraft, that last data point could have
occurred and a completely different set of events could
have then followed. You have no data that would show you
conclusively that that didn't occur.
Foley: We have nothing conclusive, but I can't imagine why any
pilot would be looking at flying an aircraft with descent rates
between 13,800 feet a minute and 25,000 feet a minute.

When Patrick began to focus in on the claims by Vance, the exchange took a curious direction.

Patrick: In the news media, people have referred to Swissair
Flight 111 and the results of the aircraft going into an
uncontrolled drive. Basically they say that the damage to the
flaperon is not consistent with what happened in the Swissair
111 flight.

Foley: You're talking about Larry Vance?

Patrick: Yes, I am talking about Larry Vance.

Foley: And you're talking about Larry Vance's book?

Patrick: I haven't seen the book.

Foley: I have.

Patrick: I had only the news reports, so I'm in the same position
as you.

Foley: No, I've actually read the book. Mr Vance provided me with
a copy last week. The flaperon came ashore in July 2015. Of
course, at that time, everyone looked at the trailing edge damage
and they made all sorts of conclusions based on just that trailing
edge damage. We also thought long and hard about that. We
didn't have access to it. The French judiciary took it to France
for analysis. One of our analysts went, but he wasn't allowed to
actually do anything meaningful in the analysis of the flaperon.

There are many scenarios that will damage the flaperon.
For example, it sits right over the top of engine and in most
crash scenarios you're going to liberate the engines and they'll
come adrift. If your wings are reasonably level, there is going
to be consequential damage, and you can't conclude from a
missing trailing edge on a flaperon that it was deployed at that
time. So we didn't make that conclusion.

Patrick picked up the curious turn in Foley's argument – having
always insisted that MH370 was in a spiralling, high and accelerating
rate of descent at the end, with no pilot to keep the wings level,
Foley now seemed to be talking about the wings being 'reasonably
level' when the aircraft hit the water.

Patrick: This wasn't a wings-level event, in your view.

Foley: We don't know – that's the whole point.

Patrick: You were pretty sure before what happened.

Foley: We've never speculated on the speed of the impact. What we've said was it was between 20,000 and 30,000 feet when those two final transmissions occurred – the aircraft was in a high and increasing rate of decent, and likely to be in a phugoid.

The 'phugoid' was an element in the ATSB's end-of-flight scenario which had seemed to creep in as the debate developed over the years, and enabled the bureau to express more ambiguity about what speed the aircraft might have been travelling when it hit the water and what attitude it was in at that point. A phugoid is an up-and-down repetitive pattern in which an aircraft which is not under the control of a pilot, stalls or comes close to a stall. It then descends rapidly, but then as the airflow speeds up over the wings the aircraft starts to level off or climb again, slowing down until approaching a stall the cycle is repeated.

Patrick asked how much interaction the ATSB had had with pilots Keane, Bailey and Hardy, and Foley replied that their views had been considered.

Foley said he had had 'lots of interactions' with Hardy, and claimed he had sent the search ships at least some way towards where the British Boeing 777 captain said he thought MH370 might be.

'We went a long way to the east in that search area.'

Then Patrick went down a very interesting line of inquiry which, effectively, got Foley to say for the first time explicitly what he had probably always wanted to say, but had for years been reticent about due to diplomatic considerations.

Patrick: Working back to your analysis or your conclusion that the aircraft wasn't piloted, at what point in the flight do you say it became a pilotless aircraft?

Foley: It's absolutely evident. We've always been in agreement
with the notion that an aircraft doesn't turn itself. I mean, there
must have been someone in control of that aircraft, probably
until about 18:25 or thereabouts. [Foley was referring to
Universal Coordinated Time, or UTC, equivalent to 2:25am
local Malaysian time.]

Although to every man and his dog in the aviation business, what
Foley had just told the Senate committee was a no-brainer, it was in
fact significant. It was effectively saying the ATSB believed a pilot had
hijacked the aircraft, and had flown it for about two hours – even if,
as the ATSB maintains, he or she was not flying it at the end of the
flight. Hood then jumped in.

Hood: Once again, we're not saying it was the pilot either; we're
saying that control inputs were made, because we've got no
evidence to suggest that it was the pilot.
Patrick: Respectfully, control inputs –
Hood: Yes, we're saying control inputs.

Then Patrick went to the next point of logic in what was an
exquisite cross-examination: if Foley was so sure a pilot was flying
MH370 in a deliberate fashion for about the first two hours of the
flight, why was he so equally sure a pilot was not flying it at the end?

Patrick prefaced the question by saying, 'I know you're an experienced crash investigator. I'm even more dangerous because I've got
a private pilot's licence.'

He then said, 'I'm just curious. You can't explain how a pilot
might do very strange things at the end of a flight, but somehow it's
reasonable that the pilot did some very strange things at the start of
the flight.'

Foley then came up with what he called a 'plausible scenario'.
He recounted a 1994 case investigated by the US National

Transportation Safety Board in which a cargo aircraft took off, but due to a problem with one of the doors the crew could not pressurise the cabin. The captain, despite the objections of the rest of the flight crew, elected to fly on after donning oxygen masks.

'Shortly after level off, the captain became incapacitated from decompression sickness. The first officer took command – and they landed the plane.'

Although the point of Foley's line of argument was not completely clear, it seemed to be to try to counter Vance and other proponents of the 'pilot to the end' theory, by saying while a rogue pilot could have donned an oxygen mask to counter hypoxia, he or she would eventually succumb to decompression sickness, or what happens to mountain climbers with altitude sickness.

Senate Committee Chair O'Sullivan wrapped up the session with the ATSB soon after that. But O'Sullivan made a parting observation: 'With your efforts over the four years, it's got to torment your soul, as much as anything else.'

Foley: 'It certainly does.'

The cross-examination of Foley had not lasted all that long, about half an hour, but it was the first time he'd had to address several key questions about the ATSB's failed search for MH370 before a public audience. He had repeatedly outlined the ATSB's fundamental argument that it had devised the search strategy based on what solid evidence it believed was available. He had again insisted the ATSB's analysis of the flap indicated it had been retracted. He had posited an intriguing new 'plausible' scenario in which Zaharie might have depressurised the aircraft and stayed on oxygen, but unwittingly allowed himself to be overcome by decompression sickness.

But under questioning from Chisholm and Patrick, Foley had made a few key concessions: among them, he admitted he couldn't really say how the flight ended because he didn't have the data of the final minutes. And, like Dolan, Foley had delicately crab-walked to a position where he had effectively stated the plane was hijacked by a pilot, who might in fact have flown it to the end of the flight after all, even though such a scenario was, he said, unlikely.

'We haven't ever ruled out someone intervening at the end,' Foley had said.

The bet-each-way messages from Foley led the media to focus on different interpretations.

'Australian investigators have defended their search ... saying it was unlikely the pilot performed a controlled ditching,' the Australian Associated Press reported.

By contrast, the Chinese official news agency Xinxua's headline was: 'Australian search chief admits MH370 "rogue pilot" possibility.'

It wasn't long before Foley's testimony before Senate Estimates started to be dissected by the professional aviation community. The curious new line from Foley about a pilot suffering from high altitude 'decompression sickness' was branded a red herring by, among others, Mike Keane, who told me: 'Suffice to say that "altitude sickness" is totally irrelevant to the MH370 event.'

Bailey said, 'I have done explosive decompressions in the RAAF pressure chamber and experienced an actual event in a fighter at 40,000 feet but never had any decompression effects.'

Simon Hardy countered the claim that the ATSB had fully explored the area farther south off the Seventh Arc that he and the other pilots had recommended. 'Mr Foley tried to accommodate my workings by going 42 nautical miles and not 100 nautical miles,' Hardy told me. 'When I visited the ATSB in May 2015 I was aware that the offices were five miles from Canberra airport. Had I tried to accommodate Mr Foley by going only half of that distance, I would not have found the ATSB. In the same way, Mr Foley has not found MH370.'

Vance suggested the idea that MH370, with no pilot in control, somehow managed to land on the water, wings level, at a comparatively low speed so that the flap and flaperon managed to remain largely intact, was absurd. The chances of an out-of-control spiralling aircraft being in that precise attitude just when it arrived at the surface of the ocean were infinitesimal, he said, but in any event, the logic of the phugoid would not make it possible for it to be at low speed. The high-speed dive portion of a phugoid cycle would indeed be followed by a climb and slowing of airspeed, but the aircraft had to go down fast to build up speed before it could come back up, and it could not come back up once it hit the water.

'Foley's scenario of the aircraft being on the slowing, climbing part of the phugoid cycle at the end would require it to go underwater first, and then fly up underwater back to the surface,' Vance said.

Apart from the Senate Estimates appearance, the ATSB did not publicly take any steps to further counter the material exposed by Vance. What it did in the shadows to try to suppress media coverage was extraordinary.

In the days after *The Australian* published extracts of *MH370: Mystery Solved*, the newspaper ran follow-up stories with comments from, among others, Mike Keane, saying it was time for the ATSB to accept Vance's theory was right. Otherwise, the former easyJet chief pilot alleged, Australia would be part of an overall international failure to do everything possible to get to the truth of what he claimed was on circumstantial evidence a mass murder.

Again, as usual, I gave the ATSB the chance to comment on Keane's claims before going to press, and again, as usual, it passed up the opportunity. But behind the scenes, the reaction of the ATSB to this and other stories in the wake of Vance's book was its most extreme to date. At considerable expense to Australian taxpayers, the agency hired a big-end-of-town legal firm to issue warnings to the editors of *The Australian*.

'Our client requests that you refrain from publishing any further articles regarding this incident or our client without first considering the concerns raised in this letter, particularly with respect to naming individual employees,' MinterEllison wrote to the editors and the newspaper's legal counsel in a letter dated 18 May 2018. In particular, the law firm expressed concern that Sadler, who signs his emails as the ATSB's Senior Media Advisor, and Foley, who has appeared before public Senate Estimates committee hearings as head of the search for MH370, were named in the articles as not commenting.

The reaction of the editors of *The Australian* was, once again, to reject the warnings from the ATSB and its lawyers, and instruct me and other reporters on the newspaper to write more, harder stories to reveal the truth about MH370 and the role of the ATSB, the JACC, and their officers.

In late October 2018, *The Australian* revealed these failed efforts by the ATSB to restrict the newspaper's coverage using MinterEllison to issue warnings to the editors.

Accompanying the news story was a comment piece by Byron Bailey, who wrote that the bureau's 'attempts at using high-priced lawyers to suppress coverage of its failures in its search for Malaysia Airlines Flight MH370 are a disgrace, and a threat to the democratic principles of free speech and press freedom'.

Bailey called on Transport Minister Michael McCormack to 'hold the ATSB to account.'

Businessman and aviator Dick Smith, himself a former publisher who established the highly successful magazine *Australian Geographic*, described the repressive behaviour of the ATSB towards the media as 'outrageous'.

'They are basically a secret, secret organisation. They are so insecure.'

Smith, a former chairman of the Civil Aviation Safety Authority, said he believed it was time for the minister to take charge and demand the ATSB bring itself up to the levels of efficiency, timeliness and transparency that Australians expect for their taxpayer dollars, and in a fashion consistent with a democracy that values both free speech and freedom of the press.

THEORY FIVE:
RAPID DECOMPRESSION

Zaharie Ahmad Shah had enjoyed several non-alcoholic drinks with his latest mistress at his favourite Kuala Lumpur nightspot earlier in the evening.

So, 40 minutes into the flight, with co-pilot Fariq Abdul Hamid well settled and in control as part of his training, and after signing off to Kuala Lumpur controllers with 'Good night, Malaysian Three Seven Zero', Zaharie decided to leave the flight deck for a 'biological break'. Just a minute later, faulty cabin door seals broke and the aircraft suffered rapid decompression. Fariq, well trained to deal with such an emergency, immediately put his oxygen mask on, but the young co-pilot was unsettled at the rush of air out of the cockpit, the cold creeping in, the fogging up of the cockpit, and the fact his veteran and trusty captain was not there.

His first reactions were professional; he knew the drill – aviate, navigate, communicate, in that order. With his oxygen mask on, and having established the flight controls worked normally, Fariq turned the aircraft around on a heading to Kota Bharu, with a view to making an emergency landing there. But the first officer's oxygen mask had an undetected fault which prevented him from getting the full supply. His brain got some oxygen but not enough to work properly, leading him to still fly the aircraft but make irrational decisions such as not making a distress call. With the flight deck thrown into confusion, Fariq tried to send a distress signal on the radar transponder, but instead accidentally switched it to 'standby', which effectively turned it off.

Zaharie meanwhile, occupied with the matter at hand in the toilet at the precise moment the crisis erupted, initially took a few breaths from the drop-down mask, but decided it was his duty to try to get back to the flight deck. He made a dash for it, but Fariq was already too hypoxic to unlock the cockpit door quickly enough. Zaharie started to lose useful consciousness, and tried but missed the chance to get to the portable oxygen bottles and masks, and soon passed out.

Fariq was in control, but groggy from partial hypoxia and not thinking straight. He did not put the aircraft into a rapid descent as he should have, and at 35,000 feet, the chemically produced 12 minutes of oxygen supplied through the drop-down masks for the passengers ran out before the aircraft got back over land and into mobile coverage. Fariq, thinking in the fuzzy-headed way of partial hypoxia that he was dealing the emergency magnificently, flew MH370 first towards Penang, then in the general direction of Langkawi where he had done flight training and met his girlfriend, then tried to vaguely turn around, but ended up setting the aircraft on a course almost due south before he passed out altogether. And with that, MH370 became a ghost flight.

This scenario is based on a theory developed by Christine Negroni, an American aviation journalist, who in 2016 published *The Crash Detectives*. As mentioned, there have been several precedents of hypoxia on commercial flights – Helios Flight 522 being the all-time classic. In that case, there was a period, though only a short one, where the pilots were still conscious, but not making rational decisions or communicating sensibly with the engineer on the ground. In some cases, air traffic controllers have recognised by the slow and not quite right tone of pilots that they are partly hypoxic, and successfully persuaded them to take corrective action.

Negroni has also written that in private aviation there have been several hypoxia cases including the ghost flight of a Socata TBM 700 that killed Laurence and Jane Glazer in 2015. The Glazers, prominent American real estate developers and philanthropists, had taken off from Greater Rochester International Airport heading for Naples,

Florida, where they had a holiday home. Laurence Glazer was an experienced pilot, and flying the plane at 28,000 feet, he radioed air traffic controllers to report 'an indication that is not correct in the plane' and asked to descend to 18,000 feet. Controllers initially cleared him down to 25,000 feet, but when they instructed him to descend to 20,000 feet a few moments later, his speech had become slurred and he didn't respond.

Faulty oxygen delivery systems are a notorious problem facing military pilots including when they get some supply, but not enough.

There are also some pretty spectacular cases of rapid decompression: one which beats them all for drama is British Airways Flight 5390 which left Birmingham Airport in England for Málaga in Spain on 10 June 1990. All of a sudden, a windscreen panel for which an aircraft mechanic had used the wrong bolts to install blew out, along with the captain, who was sucked half way out of the cockpit and was flapping around on the roof. A quick-acting flight attendant who happened to be in the cockpit grabbed the captain's belt and held on, while the co-pilot put the aircraft into rapid descent.

In the intense cold the cabin crew took turns holding onto the captain. They all thought he must be dead – his head could be heard banging around against the fuselage in the slipstream, but the co-pilot wanted to keep him frozen on the roof rather than let go because his body could have taken out the left engine if it were sucked in and got gobbled up. The co-pilot performed an emergency landing at Southampton Airport and all 87 on board survived – including, extraordinarily, the captain, who after several months' recovery flew again.

Again, several moving parts have to operate in unison here to make Negroni's theory work, but there have been a number of cases of rapid decompression of one sort or other, and it is the case that there is a period, though not usually long, where pilots can be partly hypoxic and have a degree of consciousness to fly the plane but not rationally. So it's another theory with elements of solid precedent.

TWELVE

'YOU CAN ALWAYS GO IN WITH A KNIFE'

The day MH370 vanished, Kok Soo Chon was at the cinema in Petaling Jaya with his wife, watching the new airline hijack movie *Non-Stop*.

Non-Stop features heaps of action and excellent acting by Liam Neeson, who courageously saves this otherwise ridiculous film. A world-weary US federal air marshal, alcoholic Bill Marks played by Neeson, boards a British Aquatlantic Airlines Boeing 767 from New York City to London. As one would expect if you fly an airline with such a silly name, after take-off Marks receives a text on his secure phone from an unidentified hijacker claiming someone will die every 20 minutes unless a $US150 million ransom is paid into a specified overseas bank account.

The movie has every conceivable violent and spectacularly dramatic aviation crisis imaginable. Someone uses a blowpipe to fire a tiny poison dart from a hole in the first-class bathroom to kill the captain. There are onboard gunfights, a bomb, an RAF jet fighter interception threatening to shoot down the airliner with rockets, and stabbings and martial arts galore. The bad guys plan to parachute out of the plane, there's a big bag of cocaine in a briefcase, and somebody shoots out a window causing rapid decompression and the oxygen masks to drop down. There's a conspiracy to frame Marks and discredit the federal air marshal service because it let the 9/11 attacks happen, and, of course, Marks still has time in all that for what in the film industry is called a 'meet cute' in which he finds the new love of his life. All of this and more in just 106 action-packed minutes.

As this chapter will explore, one wonders whether four years on from watching *Non-Stop*, that plot was still in Kok's mind when as chief investigator into the disappearance of MH370, he brought down the Malaysian government's final report of his safety investigation.

Kok had a pretty good resumé for the job. He had an engineering degree, and also a law degree from the University of London and a practising certificate from the Legal Board of Malaysia. Kok had joined the Malaysian civil service as an electrical engineer in a hospital, and had enjoyed a stellar career from there, including spending four years as general manager for the construction of Kuala Lumpur International Airport where he also helped build air traffic services. From 1999 to 2007 he was director-general of the Department of Civil Aviation, and had been a former permanent representative of the International Civil Aviation Organisation council in Montreal.

So when MH370 disappeared, Kok, who had technical and legal knowledge, a solid grounding in aviation, and an impeccable record of public service, looked to be the logical choice to lead the Malaysian government's ICAO Annex 13 aviation safety investigation into the disappearance of the Malaysia Airlines Boeing 777 registered 9M-MRO.

As mentioned, the way such Annex 13 investigations work on big international cases it's usual practice for the host nation to invite experts from other countries to appoint what are called 'accredited representatives' to the investigation panel. This case was just about as big, as well publicised, and as difficult as it gets, and so the Malaysian government established a substantial panel with accredited represent-atives from the ATSB, the US National Transportation Safety Board, China's Aircraft Accident Investigation Department, Britain's Air Accidents Investigations Branch, France's BEA, Indonesia's National Transportation Safety Committee and Singapore's Transport Safety Investigation Bureau.

An important part of the Annex 13 system is that the accredited representatives don't have to go along with the final report; they can write comments or even a dissenting report. The preferred option for the host government, though, is to reach a consensus with all the accredited representatives supporting the final report without comment. That was one of Kok's key goals as he took up the reins of the complex task.

While there was to emerge significant controversy about the findings and conclusions of Kok's investigation, all the evidence suggests it was by the book and technically ticked off all the boxes of international air crash investigation procedure.

Apart from the seven foreign accredited representatives, Kok had 19 Malaysians on the investigation team – airline captains, medical doctors and other professionals from different fields. Kok and his team homed in on seven areas of investigation.

They looked at the airworthiness and maintenance schedule of the Boeing 777-200 to see if there were any mechanical issues which could have caused the strange developments on the flight. This found that repairs had been made to its wing tip after it got sliced off on the tail fin of a China Eastern Airlines A340–600 in Shanghai in 2012.

With the help of a report by the Royal Malaysian Police, the team delved into the background of the pilots and cabin crew, their medical and professional records, and looked for any anomalies around the time of the flight.

The investigators looked at the air traffic control transcripts.

They assessed the cargo on the flight, particularly what constituted about half the total: 4566 kilograms, or what some might call a lifetime supply, of fresh mangosteens, and 221 kilograms of lithium-ion batteries.

Kok's team delved into the military radar data.

They worked with Inmarsat on the seven satellite handshakes.

They looked at the organisational structure and information management of the Department of Civil Aviation and Malaysia Airlines.

The investigators interviewed more than 120 people – pretty much anyone who might have had something vaguely relevant to say. That included aircraft refuellers, administrators in the Department of Civil Aviation, caterers, cargo loaders, freight-forwarders, airline officials, mangosteen growers, cleaners and, of course, the crew's next-of-kin. (The Royal Malaysian Police had also interviewed Zaharie's various women friends including Fatima Pardi, and the ones he hoped in vain would be his friend, such as the 18-year-old twin model Jasmin Min.)

The pilots on the team got into Boeing 777 simulators and tried out the flight as it was known, and all the scenarios that might have befallen the aircraft.

Kok and his team, by all reports including his own, did a lot. To stay in touch with the accredited representatives and Boeing and Inmarsat in the other time zones, Kok told the Malaysian news agency Bernama, he had to work all hours – in fact, non-stop.

'We are trying our best to find whatever truth we can find in our report so that everyone will know what happened on that fateful day,' he said.

The release of the final report of Kok's Malaysian-led ICAO Annex 13 Safety Investigation had been hugely anticipated, but when it came to the next-of-kin in Australia, it was pretty poorly organised. The date, 30 July 2018, was set and announced publicly weeks in advance, mainly to give the international media time to prepare and fly to the Malaysian capital for the press conference if they so chose, and to give next-of-kin the chance to attend their own briefing.

Danica Weeks would have gone if Malaysian authorities had got their act together a bit sooner. She was told about a week in advance by a Malaysian support group that the report would be coming down, but she was informed at that stage that next-of-kin would have to pay for their own airfares and accommodation. Then, the Thursday before the Monday the report was to be released, an offer came through to pay her way, but that just didn't allow enough time for the single mother to organise such a trip.

'I wanted to be there, to be briefed on the report, I've been waiting to see what is in it,' Danica told the ABC. 'I'm very angry, that this offer came with only 48 hours to get over there. I would have jumped at the chance to ask questions.'

Quite a few families did head to the Malaysian administrative capital Putrajaya on 30 July to accept the government's offer to be briefed on the report in the morning, ahead of its public release and media briefing in the afternoon. It was a long briefing – two-and-a-half hours – but at the end of it the 35 families who attended told journalists they felt let down, still had a burning gap of not knowing what had happened to their loved ones, and were angry. Some family members left the briefing in tears.

It turned out that while Kok had said early on in the investigation he wanted to 'find whatever truth we can', the truth had ultimately eluded him. Despite a massive effort, Kok told the families he had been unable to work out what exactly happened to Malaysia Airlines Flight MH370.

K. S. Narendran, whose wife Chandrika Sharma was on the ill-fated flight, told *The Australian* after the briefing there was 'absolutely nothing new as far as I can tell' from the report.

'The plane took off, it turned back and then disappeared. We don't know where it went or where it is – that is essentially a summary of this report,' said Narendran, who flew from the southern Indian city of Chennai to attend the briefing.

Journalists and MH370 club members around the world got their look at the investigation report an hour or so later when the Malaysian government put it up on the web. It comprised a main document of about 500 pages, and another 1000 pages of appendices. But it all boiled down to one sentence.

'In conclusion, the Team is unable to determine the real cause for the disappearance of MH370,' the report said.

And there was no way of determining the real cause, the report said, unless the aircraft were found: 'Without the benefit of the examination of the aircraft wreckage and recorded flight data information, the investigation is unable to determine any plausible aircraft or systems failure mode that would lead to the observed systems deactivation, diversion from the filed flight plan route and the subsequent flight path taken by the aircraft.'

The next-of-kin in Australia got a copy of the report around the same time it was publicly released. Danica dived into it, and told me a few hours later what she thought of it.

'Let's just say I'm totally deflated . . . the report has come to no conclusion, it is merely a mix of words that gives no new information on the possible location of our loved ones,' she said. 'As the report itself states, the fact there are 239 persons still missing lays bare that Malaysia is still responsible for those missing [and] has a legal and moral right to continue to search for MH370.'

Kok's report did not say nothing, though – even if it did not come to a conclusion about what happened, it did make some adverse comments and recommendations.

The investigators were highly critical of the air traffic controller for the sector in question for not reacting faster to a clear and present danger. The report said as soon as the Ho Chi Minh controllers said they had lost all contact with the aircraft, the controller in Kuala Lumpur 'should have realised that MH370 could be experiencing an emergency situation'.

'This was especially so after he had tried to establish radio communication with MH370 by making a "blind transmission" . . . without success.'

The controller should have immediately informed the watch supervisor, and search and rescue service, Kok's team said. When the watch supervisor was eventually woken up, he rang Malaysia Airlines operations, was told all was well because Flight Explorer showed MH370 was over Cambodia (which was never part of the flight plan), and, satisfied, went back to the rest area.

The report made one absolutely undeniable observation: the disappearance of a big commercial jetliner should not be allowed to happen again.

'In this technological epoch, the international aviation community needs to provide assurance to the travelling public that the location of current-generation commercial aircraft is always known. It is unacceptable to do otherwise.'

The final report did, in fact, exhibit that a lot of hard work had been done, and the findings had effectively excluded a number of possible causes.

There had been a lot of speculation that the two main items of cargo, the lifetime supply of delectable mangosteens and the lithium-ion batteries, had somehow found a way between them to start a catastrophic fire. There are scores of cases where lithium-ion batteries have caused fires of various sizes on aircraft. They are the chief suspect, though not convicted beyond reasonable doubt, of taking down a Boeing 747 cargo plane in 2011.

On 28 July that year, Asiana Airlines Flight 991 departed Seoul-Incheon International Airport on a flight to Shanghai. Just under an hour later, the co-pilot radioed in. 'Shanghai control,

Shanghai control, AAR991 request emergency descent, emergency, declare emergency due to fire main deck. Request descent, and descent to one-zero thousand.' This request was approved, but the aircraft never made it. Like Swissair 111, the fire spread very quickly, and the pilots started losing control.

'Rudder control . . . flight control, all are not working,' the captain radioed in.

One of the pilots issued the words, 'Mayday, Mayday, Mayday', and the last transmission from the first officer, 19 minutes after first declaring an emergency, was 'altitude control is not available due to heavy vibration, going to ditch . . . ah'.

The aircraft crashed down at high speed into the sea off Jeju, South Korea. The origin of the fire was never definitively established, but a lot of attention focused on the mix of flammable materials, including the lithium-ion batteries, along with paint, amino acid solution and synthetic resin.

The MH370 investigators asked, could mangosteen juice and lithium-ion batteries have hooked up to form a similar deadly combination on MH370? The report said there were suspicious circumstances:

'The batteries were speculated to be a fire hazard and the mangosteens were also speculated to be out of season at that time of the year.'

It was a thorough piece of investigation.

'Contrary to speculations that the fruits were out of season, it was found to be in season in Muar, Johore and neighbouring countries,' Kok's team reported.

Both the type of batteries and mangosteens were tested to within an inch of their lives. The sponge used to keep the fruit fresh was found to have a pH value of 6 and the mangosteen juice had a pH value of 3.

'When current was passed through mangosteen extracts, the current flow indicator lit up (mangosteen extract was conductive).'

Nonetheless, the investigators tried everything to persuade the mangosteen juice make the lithium-ion batteries catch fire, but despite their best efforts, it just didn't work.

So, those suspects – the mangosteen growers and the lithium-ion battery manufacturers – were exonerated.

Mahathir Mohamad's theory of a remote electronic takeover of the aircraft was also investigated.

It turned out Mahathir was, in one sense, right: Boeing had, incredibly, devised a futuristic anti-hijack technology to this end, the investigators determined. The aircraft company had in 2003 filed, and in 2006 received, a patent 'for a system that, once activated, would remove all controls from pilots and automatically fly and land the aircraft at a predetermined location'.

The thought was that even though cockpit doors had been toughened, a captain might yield to a threat of violence from a hijacker and open it.

So the patent allowed for the aircraft to be flown automatically to a designated airport, and no-one on board would be able to stop it. This revelation, on the face of it, brought into the realm of possibility the idea of a rogue state like North Korea hacking into the anti-hijack remote autopilot to steal the aircraft or just take it down. But, the investigators found, the technology had never got beyond the patent stage.

'Boeing has confirmed that it has not implemented the patented system or any other technology to remotely pilot a commercial aircraft and is not aware of any Boeing commercial aircraft that has incorporated such technology,' the report said.

The investigators could also not find any sign of mechanical failure that could explain the disappearance of MH370 – all the maintenance records, and automatic reporting systems showed everything on board to be working fine.

The loss of communications was most likely explained by someone turning them off, the report said.

There were some other, individually intriguing bits of work done by the investigators, including looking into the eerie mobile phone log-on – just one was recorded – from the co-pilot Fariq's phone when MH370 rounded Penang. The investigators wanted to see if a telephone call could, in fact, have been made. A telecommunications expert flying in a King Air 350 over the same area during the same time of night tried three different types of mobile phone at different altitudes up to 24,000 feet – one was able to make a call at 20,000 feet.

Among the other key findings of the Malaysian investigation, a vital element related to the turns the aircraft made after it 'went dark' but was picked up on military radar. The first left-hand turn after IGARI – the 'turn back' – took two minutes and 10 seconds, according to the military radar playback. The pilots on the investigation team tried several attempts to make the turn via setting the autopilot – it didn't work, the turns took more than three minutes. Then they tried it by disconnecting the autopilot and making the turn manually. The second manual attempt, the closest to the actual time, took two minutes and 28 seconds.

It was a hair-raising turn. The maximum bank angle on autopilot is 25 degrees; this turn in the simulator was made at a bank angle of 35 degrees. The 'bank angle' warning sounded several times, telling the pilot this turn was extreme. About half way through the turn, the stick-shaker went off, warning the pilot the aircraft was in danger of stalling – the greater the bank angle, the less the lift generated by the wings. This produced one of the key conclusions of the report: that left-hand turn just after IGARI could only have been performed by a pilot disengaging the autopilot and turning the aircraft manually in a difficult, risky, even violent manoeuvre.

'The turnback was not made by autopilot, the turnback was made by manual control,' Kok told journalists in the press conference where he released the report.

The investigators said they had no evidence anyone other than the pilots was flying the plane from the turnback on, but said they equally could not exclude the possibility that somebody else was flying it.

Kok's report mentioned the simulated flight to the southern Indian Ocean flown on Zaharie's home computer, but dismissed it as irrelevant, saying the Royal Malaysian Police report 'concluded that there were no unusual activities other than game-related flight simulations'.

There was some discussion in the report of the large amount of extra fuel carried ordered by Zaharie. It said, 'a captain has the privilege of carrying extra fuel if he feels that there is justification to do so, based on expected weather forecast en route and at the destination.'

But in this case, it said, 'there was no known en route weather forecast that could pose a threat for MH370.'

The report said no more than a 'reasonable amount' of extra fuel was carried. But it says the flight plan called for enough fuel to fly to not one, but two alternative airports: Jinan Yaoqiang International estimated to be 46 minutes from the diversion point, and Hangzhou Xiaoshan International estimated to be one hour 45 minutes away.

The investigators had looked at the personal backgrounds and social situations of Zaharie, referred to as the pilot-in-command or PIC, and Fariq, referred to as the first officer or FO, and the 10 cabin crew. Reading the conclusions it appears they were an extraordinarily well-adjusted, healthy, well-behaved and happily partnered dozen.

'There were no behavioural signs of social isolation, change in habits or interest, self-neglect, drug or alcohol abuse of the PIC, FO and the cabin crew,' the report said. 'The PIC and FO as well as the crew were not experiencing difficulties in any personal relationships.'

In passing here and there, the report said how magnificent Malaysia Airlines was as a whole, including referring to 'excellent service awards won by the company's cabin staff for several years'.

Of Zaharie, the report said, 'The PIC's ability to handle stress at work and home was reported to be good. There was no known history of apathy, anxiety, or irritability. There were no significant changes in his lifestyle, interpersonal conflict or family stresses.'

Zaharie had hurt his back in a paragliding accident some years earlier, but there was no evidence he was still on prescription pain killers.

His finances all appeared to be in good order, there were no unusual financial transactions in the period leading up to the flight, and no unusual insurance policies to be found. He was healthy, and on the day of the flight, he was looking his usual calm, well-dressed, confident self.

'On studying the PIC's behavioural pattern on the CCTV recordings on the day of the flight and prior 3 flights there were no significant behavioural changes observed,' the report said.

Professionally, the report said, Zaharie had sailed through with 'flawless safety records with a smooth career pathway to his existing position'.

But at the same time the investigators picked up a couple of odd things in the radio transmissions between the controllers and Zaharie. For some reason, Zaharie said he was maintaining his altitude – 35,000 feet – twice within seven minutes: 'maintaining flight level three five zero, three seven zero'. The investigators said while this happened now and again in flying, 'it was anomalous at this time'.

More significant was that Zaharie, in the famous final transmission, 'Good night, Malaysian Three Seven Zero' in response to the Kuala Lumpur controller advising him to switch to Ho Chi Minh control on radio frequency 120.9, did not read back the frequency. This, Kok's team said, was in breach of both Malaysian and ICAO regulations, the latter of which says 'clearances or instructions shall be read back or acknowledged in a manner to clearly indicate that they have been understood and will be complied with'.

On the much-disputed question of what the pieces of MH370 found washed up on the other side of the Indian Ocean suggested,

Kok's team did not go into any great detail of the examination. The investigators said of the wreckage found thus far, 'no traces of explosion were found', eliminating a bomb or missile bringing down the aircraft.

The report did also say, as Larry Vance found, that the right flap and flaperon were in line on impact and butted into each other. But the Malaysian-led investigation stuck with the ATSB conclusions that the flap and flaperon were most likely retracted.

However, there was one startling admission which went completely the other way: that soon after the discovery of the flaperon in July 2015, the French had determined it was 'likely to be deflected at the time of impact'.

'This was primarily based on the damage observed on the trailing edge of the flaperon,' the report said – just the conclusion Vance had come to and disseminated at the time.

By 'deflected', the French meant lowered. This suggested that going right back to the middle of 2015, the French had provided evidence that MH370 had been configured for a controlled ditching, something the ATSB had not mentioned. But the Malaysian report swept this evidence aside.

'This scenario was considered a hypothesis only due to lack of corroborating information, and more importantly, it was done without the benefit of the damage information available from the right outboard flap which was found much later,' the report said.

The investigation report went into considerable impenetrable detail about last two satellite transmissions eight seconds apart, which the ATSB relied on heavily for its 'death dive' theory claiming they show MH370 at the end of the flight was in rapid and accelerating descent. Like the revelation that the French had concluded the flaperon was lowered, the report casually threw in a bombshell you would miss if you did not know the significance of it. It concluded the burst frequency offset changes could indicate rapid descent, but then again, it could mean something else altogether – something called 'warm-up drift' of the oven controlled crystal oscillator (OCXO).

The 8:19am log-on request and log-on acknowledgement could indicate 'that the aircraft was likely to be descending at this time,' the report said.

'Alternatively, it could have been due to the OCXO warm up drift, or it could have been due to a combination of uncompensated vertical velocity and OCXO warm up drift.'

This finding, buried in jargon as it is, turned out to be a critical blow to the 'death dive' theory. Robin Stevens, a British electrical engineer and later insurance executive who has been working with pilots Bailey, Hardy and Keane on developing a new search strategy, watched the MH370 saga from the start. He generously explained in layman's terms what the 'warm-up drift' issue was about, and its significance. It hinges on the fact that investigators believe there was a loss of power to the satellite data unit after the main engines ran out of fuel which would have shut it down, and then a minute or so later a re-powering of the equipment when the auxiliary power unit automatically kicked in.

'The aircraft's satellite data unit has a crystal oscillator to control the frequency of its transmissions to the satellite, and the temperature of this oscillator has to be kept within close limits to ensure as stable a transmitting frequency as possible,' Stevens told me.

'The oscillator sits inside a miniature oven. Whenever the SDU is depowered, the oven and crystal oscillator cool down. When the power is put back on, the oven heats up, but there can be a time lag of several minutes before the oscillator is at the proper temperature again. The electronics controlling this process is not particularly precise, the result being that the SDU can start transmitting before the oscillator has reached the correct temperature, and consequently, the SDU transmissions will gradually vary in frequency (drifting) before the correct temperature is reached.'

Under normal circumstances, Stevens explained, such warm-up drift was not a problem. But with MH370, he said, it was a big issue because the investigators did not know enough about how it worked under such unique circumstances to be confident about interpreting the data when the SDU came back online at the end of the flight. 'This was the worry that some of the SSWG participants evidently had,' Stevens said.

Stevens said the inclusion of the alternative explanation for the BFO offset changes was very revealing, and 'implies that a piloted glide shouldn't be ruled out'.

In its update report published in November 2016, the ATSB downplayed the warm-up drift issue, saying that if the power outage were brief, its effect would be negligible, or alternatively, small and calculable. But Stevens suggested the Malaysian investigators, to get consensus among the accredited representatives on the panel, had agreed to incorporate the lingering doubts of at least some of the international experts.

'There were certain members of the Search Strategy Working Group who were never totally happy with the descent rate explanation, and they appear to have gotten the Malaysians to spread their bets,' Stevens said.

If Stevens is right, this could also explain the strange deletion of the 'consensus' line from the JACC bulletin of 27 June 2016, and provide a motivation for why the ATSB suppressed the opinions on the satellite data when I sought them under FOI.

Stevens is another expert and close observer of the MH370 saga who believes the ATSB, at least subconsciously, fell into the trap of bias against the 'rogue pilot to the end' theory for fear of upsetting the Malaysians, displaying motivated cognition in how it interpreted the available data.

'The Malaysian authorities have, from day one, consistently played down or ignored any suggestion of deliberate, pre-meditated pilot involvement,' Stevens said. 'Any suggestion of a piloted, end-of-flight glide was and still is strictly taboo. The ATSB were thus constrained by outside political influence, to assume an unpiloted final descent, and so naturally enough they were happy to interpret the final BFOs as a death dive. It was convenient to the narrative.

'If this was the way the flight ended, then the ATSB search would have found the aircraft near the Seventh Arc.'

So, at the end of the day, the Malaysian-led ICAO Annex 13 safety investigation report into the disappearance of Malaysia Airlines Flight MH370 contained – almost between the lines – two major findings which seriously weakened the theory that the aircraft went down unpiloted in a rapid, uncontrolled descent. Firstly, that the French analysis of the flaperon had determined it had been deployed for a controlled ditching. Secondly, that the last two satellite trans-missions might have indicated MH370 was in a rapid and increasing descent, but might not have indicated that at all, but rather the quirk of warm-up drift.

So, in the end, Kok's team decided that without the wreckage and the black boxes, they could not say what happened to MH370 – neither mechanical nor human factors had presented as decisive explanations. The report itself said somebody deliberately made the turn back, did not exclude pilot hijack, but just said there were no signs pointing to it, and also did not rule out hijack by someone else. But the way Kok presented it at the press conference, the impression was left that the investigators had cleared Zaharie and Fariq, and were more inclined towards external intervention.

Kok employed a similar approach to what the defence lawyer in O.J. Simpson's murder trial, Johnnie Cochran, famously used: 'If it doesn't fit, you must acquit.'

Kok said the investigation had found there was no evidence pointing to motive or mental instability that would have led either Zaharie or Fariq to commit mass murder.

'We are quite satisfied with their background, with their training, with their mental health, mental state,' Kok said.

And as for Zaharie:

'He was a very competent pilot, almost flawless in the records, able to handle work stress very well. We are not of the opinion it could be an event committed by the pilot,' Kok told journalists.

So, the question had to be asked: since the investigators had concluded a pilot flew MH370 off course, who, if not Zaharie, made that first steep manual turn and flew on? That's where Kok came up with the clincher in the thriller-like narrative: it could have been the Third Man. He said the investigators could 'not exclude the possibility that there's unlawful interference by a third party'.

'We cannot deny the fact that there was an air turnback,' Kok told the press conference. 'We cannot deny the fact that, as we have analysed, the systems were manually turned off with intent or otherwise. So we feel that there's also one possibility that could account for all these . . . No matter what we do, we cannot exclude the possibility of a third person or third party or unlawful interference.'

One wonders how many times Kok watched *Non-Stop*.

'Even if you don't fly a plane, you can still engage in unlawful interference,' he told the press pack. 'You can always go in with a knife.'

But asked what was known about the passengers, Kok said all had been checked and cleared.

Kok insisted the conclusions were not the Malaysian government's alone, noting that because the investigation was held under the auspices of the Annex 13 convention, the seven international accredited representatives had to sign off on it. None, including the ATSB representative, had dissented from the main report or even made their own comments, as they could have under the convention.

'Maybe it will not be satisfactory to a lot of people,' Kok admitted, but added, 'I have seven stalwarts in aviation who are with me. We have finally reached consensus.'

A lot of professionals in the aviation industry, including those who see some deficiencies in the investigation, take the view that the Malaysian-led team's failure to arrive at a conclusion was fair enough. Veteran US airline captain, air crash investigator and aviation safety expert John Cox, mentioned earlier, said he thought more work could have been done to establish where the aircraft came down, and a more thorough examination of the washed-up pieces of the aircraft would have provided more transparency. But he said: 'The criticism of the report and the investigators in some cases is driven because there is not irrefutable proof of the cause of the event, nor was the aircraft located.'

Where the Malaysian investigation got into real trouble in terms of credibility was how Kok spun his conclusions beyond the report itself.

'One needs to draw a distinction between the report and the person that presented it,' Cox said. 'There is criticism of how the Chief Investigator explained it. When reading the report, the reader must draw their own conclusions, which may differ from the Chief Investigator.'

Many people in the professional aviation industry did just that, and came to very different conclusions as to what happened on MH370.

THIRTEEN
REACH FOR THE SKY

When Mike Keane was growing up in Hamilton, New Zealand, he read the classic fighter pilot book *Reach for the Sky*, the remarkable true story of Battle of Britain hero Douglas Bader.

Bader, by all accounts an extraordinarily skilled pilot, joined the RAF, and took up a dare to do some low-level aerobatics one day in 1931. He made the following entry in his logbook after that exercise. 'Crashed slow-rolling near ground. Bad show.'

It was the ultimate in the English art of understatement. In fact, Bader lost both his legs and nearly his life in the accident and for a period was invalided out of the RAF.

But he was recommissioned at the start of World War II and, with no legs, was able to withstand greater G-forces without passing out. He emerged one of the most successful fighter aces and top RAF leaders of the conflict.

After 24 confirmed victories, Bader's Spitfire was chopped in two by a German ME 109 fighter in a mid-air collision, and he tried to bail out. One of his prosthetic legs caught, and he was half-outside the cockpit as the aircraft plummeted down in a slow spin at disturbingly low height above the ground. Bader pulled the rip cord, his parachute opened, and the force ripped the retaining strap on the prosthetic leg and Bader and his one remaining leg were free. Despite a few escape attempts, Bader spent the rest of the war as a POW, including in the famous Colditz Castle.

After the war, Keane got to meet his boyhood flying hero. In the intervening three decades, Keane had enjoyed a successful military flying career himself.

'None of my family had ever flown, but my siblings said I was lucky because I knew what I wanted to do,' Keane said. 'I wanted to fly an aircraft.'

Keane joined the Royal New Zealand Air Force in 1960 but, he said, having wanted to be a pilot, 'I mistakenly put down a second choice, navigator'.

He spent six years as a navigator in the RNZAF, including three years based in Singapore and dropping supplies to British forces during the conflict between Malaysia and Indonesia known as Konfrontasi, and he also engaged in 'taking stuff up to Vietnam'. He spent six months at a base in Thailand used by the US Airforce in strikes against North Vietnam.

'This gave me my first flight in a jet aircraft, the F105 fighter. Among other things we did strafing and dive bombing and a super-sonic run. I was hooked, I wanted to be a fighter pilot.'

The problem, Keane explained in an interview with me at his home in the hinterland of Queensland's Sunshine Coast, was that 'they told me, "wait another two years – subject to a flight grading". I thought stuff that, and I applied to the RAF, and they accepted me as a pilot.'

In 1970 he started flying Phantoms which the RAF had recently brought into service. By 1974, Keane was in charge of a flight of four Phantom fighters at the RAF base of Bruggen in what was then West Germany. There had, Keane said, been a few problems with the British version of the Phantom; the RAF had wanted to use

British Rolls Royce Spey engines rather than the standard American General Electric J79 turbojets.

The Spey had been a very reliable engine in civil aviation, but in a military fighter bomber it was subjected to far more frequent and dramatic throttle changes including to full power, and the pressures on it were far more intense and it had trouble coping.

Keane found that out one grey Cold War November morning when he took off from Bruggen leading his flight on a low-level ground attack training exercise.

'We had just become airborne when a loud explosion rocked the aircraft. In less than 10 seconds the fire lights were on for all three sections of the engine. The aircraft became difficult to fly and there was a total loss of electrics, including the radio and intercom. I knew we were in trouble in a big way. I pushed a button, which was powered by a torch battery, that illuminated an EJECT light in the back seat. My navigator promptly ejected.'

The Spey engine had exploded and the disintegrating turbine blades tore into the fuel tanks and the aircraft caught fire. Keane guided the crippled plane away from built-up areas, but soon after reaching open countryside it pitched and rolled into a steep inverted dive.

'I pulled the bottom ejection handle, and nothing happened. I could see the ground through the cockpit canopy coming up. I pulled it again, nothing happened, I went for the top handle and pulled, nothing happened. Just before the aircraft hit the ground the seat fired and a fraction of a second later there was stillness as the parachute opened. The whole aircraft was just a ball of fire from the cockpit back and it exploded in a black and orange ball of fire on impact.'

An hour later a German helicopter picked Keane up. He was later awarded a Queen's Commendation for staying with the aircraft long enough to steer it out of built-up areas.

The failure of the ejection seat, Keane said, was caused by the fact the navigator had ejected first, and the combination of the aircraft manoeuvres and the suck from the vacant cockpit prevented the canopy from separating. Without separation the seat could not fire. American Phantoms had explosive bolts to 'punch' the canopy off, but as a cost-saving the UK Phantoms did not; however, as a result of this accident all RAF Phantoms were retrofitted with explosive bolts.

As it happened, Keane's hero Bader came to visit Bruggen a couple of weeks later – after a career as an executive with oil company Shell, flying himself from job to job, Bader had begun visiting RAF bases and was much sought after as an inspirational figure. The station commander introduced the two spectacular bail-out survivors to each other.

'Bader said to me, jokingly, "So I hear you're the lily-livered chap who bailed out",' Keane said.

Keane continued to do well in the RAF, rising to squadron leader and commanding a squadron at the Advanced Training Flying School. He took a course in intelligence and, as a secondary duty while still a fighter pilot, served as an intelligence officer.

As he approached the age of 38 – which in the RAF is a decision-point of whether to leave with an honourable discharge or carry on, normally to age 55 – he was offered the chance to rise to wing commander. But that, Keane said, would have involved taking up a desk job in the Ministry of Defence.

Keane decided he wanted to keep flying, left the RAF, and joined Orion Airways to fly Boeing 737s.

Before long he was fleet captain in charge of the B737s before going on to fly Boeing 757s and 767s. Then a head-hunter approached Keane: would he be interested in taking up the post of chief pilot at a start-up airline, easyJet?

It was then a fledgling operation – 35 pilots and three aircraft – but, although the money was pretty much the same, there was an equity stake on offer and Keane liked the business model. He accepted, and what followed was, he said, 'seven years of sheer, bloody, grinding hard work'.

It was, at the same time, exciting and professionally challenging. The growth of easyJet was exponential; including in the number of aircraft and pilots. It was difficult to find experienced pilots who would join a start-up airline, particularly those who were qualified civil aviation examiners, and Keane found himself doing a considerable amount of training and checking of easyJet pilots, in addition to a demanding office schedule.

'I just wanted to make sure nothing went wrong, safety was paramount,' Keane said.

By the time Keane retired from easyJet it had become the biggest airline in Britain – with further expansion, it has today over 250 aircraft and 3000 pilots. Keane had clocked up 25,000 flying hours by the time he, his Australian wife Judy and their children, moved to the Sunshine Coast and built a magnificent house on 15 acres of beautifully landscaped hilltop with a lake, orchard and garden. He'd had 45 years in aviation, as a navigator, fighter pilot, intelligence officer, airline pilot and chief pilot.

So when he saw the ATSB come up with its theory that by the end of the flight MH370 had no responsive pilots, his experience told him it was wrong. He also thought the various theories about some sort of accident like a fire or rapid decompression simply didn't stack up against the known facts.

'I followed this right from the very start,' Keane said. 'I said in the first couple of weeks to Judy, "It's almost certainly a hijack by the captain".' Keane had been involved in one air crash investigation himself, involving a Red Arrows Gnat aircraft on a training flight. The engine had 'run down' forcing both pilots to eject. Keane was one of the three officers on the Board of Inquiry into the accident. At the time he was a squadron commander flying the Gnat and his selection to the Board brought firsthand knowledge of the aircraft and its systems.

The first few weeks were dominated by interviews of the two pilots and dozens of others who were involved directly or indirectly with the aircraft on the day and even weeks before. Eyewitnesses gave conflicting accounts which provided an element of confusion.

'Initially, we felt the most likely cause was a serious malfunction of the engine but that theory was knocked on the head after we received the engine technical report,' Keane said.

The Gnat was a small and complicated aircraft with a disproportionate number of fuel tanks and a complex feed system, with small side tanks supplying a collector tank. The technical tangle created a possible anomaly in which the fuel gauge would show the total amount of fuel in the aircraft, rather than the amount available to the engine, which could be less.

Keane talked to aircraft refuellers about how the system on the Gnat worked, and while the factors were complicated, the answer to what had happened was simple: the engine ran out of fuel, even though some fuel remained in the tanks. 'The important lesson I learnt about an investigation is to keep an open mind and consider the small detail as it often provides the pieces of the jigsaw that paint the picture,' he said.

A couple of years after the disappearance of MH370, Keane decided he had to plunge into the international debate about the mystery. He had started reading the stories Byron Bailey and others had been writing for *The Daily Telegraph* and *The Australian*, and entered the lively online comment sparring match. Keane got in touch with Bailey, a fellow former fighter pilot, and they started corresponding about MH370. At the suggestion of Bailey, on a visit to Sydney Keane met with me, and I suggested he write a feature-length piece for *The Australian* about his analysis of the facts surrounding MH370. The published piece was another top billing article on the newspaper's website, and attracted nearly 100 published comments. It came out four days before the third anniversary of the loss of MH370.

'The three-year mark is a good point to review whether the search strategy drawn up by the Australian Transport Safety Bureau was soundly based but unlucky, or whether it was established on the wrong premise and doomed from the start to fail,' Keane wrote.

Keane's approach followed step-by-step logic, going down the same pathway as Simon Hardy and Bailey before him but with several new elements and a particularly forensic approach.

Keane worked through the range of possibilities by reviewing and excluding one or another onboard emergency, the counter-indicators being that those flying the aircraft made no distress call, and flew over suitable airfields without making an emergency landing.

By contrast, Keane wrote, each clue pointed to a meticulously planned murder-suicide. The turning off of the secondary radar transponder just at the point of switching from Malaysian to Vietnamese airspace aimed to confuse air traffic controllers – and succeeded, hampering the initial search for the aircraft.

The evidence suggested Zaharie depressurised the aircraft at the start of the hijack, Keane maintained, because no-one made a mobile telephone call or sent a text during the whole of the flight.

Keane has noted MH370 took a track to 10 nautical miles south of Penang Island, where Zaharie grew up, and made a lazy turn to the right. Zaharie would have had a good view of the lights of his home town, and Keane believes that part of the flight could be interpreted as a last, emotional farewell.

The next clue was the location where the aircraft ended up, which was extremely remote, and offered a number of deep and challenging seabed features. This indicated a deliberate and well-researched plan to hide the aircraft where it would never be found.

Zaharie would have wanted to run the aircraft nearly out of fuel to avoid an oil slick for the same reason, Keane deducted, and fly the aircraft right to the end to give his vanishing-an-aircraft plan the best chance of success including being sure of placing the aircraft in one of the deep-water spots that are common in that area.

It all fitted together by powers of deduction, Keane maintained.

'The circumstantial evidence points to a pilot hijack and the most likely suspect is the captain,' Keane concluded.

As Keane observed during our interview, in many big murder cases, the accused is found guilty only on circumstantial evidence. Back in 2016, I covered the murder trial of former NSW police detectives Roger Rogerson and Glen McNamara. The two were accused of the shooting death of university student and would-be big-time drug dealer Jamie Gao. No murder weapon had been discovered, no eyewitness account or CCTV footage existed of the actual shooting inside a storage shed, the gunshot forensic evidence was disputed and inconclusive, and each man presented the court with a dramatic story about how the other had pulled the trigger.

Crown Prosecutor Christopher Maxwell QC had told the court he could not prove whether it had been Rogerson or McNamara who fired the gun, but said he did not have to. This was because, he argued, Rogerson and McNamara were part of a 'joint criminal enterprise' to murder Gao and then steal the 2.78 kilograms of the drug known as 'ice' he had brought to sell to them. The jury found both men guilty.

The corollary of Keane's analysis on MH370 was that he found the approach, and outcome, of the Malaysian-led Annex 13 safety investigation report deeply flawed in process, and in steering away from the conclusion that Zaharie hijacked the aircraft and flew it to the end.

In another feature in *The Australian* after Kok Soo Chon delivered his report, Keane took the Malaysian chief investigator's 'Third Man' hijack scenario to task. How credible was it, Keane asked, that a third party could have gained access to the cockpit, disabled the aircraft's electronic equipment, 'neutralised' the two pilots, then seated himself before flying the aircraft through a demanding turning manoeuvre in the space of two minutes?

'It beggars belief,' Keane wrote.

The report also 'conflicts with its own content', Keane observed. He noted that on page six it stated:

'On the day of the disappearance of MH370, the military radar system recognised the "blip" that appeared west after the left turn . . . was that of MH370. Therefore, the military did not pursue to intercept the aircraft since it was "friendly" and did not pose any threat to national airspace security, integrity and sovereignty.'

Keane wrote that 'in my fighter pilot days there would have been a scramble to intercept the aircraft to find out what was happening.'

But then, Keane saw, on page 337 of the report, it said:

'In interviews . . . controllers informed that they were unaware of the strayed/unidentified aircraft (primary radar target) transiting.'

The contradiction between the two statements created an element of doubt about other sections of the report, Keane believes. He says the report's dismissal of any significance in the flight path to the southern Indian Ocean on Zaharie's home computer 'makes it difficult to take the Royal Malaysian Police report as a serious contribution to the investigation'.

In regard to fuel, Keane disagreed with the report's statement that Zaharie ordered no more than a reasonable amount, saying an experienced captain would not have imposed the extra cost on the airline of carrying 3000 kilograms of additional fuel above what was required, which equated to a further 30 minutes of flight and an extra range of 250 nautical miles.

Keane observed that Zaharie was said to be upset about Anwar Ibrahim's conviction on sodomy charges on the eve of the flight, but there was no weight or even serious consideration given to Zaharie's involvement in politics.

For Keane, if the pilot hijack theory were correct – and he believed the circumstantial evidence proved it was beyond reasonable doubt – it meant MH370's resting place had to be treated as a crime scene, and finding it should be a matter of priority for a criminal investigation of a prima facie case of mass murder of 238 people.

Keane claimed the ATSB was complicit in what he called the 'deeply flawed' Malaysian government MH370 safety investigation, by granting Australian government endorsement to the final report without comment.

He concluded: 'Transport Minister Michael McCormack should demand the ATSB publicly account for why it did so – the families of the six Australians on board MH370 deserve nothing less.'

Keane was joined by other highly experienced aviation and other experts around the world in pointing to deficiencies in the Malaysian–led, Australian–endorsed report.

Larry Vance who is, once again, one of the world's most experienced air crash sleuths, called for a new, independent international investigation to be established by ICAO.

'This deficient investigation cannot be allowed to stand as the last word on what happened to MH370,' Vance said.

In correspondence, Vance told me the report was not all bad. It had put to rest some of the more 'far out there' theories that have circulated about what might have happened, such as a battery fire or remote act from outside the airplane. Conversely, Vance said, it made clear the disappearance of MH370 was the result of human intervention.

The key weakness of the Malaysian–led investigation, Vance said, was its 'failure to properly assess the physical evidences on the recovered pieces of wreckage, and to put an analysis together that explains that the flaps were extended during a controlled ditching'.

'That makes this report a tremendous disappointment, and a disservice to the industry and to those who perished, and their survivors.'

Vance noted that the report revealed for the first time, publicly, that the French had determined the flaperon was lowered, consistent with his findings and the 'controlled ditching' theory.

The only people who are confirmed as being engaged in an on-going criminal investigation into the disappearance of MH370 are the French. A few days after the Malaysian investigation report came out, the big French daily newspaper *Le Parisien* reported that, while all the other countries which lost nationals on MH370 had given up, France's 'gendarmerie des transports aériens', or aviation transport police, were renewing their efforts to investigate the death of the four French citizens.

'As of this day, France is the only and last country to try to understand how Malaysia Airlines Flight MH370 could have disappeared on 8 March 2014,' the newspaper suggested.

Le Parisien described French authorities as viewing the Malaysian report as 'imprecise and ambiguous' for downplaying the possibility of pilot hijack. In particular, *Le Parisien* said, French investigators wanted to review the satellite data from Inmarsat, to independently determine the likely flight path of the aircraft, and the British satellite company later confirmed it had been approached and was cooperating.

There were some immediate consequences flowing from the report within Malaysia. The country's civil aviation chief, Azharuddin Abdul Rahman – he who had famously not waited for his phone to charge up on the night MH370 went missing and told his wife the next morning 'something is not right' – fell on his sword over the failings of the Kuala Lumpur air traffic control centre he was ultimately responsible for, and resigned.

Transport Minister Anthony Loke said he had established a committee to investigate and take action against any misconduct based on the report findings, focusing on the controllers.

But the international aviation community, and many beyond it, say while those actions relating to air traffic control are correct and appropriate, the issue remains that the MH370 mystery will not finally be solved until the aircraft is found and the wreckage and black boxes recovered. Another famous air crash investigator in the US, John Goglia, told me the recordings from the flight data recorder and cockpit voice recorder would still be recoverable – they are designed to last, and at great depth the cold and lack of oxygen would help preserve them. The most important thing, aviation professionals say, is to keep looking. Ocean Infinity maintains it would like to have another go one day; presumably it would want a further 'no find, no fee' deal with the Malaysian government. Ocean Infinity, incidentally, went on to solve another mystery: it was employed by the government of Argentina to look for its lost submarine ARA *San Juan*, and in November 2018 found it in the Atlantic Ocean at a depth of 800 metres.

An interesting issue when it comes to mounting a new search is who might fund it. One fact revisited by *The Weekend Australian* in early 2019 was that the two-year undersea hunt for Air France 447 was largely paid for by the manufacturer of the A330 aircraft, the European aviation giant Airbus. It put up 12 million towards the seabed search, plus technical and logistical support, such as supplying a transport plane and ship.

Danica Weeks launched what snowballed into a major international law suit against Boeing in the US that failed in November 2018 on jurisdictional grounds. She says she only took the action to get Boeing to do for MH370 what its arch rival Airbus did for AF447.

'What I wanted was for Boeing to say, okay, we want to prove we are not negligent, we are going to go out and find this plane,' Danica told me in January 2019.

Boeing's strategy when it comes to its Boeing 777, which flew Malaysia Airlines Flight MH370, has been to do and say as little as possible beyond insisting it has provided full technical support for the investigators.

Asked if Airbus thought Boeing should follow the lead Airbus set with AF447 and cough up some millions in cash towards a new search, Airbus spokesman Justin Dubon said: 'It is imperative for the entire aviation sector to learn as much as possible from accidents by understanding the root causes of these events in order to prevent them from ever happening again.'

At the time this book went to press, the pressure to renew the search was building in the lead-up to the fifth anniversary of MH370's disappearance.

There was a foretaste of a renewed international campaign in Malaysia in late November 2018, when next-of-kin presented Malaysian Transport Minister Anthony Loke with what were said to be five new pieces of MH370 wreckage found off Madagascar.

Grace Nathan, whose mother Anne Daisy was on MH370, said at the time: 'The fact that debris is still washing up now means that the investigation should still be live . . . it shouldn't be closed.'

In January 2019, it was reported Malaysian authorities had declared at least one of the pieces was likely from MH370, a section of floor panel.

The Malaysian government says it is not unsympathetic to re-opening the search, but insists it would need something new to go on.

'We are open to proposals, but we must have some credible leads before we decide,' Loke said at the November 2018 media event.

The question, if a new search for MH370 were to be launched, would be where to look.

The best piece of information on where to find MH370 remains the satellite burst timing offset data which produced the seven handshakes and the Seventh Arc. The reverse drift-modelling is also of use, but that has proved to be a rather inexact science. One obvious option would be to search a progressively wider stretch around the Seventh Arc beyond that already covered. The hunters could also go farther north along it, and maybe a bit farther south-west, though the aircraft's endurance is finite and there is no point searching too far in that direction.

The problem with such an approach is that it would still be based on the ATSB's same assumptions about how the flight ended, which have been progressively challenged by new facts and independent expert analysis.

Between the ATSB-led search, and that of Ocean Infinity, about 250,000 square kilometres of seabed in the southern Indian Ocean were covered, based on the bureau's insistence that no pilot was flying the plane at the end. An increasing number of aviation professionals are asking: since the search based on the ATSB's theory failed to find the aircraft, why not consider a new hunt based on the alternative scenario that Zaharie flew the aircraft to the end, which its proponents say would involve covering no more than about 7000 square kilometres or less?

As the former ATSB boss Martin Dolan eventually conceded on the *60 Minutes* episode, there are 'two viable theories' and if the plane were not found based on the bureau's 'unresponsive crew/hypoxia' theory, 'then the conclusion is that we focused on the wrong set of priorities'.

Pilots Bailey, Hardy and Keane; engineer Stevens; and air crash investigator Vance have been liaising for years now on MH370. Vance, as discussed earlier, has doubts about the merits of continuing to search at all because if a pilot flew the aircraft to the end, it could have been over an unmanageably wide area. But he said if he had to search, he would next go where the others propose.

That is in an area just outside of where the ATSB search along the southern end of where the Seventh Arc ended. Hardy identified this search zone in 2015. He used the same radar and satellite tracking data to develop a mathematical formula based on similar calculations of speed, wind, direction and endurance along the Seventh Arc as the ATSB employed, but with the additional assumption of a controlled glide or engines-running descent of about 100 nautical miles at the end and a ditching by Zaharie. Hardy said whether this was done after fuel exhaustion, or with a small amount of fuel left and the engines just barely turning over to keep them alive if needed, made little difference to the modelling.

Hardy spoke with me from Mumbai, where he had arrived after piloting a Boeing 777 from London. In addition to his extensive flying experience, he also has a large amount of engineering and track-plotting expertise. He took up a Royal Naval flying scholarship aged 17, and the navy put him through university to earn a design engineering degree.

He served as a senior design engineer working on torpedo guidance systems. He came up with his analysis of where MH370 ended up using the same sort of simple draughtsman techniques he had acquired.

There is a fascinating three part YouTube video series in which Hardy describes exactly how he made the calculation of where he believes MH370 most probably is, easily findable on the web. In it, Hardy is very logical and persuasive. Using the same basic information as the ATSB had, he combined the basic skills he learnt as a naval officer, engineering design draftsman, and pilot to draw it all out on a series of big charts with a ruler, rather than enter it all into a computer.

Hardy's process followed basic geometry, solving simultaneous equations, and fundamental navigation techniques such as taking three bearings to work out a position. He used the seven arcs to make calculations of simple logic of distances and speed. Like the geometry one learns as a school boy or girl, Hardy's analysis had a very satisfying end: a logical 'Q.E.D.' showing MH370's likely resting place.

Hardy said that when Ocean Infinity chief executive Oliver Plunkett arrived London to talk with key staff and the ATSB, Hardy outlined his calculations over two-and-a-half hours.

'He was pretty impressed with it, but then he saw the ATSB people who put him off.'

Hardy says for his part, he would 'not bet my house' on whether the pilots' preferred new search zone would find the resting place of MH370. But he thinks it has an excellent chance, and statistically has a vastly better probability of success than the vagaries of the drift-modelling.

Hardy's reckoning puts the most likely coordinates of the aircraft at 40 degrees South, and 086.5 degrees East. But allowing for some elasticity in the variables, Hardy still proposes a search area of 7000 square kilometres.

Keane likes the idea of searching the deep underwater canyons known to be in this area, where he thinks Zaharie would have tried to sink the plane, including the Geelvink Fracture Zone. His best guess is 38 degrees 15 minutes South, 86 degrees 48 minutes East.

Byron Bailey, for his part, thinks he could narrow down the area even more on his variation of the end of flight which involves a ditching even closer to the area searched by the ATSB, based on Zaharie turning into the south-westerly wind a little earlier. He points out he and his colleagues' calculations are not much different from that of the ATSB early search plan based on the Defence Science and Technology Group's original 'hot spot' of probability. The pilots' estimate just puts MH370 gliding a bit further along a true track of 188 degrees South. Bailey puts MH370 at 39 degrees, 10 minutes South, 88 degrees 15 minutes East. The original DSTG hot spot, the track, the pilots' preferred search area, and just where Bailey, Hardy and Keane believe to be the most likely location of the aircraft is, are shown in the picture section.

If a new hunt were launched of their proposed 7000 square kilometres, and they are right, MH370 could be found in a week at the rate Ocean Infinity searched.

There's no guarantee of success – there are still too many unknowns in the equation. But thus far the searches based on other approaches have failed. At the time of writing the pilots had the most developed and authoritative alternative theory of where to look. With the expertise of people like Vance and Stevens added in, they have a vast range and depth of practical and professional experience in aircraft, navigation, engineering, aerodynamics and air crash investigation.

In the absence of any national government agency from Malaysia, Australia or anywhere else having a new search plan, and with the fifth anniversary of the loss of MH370 approaching, that informal professional team makes a compelling case that their analysis deserves a shot to offer hope of closure to the families where others have tried and failed.

For those who might lose hope MH370 will one day be found, let's finish with the story of the Australian submarine HMAS *AE1*. The boat and the 35 men on board disappeared at the start of World War I on 14 September 1914, patrolling for German Imperial Navy warships in the waters of what was then German New Guinea. The first search, by Allied warships, started within hours of *AE1* not returning to base at its appointed time.

For another 60 years, *AE1* and its secrets lay dormant. But then a whole series of individuals and organisations could not resist the attraction of trying to solve it. In the 1970s a Royal Australian Navy officer who had been posted as deputy defence attaché at the Australian High Commission in Papua New Guinea, Commander John Foster, took an interest in the *AE1* saga.

Foster trawled through Australian archives to try to work out where *AE1* might have gone down. In 1976, having come up with a target area, Foster persuaded the RAN to let him lead an expedition to examine it with side-scan sonar deployed from the hydrographic survey ship HMAS *Flinders*. This was four decades ago, and such equipment was not what it is today. That effort was unsuccessful, although *Flinders* continued to do some ad-hoc searching when it was deployed in the region.

Then the world-renowned French undersea explorer Jacques Cousteau's curiosity was piqued, and in 1990 he conducted a hunt with his famous research ship *Calypso*, but ran into technical problems. A number of other searches followed, one involving a Royal New Zealand Navy vessel and some organised by Foster in collaboration with a film company, and another with the Australian

Broadcasting Corporation. By this stage, Foster had been working on a new angle: talking to locals to seek oral history which might provide new leads.

He heard reports that two locals, while diving for shells on Mioko Island's Wirian Reef in the Duke of York Islands group, had discovered a wrecked submarine. In 2003 scuba divers under Foster's direction went hunting for *AE1* from a utility boat owned by the Rabaul Hotel, but got warned off by big sharks. Then Foster heard of another local legend: Mioko islanders talked of a gigantic 'Devil Fish' which had appeared one night at the time of the loss of *AE1*, then hid back in the sea.

Various other searches led by Foster or the RAN looked unsuccessfully for *AE1* over the years – one in 2007 based on reports of a sighting of a submarine wreck which turned out to be just a geological formation, then another search in 2009.

Foster died in 2010, but the legacy of his dogged efforts to find the submarine was carried on by a group of researchers and supporters who set up the organisation Find AE1 Ltd. The RAN had another unsuccessful search for *AE1* in 2014.

Then in 2017 a group including serving and former RAN officers, members of Find AE1 Ltd, and maritime archaeologists from the Australian National Maritime Museum, had another look at all the evidence. In December that year, with financial backing from the federal government and corporate donations, the group launched its expedition – the thirteenth search for *AE1*. The expedition chartered a ship owned by the Dutch Fugro undersea survey group, *Fugro Equator*, one of the vessels used in the unsuccessful underwater search for MH370. It was equipped with an autonomous underwater vehicle.

A century and three years after it disappeared, the undersea robot found *AE1* in the first hours of its pre-programmed passes around the Duke of York Island group. The crystal-clear pictures of the wreck, with the odd pink fish swimming around it, captivated world attention. Not only did they find it, but the searchers carried out meticulous underwater photography and three-dimensional scanning of the submarine, bringing the material back for examination by naval experts.

The analysts concluded that *AE1* suffered a catastrophic failure, probably during a practice dive, and at high speed struck a rocky bottom at a depth of 300 metres. The structure of the damage indicated the forward compartment had imploded when the submarine descended below crush depth, which would have meant a sudden death for the crew.

'When the end came for the men of *AE1*, it would have been very fast; they may well have not known what hit them,' expedition leader Rear Admiral (retired) Peter Briggs told *The Australian*.

It might have been luck in part, but mostly the discovery of the *AE1* hinged on the searchers coming up with the right theory of what happened to the submarine. They worked on a new scenario: not that it had been destroyed on the surface by gunfire, for example, because no survivors or flotsam had been found by the first search, nor any prisoners of war taken. Rather, they designed the hunt on the premise that *AE1* had suffered a diving accident after it was last sighted by a companion Australian warship on the patrol.

Most professionals in the aviation community believe someone or some group will, similarly, yet again review the available material, or find new information, and establish what happened to MH370.

Using powers of deduction, just as the searchers for the *AE1* did, they will work out where to look in a new area which has not been searched already, mount a new hunt, find the aircraft, and unlock its mystery.

That's going to be as important whenever it happens as it has been since 8 March 2014 when MH370 and the 239 souls aboard vanished into thin air.

Finding the aircraft will enable air crash investigators to work out what happened and develop strategies to stop whatever it was from happening again. That's what air crash investigation is all about, and after about a century of passenger aviation it has made flying the safest form of transport on earth.

Secondly, cracking the mystery of MH370 will resolve the controversy of whether the ATSB did or did not adopt a strategy based on a false premise, possibly due to political concerns, resulting in the waste of $200 million of Australian, Malaysian and Chinese taxpayers' money on a search which had little chance of succeeding. By extension, it will reveal whether the ATSB's and the JACC's secrecy and failed attempts at repression of journalistic endeavour were motivated by fear of exposure of what they knew to be their errors.

Finally, the discovery of the resting place of the Boeing 777 registered 9M-MRO will help bring closure to the families of the 239 missing, easing a travail which continues to this day.

EPILOGUE

In the living room of her home in Brisbane, Jeanette Maguire has a small shrine, of sorts, to Cathy and Bob.

The little collection has a photo of her sister and brother-in-law on their wedding day, a couple of purple candles, and one of the China dolls Cathy used to collect. A small wooden plaque has the word 'Sister' on it and the words, 'God made us sisters, our hearts made us friends'. There is also a small hand-painted candle-holder showing butterflies darting around flowers, and the words 'Butterfly Wishes . . . believe in the beautiful, amazing woman you are'.

The candle-holder was, Jeanette said, what 'one of my beautiful old work colleagues bought me for Christmas in 2014 after Bob and Cathy's disappearance. It was an amazing present and represented all that she saw me go through that year.'

Those MH370 next-of-kin I've interviewed have carried on, coping with their grief and lack of knowing, each in their own way. As a family, Jeanette said, 'we are very loving, very strong.'

'To get through in our world, we have a lot of humour between us.'

But the MH370 families still struggle every day with the unhealed emotional wounds.

'I am still gutted inside,' Jeanette said. 'A big part of me is lost with them. Bob was like my big brother. I was 11 when Cathy met Bob.'

In her case, Jeanette's job as a payroll manager has been her refuge.

'My safe haven was to go to work and lead a different life.'

But, Jeanette said, she just cannot escape MH370.

'Dealing with Cathy's girls and grandchildren . . . I am here, but I am not here. At least if we know where they are, at least we have their burial area,' Jeanette said. 'At least we will have the place.'

In the latter part of 2018, I met with Danica Weeks at the Maleny Hotel on the Sunshine Coast to talk about her life and MH370. She did not want to meet at her home because the discussion would upset her two young sons, Lincoln, now aged eight, and Jack, five.

'You can't let it go. As much as you can take little breaks from it, it never goes away,' Danica said. 'It's a surreal world.'

Danica stuck it out in Perth for a couple of years, but then decided to move to the Sunshine Coast to be near her mother and live in a place which is, more than anywhere else, home. She has returned to full-time work as finance manager for Suncoast Gold Macadamia Nuts in Gympie – she says the honey-roasted ones are particularly delicious and the process makes them smell great.

At the time of writing, Danica had not been able to sell the Perth house she and Paul bought due to a legal snarl – she lacks a death certificate for him, and she needs one for the deeds.

'The Western Australian coroner can't give me one, he's not running the investigation,' Danica said.

Asked if she could get one from Malaysian authorities, Danica said: 'I am not going to ask for a death certificate from the government of the country that killed my husband.'

Danica has various health issues; she has been prescribed anti-depressants and sleeping pills, and has no problems letting this be known.

'At the end of the day, it is what it is,' she told me. 'I have no qualms in saying yes, I have to get help. I have nothing to hide.'

Danica can't get over the fundamentally bizarre quality of MH370.

'The logic of a Boeing 777 just disappearing . . . loved ones being sent off on a commercial plane, and they just disappear.'

She says she imagines Paul would have thought the same thing.

'As a mechanical engineer, he was never deluded that planes don't crash, but he could not have believed that one could never be found.'

Danica says she knows she is far from an island in experiencing tragedy; other families who lose a loved one by sudden misadventure such as a car accident suffer shock, grief and dislocation. But, she said, at least they know what happened, and can reach closure.

'With MH370, we don't get to, because there is no finality,' Danica said. 'It's very hard to come to grips with it because there are no facts. It's that not knowing.'

The purple candles in Jeanette's shrine to Cathy and Bob came from the memorial service the federal government put on in Brisbane – in keeping with most of the Australians on the flight and their relatives being Queenslanders – on 8 March 2017. The date marked the third anniversary of the loss of MH370, and followed the end of the ATSB-led search a couple of months earlier.

Transport Minister Darren Chester and Angus Houston were among around 100 who attended the private ceremony at St John's Anglican Cathedral, along with diplomats from Malaysia, China and New Zealand. It was not a particularly easy task for Chester to get the message and tone right; many next-of-kin resented his place among the trio of Australian, Chinese and Malaysian ministers who had decided not to continue the search for the aircraft without new evidence of its location.

'While to date we have been unsuccessful, we remain hopeful that at some stage in the future, there will be a breakthrough, the aircraft will be found, and we will be able to answer more of your questions,' Chester told the congregation.

Sadly, however, the ATSB and the JACC still show no inclination to answer questions about MH370 which might help the families at least know more about what happened in the hunt for the aircraft and what might be done in a new one. In the lead-up to writing this book in mid-2018, I contacted ATSB head Greg Hood, ATSB search leader Peter Foley, and JACC head Judith Zielke asking each for an interview, pointing out that with the Malaysian government Annex 13 safety investigation completed, there could be no residual concern of compromising it. Hood, Zielke and Foley did not respond.

I also advised dozens of middle-ranking and junior ATSB and JACC officials that the book was coming out, where relevant outlining how they fitted into it, and asked if they would like to present their side of the story. I asked Hood and Zielke if they would support any staff who did grant an interview, or threaten sanctions against them. Zielke did not respond. Hood had Patrick Hornby, the ATSB's chief legal officer, do so on his behalf.

'As this is a legal issue, I am responding,' Hornby wrote in an email to me. 'I refer you to previous correspondence and the ATSB's correcting the record posts on its website.'

The latter element refers to the bureau's diatribes against *The Australian* in its 'Correcting the Record' website section. Hornby would not say what the legal issue was, nor what specific correspondence he was referring to.

I also reached out to Neil Gordon, the distinguished mathematician from the Defence Science and Technology Group who had led the sophisticated work on the satellite data. Gordon initially indicated he thought it would not be a problem, but said I had to contact Defence Media, who turned down the interview request without explanation in an unsigned email. Defence Media did not respond to emails asking why, who I could talk to, or who the head of the unit was. I tracked that last piece of information down through a source, and rang the head of the unit, Amy Hawkins, who would not say why Gordon could not talk to me but said the decision had been taken at a high level.

I also approached Fugro's Paul Kennedy, who had always been happy to talk in the past, who told me he had to ask the ATSB for permission to speak to me for the book. A few days later Kennedy told me he'd been gagged, but ATSB spokesman Paul Sadler would not tell me why. Around this time Teresa Liddle decided something had to be done about the ATSB's culture of secrecy when it came to MH370. For years since the aircraft vanished with her sister Mary Burrows on it, Teresa had delved into everything about the flight. She taught herself how to read aviation charts by finding a manual about them. She pored over each and every report from the ATSB and the Malaysians, looking for inconsistencies – and often found them. In the process, she had her own run-ins with the ATSB. She was outraged at the refusal of the ATSB to meet some of the key FOI requests I'd made. In the middle of 2018 Teresa called for an inquiry, possibly a royal commission, into the ATSB's failed search and its handling of MH370 issues, and condemned its suppression of information.

'They should not hide behind Freedom of Information [exemptions] and not provide the documents on the basis that they did not want to upset Malaysia,' Teresa said, quoted in *The Australian*.

'It is critical to the aviation industry.'

To all those at the ATSB, the JACC, Defence, the Search Strategy Working Group, the organisations making up the panel of Annex 13 accredited representatives and of course the Malaysian investigation itself: if you have been discouraged from revealing the truth, it is not too late to do so. I will continue to investigate MH370, write stories about it in *The Australian*, and there may be a second edition of this book. I encourage those who know more to come forward. It's an invitation to get on the right side of history, and democracy.

As with the Pentagon Papers, government agencies can try to restrict and threaten the press, but the pattern is that the press prevails and the truth finally comes out. Anyone who has watched the excellent movie *The Post,* about *The Washington Post*'s courageous campaign to publish the Pentagon Papers against legal action from the Nixon administration, can see the analogy. Ultimately the US Supreme Court upheld freedom of the press. Hugo L. Black, one of the Supreme Court justices, wrote in an opinion supporting *The Washington Post* and the *New York Times:*

'In revealing the workings of government that led to the Vietnam War, the newspapers nobly did that which the Founders hoped and trusted they would do.'

There are little private shrines to those lost on MH370 in the homes of next-of-kin all over the world.

Intan Maizura has one to her husband Mohammed Hazrin. Knickerbockerglory's brilliant documentary *MH370: Inside the Situation Room* had some particularly moving interview segments with Maizura, a Malaysia Airlines flight attendant who had fallen in love with and married Hazrin, a flight steward on the airline, and had two children with him. Like Danica Weeks, Maizura had driven her husband to the airport to board MH370.

'And that was the last kissing . . . Oh my God, I have not felt this feeling for a long, long time . . . sad,' Intan told the interviewer, as her face shone from the blend of happiness of the memory and the pain that it was just that.

Also like Danica, the disappearance of MH370 left Maizura a

single mother bringing up two young children. 'All I can remember that day I just cry and cry and cry and cry,' Maizura said in *MH370: Inside the Situation Room*. 'That's all I remember on 8 March.'

The cluster of memories at Intan's house includes a photograph of Hazrin formally kissing Maizura on the forehead on their wedding day, two of the couple's old Malaysia Airlines identification cards, a little pottery item of an airliner and another saying 'No. 1 Dad'. There are two small heart-shaped pictures of each of them.

'That's when he gave me "I love Intan",' Maizura said. 'He is very romantic, yeah, who didn't fall for that, right?'

Like Jeanette, Danica and Teresa, it's the not knowing that intensifies the pain.

'I still have so many questions, sometimes I burst into tears because I don't have the answers. My heart says, something is wrong somewhere, this thing is weird.'

Speaking of her young daughter, Maizura said, 'And sometimes she will ask, "Where is Papa's grave?" What to say? You know, even though the truth might be painful, we do want to know the truth, that's all.'

After briefing families and journalists in Putrajaya on the Monday on his safety investigation report on the disappearance of Malaysia Airlines Flight MH370, Kok Soo Chon took the roadshow to Beijing to tell Chinese families that after four-and-a-half years of investigation he had not been able to work out what happened to the aircraft.

About 100 next-of-kin, some from poor rural families, made the journey to the Chinese capital, some travelling 10 hours paying train fares they could not really afford. Farmer Li Eryou, 62, came from rural Handan in Hebei province with his wife, hoping to find out something about the disappearance of their son who had been one of the few from his village to attend university, and who had been working in Malaysia for Chinese telecommunications equipment company ZTE.

Li told *The Global Times*: 'My child is a telecommunication worker who has to travel all year around. Though he is missing now, I still feel that he is working far away. It's the same as before.'

After the briefing, *The Global Times* reported, Li and his wife slept overnight at Beijing Railway Station to catch the first early train home. His wife put the thick investigation report under her head as a pillow. During the year after the accident, Li's wife had to take Valium every day. She often cried in her sleep or smashed things, like her mobile phone, for no apparent reason. In the summer of 2015, she was diagnosed with major depression.

At the briefing in Beijing, some of the family members wore T-shirts with a drawing of MH370 and the words 'Search ON'. They rose in an angry chant:

'This report is not enough at all! It's fooling everyone here. We need to keep investigating. Keep searching!'

The MH370 next-of-kin want to honour their missing in their own way, not have politicians do it for them.

In late June 2018, after continuing protests from families around the world, the Western Australian and federal governments finally cottoned on. In a joint statement, Premier Mark McGowan and federal Transport Minister Michael McCormack announced that 'after careful consideration', it would be 'inappropriate' to go ahead with a permanent memorial in Perth to those lost.

'We are very confident, after consulting with the Australian relatives, that we have made the right call,' the statement said.

It was a victory for the families over the politicians and senior bureaucrats, and for sensitivity and common sense.

'When they find the plane, then we at least know where they

are, and we can make a decision about where to build a memorial,'
Danica told *Perth Now* at the time.'We should not have wasted energy
on this – that energy should have been spent on finding the plane.'

Apart from the Lawtons and the Burrows, there were two other
Australians lost on MH370, and they had two children.

Unlike the relations of the Lawtons and the Burrows, those
children are just too young to be interviewed. But as they grow up
they will be wanting to find out what happened to their parents just
as much as the children of the Lawtons and the Burrows, and they
have the potential to be haunted by not knowing for a lot longer.

The third Australian couple to travel on the missing Malaysian
flight were, as mentioned in Chapter One, Gu Naijun and Li Yuan,
from Sydney. Gu, 31 and Li, 33 came from China but, it's understood,
met in Sydney. They were a couple who, like many in modern China
and Australia, juggled their lives between the two countries. Li was
a partner in software firm Beijing Landysoft Technology, and the
couple also owned a petrol station in southern Sydney.

Gu and Li had two 'little princesses', as they called them on
social media. The western media, at least, does not appear to have
established their names, nor their ages, though they look from
photographs no more than one year old, and three, at the time their
parents went missing on MH370. Gu posted some photos of her
family on Weibo – a popular Chinese social media website – and in
the days following the disappearance of MH370, journalists tracked
down the bright and innocent snapshots of the girls going swimming at a pool, having lunch and parading around in costumes.

Gu shared the posts with Li, who was on the road a lot.

'Dad, I'm playing on the slide now,' the caption said in one scene
at a playground.

'You'll be rolling all over the floor,' was the reply.

The families and friends of Gu and Li did not speak much to the media; it was a pretty shocking case of two very young girls suddenly and tragically made orphans. But a few days after MH370 vanished, the *Sydney Morning Herald* tracked down a high-school classmate of Gu who said she kept in touch after her friend went to university in Sydney.

'I only hope she can safely return,' the friend, who only wanted to be identified as Shelly, told the newspaper. 'If not, it's just too sad for her children and parents.'

At the Maleny Hotel, it only took an instant for Danica Weeks to find the last email exchanges with her missing husband which she keeps close, in the electronic folders on her phone, and to her heart. The last one was sent about three hours before MH370 took off. They are reproduced here, verbatim, with the odd typo unchanged.

From: Paul Weeks
Date: 7 March 2014 at 5:20:15 pm AEST
To: Danica Weeks
Subject: Miss you all already
Hi Puppy,
    Hard to say good by; I was choking back the water works, however the 28 days will go fast send I will be back. Give the boys an extra big hug and kiss from their Dad.
    Those two monkeys are my world (as are you).
    In the lounge getting my fill (as only a noohs can), so hit me back a message, will be here for another 1/2 hour.
    Love
    PAULY

Date: 7 March 2014 at 9:11 PM, Danica Weeks wrote:

Hi Sweet,

Sorry was at soccer.. then we went & had dinner at Sam's, boys all had showers & baths togther & now fast asleep.. me watching escape to country with cup of tea & ginger nut:)

Was the flight good? i miss you heaps cried most of the way to soccer had to wear sunglasses!! Linc still thinks your coming home late so going to hit him quite hard, but he's looking forward to skyping you.

Love pp xox

Date: 8 March 2014 at 12:53:04 am AEST

Hi honey,

Yes I was fragile for quite some time; mostly thinking about how Lincoln would feel when he realises that I am not going to be home for 28 days. Maybe you can use your fridge calendar to help him visualise when I will be home.

I am at Kula Lumpur at present, leaving here in two hours, then six hours to Beijing.

Glad to hear you caught up with Sam; now that you are both FIFO wives, you can lend a shoulder to each other when you are feeling down.

I don't know if I will be able to Skype you until I get to U.B, the bandwidth here in K.L is crap; barley opens a webpage, let alone Skype anyone, still. I will try once I get there.

Byway pokey, this counts as day 1, so cross it off the calendar – only 27 more to go.:)

Lots of love\

Paul

When I asked Danica what she does for fun these days, she said: 'A fun night generally is a fire outside, a pizza and a family movie.

When this happened, life became precious.'

Danica said by raising her two boys, in one sense, her missing husband was always there.

'The kids, they have Paul in them,' she said. 'I just need to look at Jack, and I can see Paul. Lincoln talks like Paul. There is always a part of him with me.'

But, Danica said: 'I will only be released when they find him.'

GLOSSARY

ailerons: Aircraft control surfaces on the wings that control roll, used to bank the aircraft.

Air Accidents Investigation Branch: The British government's air crash investigation unit.

Aircraft Communications Addressing and Reporting System (ACARS): Digital datalink system for transmission of short messages between aircraft and ground stations including automatic relay of data about aircraft performance and activity.

airway: Defined flight route upon which commercial aircraft are usually required to travel.

Australian Maritime Safety Authority (AMSA): The national body in charge of marine search and rescue operations.

Australian Transport Safety Bureau (ATSB): The federal government agency that investigates air crashes and other transport accidents.

autonomous underwater vehicle (AUV): Torpedo-like un-manned miniature submarine equipped with cameras, side-scan sonar, multi-beam echo-sounders and other devices, which are programmed to scan, chart and photograph underwater topography and objects on it.

auxiliary power unit (APU): Generator that can provide electrical and hydraulic power to an aircraft when the main engines are not running, operated by a small jet engine usually in the tail.

black box: *see* flight data recorder *and* cockpit voice recorder.

blind transmission: In air traffic control, a radio call from controllers to an aircraft, which is thought to be in flight, to establish communications.

Broken Ridge: Large underwater escarpment rising from the sea floor in the southern Indian Ocean off the coast of Western Australia.

Bureau of Inquiry and Analysis in Civil Aviation Security (BEA): The French government's air accident investigation agency.

burst frequency offset (BFO): Measure of changes in frequency in electronic 'handshakes' between a satellite and an aircraft's satellite data unit, used to calculate speed.

burst timing offset (BTO): Measure of changes in time, and hence distance, in electronic 'handshakes' between a satellite and an aircraft's satellite data unit.

cockpit voice recorder: The aircraft 'black box' that automatically records voices and sounds from the plane's flight deck.

Defence Science and Technology Group (DSTG): A branch of the Australian Department of Defence that provides specialised knowledge and analysis of military-related matters. Previously known as Defence Science and Technology Organisation (DSTO).

ditch: The act of landing an aircraft on water in an emergency.

elevator: On an aircraft, the control surface on the tail that controls pitch, or up and down movement.

first officer: The co-pilot on an aircraft.

flap: Moveable surface on the rear of an aircraft's wing that can be deployed to change the airflow for more lift and reduced speed.

flaperon: Moveable surface on the rear of an aircraft's wing which can be deployed as a flap for take-off and landing but acts as an aileron during cruise for controlling bank.

flight data recorder (FDR): The aircraft 'black box' which automatically records hundreds of flight parameters including pilot control inputs, altitude, speed and other factors.

Flight Information Region: The large global division of airspace in which air traffic control centres take responsibility for guiding air traffic.

flight management system: The computer system which guides a flight automatically according to instructions from the pilots; the autopilot.

flutter: The potentially dangerous out-of-control flapping of a control surface such as a rudder, aileron or elevator, or a flap, in flight.

Freedom of Information (FOI): In the Australian federal public service, the statutory process guided by the FOI Act in which individuals can seek documents from federal departments and agencies.

hypoxia: Lack of adequate oxygen which can cause grogginess, unconsciousness, brain damage and death, in civil aviation usually caused by accidental decompression of an aircraft at high altitude.

Inmarsat: British satellite company that owned and operated the satellite over the Indian Ocean that relayed automatic electronic 'handshakes' from the satellite data unit of MH370 to a ground station.

International Civil Aviation Organisation (ICAO): The Montreal-based specialised agency of the United Nations that develops and guides international protocols for air navigation and administration, including, under what is known as Annex 13, air crash investigations.

Joint Agency Coordination Centre (JACC): The administrative body established in early 2014 by the Australian federal government to coordinate the response of agencies and departments to the disappearance of MH370, including communications with the media, next-of-kin, and foreign government officials.

knot: Measure of speed in maritime and aviation navigation: one knot is one nautical mile per hour, roughly equivalent to just under two kilometres per hour.

National Transportation Safety Board (NTSB): The US government agency that investigates air crashes and other transport accidents.

nautical mile (NM): Measure of distance in maritime and aviation navigation, roughly equivalent to just under two kilometres.

Ocean Infinity: British-owned, Houston-based underwater marine survey company that conducted the second seabed search for Malaysia Airlines Flight MH370.

phugoid: A cyclical aircraft motion, usually when it is unpiloted or under only partial control, in which it naturally climbs or goes level until it slows down and approaches a stall, then dives, picks up speed, and climbs again.

pilot-in-command (PIC): The flight officer in charge of an aircraft on a flight; the captain.

primary radar: In aviation, radar which detects and tracks aircraft through the return and analysis of electronic pulses bounced off them.

ram air turbine (RAM): Device which automatically deploys from the fuselage of an aircraft into the slipstream during total engine failure to provide a bare minimum of hydraulic and electrical power to run control surfaces and essential instruments.

rapid decompression: Fast loss of pressurisation of an aircraft at high altitude, usually due to an accident which damages the integrity of the fuselage.

rating: A qualification for a pilot to fly an aircraft of a certain type or in particular conditions.

rudder: The control surface on an aircraft's tail which controls left-or-right direction, known as yaw.

satellite data unit (SDU): The electronic unit on an aircraft which transmits and receives data and telephone and fax communications via satellite relay to ground stations. Also known as SATCOM.

Search Strategy Working Group (SSWG): The panel of international experts from overseas government air crash investigation bodies, British satellite company Inmarsat, and US aircraft manufacturer Boeing which advised the ATSB in its search for MH370.

secondary radar: Radar that detects signals emitted from an aircraft's transponder which broadcasts its identity, position, altitude, and speed, used by air traffic controllers to keep track of flights and guide pilots.

Seventh Arc: The band in the southern Indian Ocean upon which MH370 is thought to have come down after running out of fuel. It is based on the last of seven notional rings around the Asia-Pacific region upon which MH370 is thought to have been flying at the time of each of seven roughly hourly automatic electronic 'handshakes' between MH370's satellite data unit and an Inmarsat satellite over the Indian Ocean.

sonar: System used to detect, map and produce images of underwater objects and topography by analysing the return of electronic signals bounced off them through the water, much like radar does in the air.

sortie: An aerial mission – a departure, flight and return of an aircraft – such as on a search and rescue operation.

stall: The aerodynamic fail point for an aircraft where it slows to the point where the airflow over the wings is no longer fast enough to produce enough lift to keep it in the air, and it starts to fall from the sky.

towfish: The devices towed by ships on a long tether which carry side-scan sonar used to search for objects on the seabed.

trailing edge: The rear part of a wing, flap or control surface on an aircraft based on the orientation it is flying forward through the air; the opposite position to the 'leading edge'.

transponder: Electronic device on an aircraft which transmits a signal to air traffic control radar on the ground with the plane's identity, position, altitude and speed in real time.

Transportation Safety Board (TSB): The Canadian federal agency which investigates air crashes and other transport accidents.

underwater locator beacon ('pinger'): The electronic devices attached to an aircraft's black box flight recorders that automatically emit an acoustic signal when submerged, enabling searchers with 'pinger locator' equipment to find aircraft that have crashed in bodies of water.

waypoint: Points of latitude and longitude on airways used as reference points for air navigation and air traffic control purposes, whose names are all composed of five capital letters.

witness marks: In air crash investigation, damage marks on aircraft wreckage like cracks, tears, smudges, burns and scratches that provide clues to what caused an accident.

9M-MRO: The registration of the Boeing 777 which flew MH370.

FURTHER READING

- **MH370: *Mystery Solved*.** This concise book, by Canadian veteran pilot and air crash investigator Larry Vance, provides a forensic and highly engaging analysis of the factual evidence surrounding the disappearance of MH370, concluding the aircraft was flown to the end and ditched. It's a must for anyone following the debate. For more information, see: hvsaviation.com
- **MH370 Safety Investigation Report.** This study by the Malaysian government's ICAO Annex 13 safety investigation team, while controversial in its conclusions, provides a wealth of information about the flight, the circumstances surrounding it and analysis of what's known. It comes with a huge array of diagrams, maps and appendices. It can be downloaded at: mh370.mot.gov.my
- **Australian Transport Safety Bureau documents.** The ATSB published several reports, maps, photographs, and many bulletins and other material over the three years it was involved in the hunt for MH370. They can be found at: atsb.gov.au/mh370/ In particular, the ATSB's final report, designated on the web page under 'reports' as 'The Operation Search for MH370', and titled *Final ATSB Search Report: The Operational Search for MH370*, provides a comprehensive account of its failed effort.
- ***The Australian* and *The Weekend Australian*.** The national daily has led media coverage worldwide on MH370, and will continue to do so through its network of investigative reporters, aviation writers, foreign correspondents and professional aviator commentators. We now have a page dedicated to MH370 including news stories, features and comment. It can be found at: theaustralian.com.au/topics/mh370

ACKNOWLEDGEMENTS

The people who contributed to this book are all, in their own ways, hunters for MH370.

Angus Houston coordinated the surface search and gave me valuable insights into the swings of hope and heartbreak.

Others have used their extensive knowledge and experience to provide a reality check on the search, including pilots Mike Keane, Byron Bailey and Simon Hardy. They devoted considerable time to help deepen my understanding of the disappearance of the aircraft and aviation generally. So too did Larry Vance, a great air crash investigator who has an extraordinary ability to make the techniques of his profession understandable to a general audience.

The editors of *The Australian*, in particular Helen Trinca, Paul Whittaker, John Lehmann and Chris Dore, showed great journalistic professionalism and determination in resisting the repeated efforts by the ATSB and the JACC to shut me down in my pursuit of the truth.

The team at Pan Macmillan – Danielle Walker, Georgia Webb and Angus Fontaine – are a talented and enthusiastic trio who were a pleasure to work with.

I am also grateful to other individuals and organisations who granted permissions to make use of their material, including my colleague on *The Australian* Amanda Hodge, and British film group Knickerbockerglory.

One must recognise close ones who encouraged me in this pursuit and kept my spirits high, including Christina, Ben, and the delightful, coquettish Lisbon.

And of course, there are those for whom the need to find answers to the MH370 mystery is most acute: Danica Weeks, Jeanette Maguire and Teresa Liddle, who let me into their unique, stoic world.